IMAGES
of America

DENAIR

ON THE COVER: "Big" John Davis settled in the area, which is now Monte Vista Avenue and Lester Road, when he purchased 327.97 acres for $2.48 per acre in 1871 from Green Baker, who had been deeded the land by the federal government in 1869. Davis soon built the home shown in this photograph in 1871 and purchased an additional 1,120 acres at the cost of $3 per acre. In January 1905, Davis sold 2,605.46 acres to Lester, Whitmore, and Dickinson, with Lester getting 622.9 acres including the home. James N. Lester added a kitchen, dining room, pantry, storage closet, and bathroom, among other improvements to the house. The home went through many different upgrades over the years and was finally burned down by the Denair Fire Department in April 1964 to make way for a new high school facility to be built on the land. The home was 93 years old at that time. (Stanislaus Region History and Culture Image Collection, Series I, Subseries 2, Box 1, Folder 17, Special Collections, University Library, California State University, Stanislaus.)

IMAGES
of America

DENAIR

James Shehan

ARCADIA
PUBLISHING

ISBN 978-1-4671-3460-6

Published by Arcadia Publishing
Charleston, South Carolina

Printed in the United States of America

Library of Congress Control Number: 2015941081

For all general information, please contact Arcadia Publishing:
Telephone 843-853-2070
Fax 843-853-0044
E-mail sales@arcadiapublishing.com
For customer service and orders:
Toll-Free 1-888-313-2665

Visit us on the Internet at www.arcadiapublishing.com

To Mom and Dad—thank you

Contents

ACKNOWLEDGMENTS

The photographs in this book come from many different sources, including Denair Unified School District, Denair Community Services District, John Chance, Carol Heans Royster, Cheryl Montgomery Cline, Denair Fire Department, Denair Post Office, Denair Lumber Company, Denair Lions Club, Alma Jean Mills Coleman, Joyce Domecq Morrissey, Louis Domecq, Patricia Moore, Hazel Wade Gomes, the Witmer family, the Kastner family, Bryan Tribble, Norma Cordova, Connecting Point Church of the Nazarene, California State University Stanislaus, and the Turlock Historical Society. Thank-yous go to everyone that contributed to this book. If I have left anyone out, I am truly sorry; it was not done on purpose.

Individuals who helped tremendously with the creation of this book and to whom I am in great debt to include John Chance, for his countless photographs and excellent memory of Denair's past; Jody Jorge at the school district, for all of her help and research; Stephen Browning, for help acquiring photographs and listening to me go on endlessly about this book; my family, for putting up with me as I received each image and recounted its history; Laura French from CSU Stanislaus, for rescanning the cover photograph just in time for the deadline; Eletha Cole, for putting me in touch with Cheryl Cline, who was a wealth of information and photographs; Cary Evans, for all of his research (I am so glad I finally found him in time); Robert Mann, for all of his help and support over the years (thanks for being a great friend); Carl Baggese, for paving the way with a great job on the Modesto books and for his support; and of course, Janice Key, my editor extraordinaire—who else could turn my chicken scratch into meaningful sentences in the blink of an eye? Without the help of these people and many others, this book would never exist.

INTRODUCTION

"It was a good land," Theodore Jessup said, when asked why he had chosen Denair as the spot to establish his dreamed-of Quaker colony. "Yes, the land was good, it was cheap, and there was plenty of irrigation water." Theodore Jessup had come from to Denair from Iowa via Kansas and finally Whittier, California. He was one of those Americans seeking the opportunity to better his condition.

But Jessup was neither the first nor the last white man to look with favor upon this part of the San Joaquin Valley. Mr. Cutler, a teacher at Denair School in 1908, had often regaled his pupils with tales of his own boyhood. His playground, he said, had extended from Stockton to Fresno. He and his horse had roamed as they pleased, spotting herds of antelope and cattle as they fed amid acres of Lupine and poppy. He had stopped nights at one cowboy camp or another.

By the time Mr. Cutler was a man, Big John Davis and Charles Sperry, among others, had plowed under the poppies and sowed barley. Still later, after Mr. Cutler's hair had thinned and turned grey, and he earned his living explaining decimals to leggy children, La Grange Dam had blocked the waters of the Tuolumne River, sending them flowing between the sandy banks of miles-long canals to the relative flat of the valley below. This flow of water changed the great barley ranches into forty-acre diversified farms. The story of the Charles E. Sperry ranch could be, with modifications, the story of the entire area.

—from "History of Denair" by Christine Chance
Streams in a Thirsty Land, 1972

Denair's story is similar to many of those of the towns along the rail lines in the San Joaquin Valley. In the early days, the town had somewhat of an identity crisis, changing names from Elmwood to Elmdale, then to Elms for a short while, before going back to Elmwood, and eventually coming to Denair. However, like in many of the other towns in the area, agriculture has remained the backbone since the beginning, from the massive barley and wheat fields during John Davis and Charles Sperry's time, to the orchards of almonds and fields of alfalfa of today. Agriculture is what built this area, and agriculture is what will remain.

On April 24, 1907, the town's name was changed from Elmwood to Denair, in honor of its most prominent landowner at the time, John Denair. Denair came to the area from Southern California after learning about plans that the Santa Fe Railway would be putting a section headquarters and roundhouse somewhere in Stanislaus County. John decided to purchase around 9,000 acres in the area of what was then Elmwood Colony for a low price and sell the land to the railroad at a profit. Unfortunately for Denair, his land prices were too steep for the railroad, which, in turn, chose to purchase land north in Riverbank for its section headquarters and roundhouse.

Born November 10, 1846, in Germantown, Pennsylvania, John Denair led an interesting life. At the age of 14, he enlisted in the Civil War with the 150th Regiment, Company B of the

Pennsylvania Infantry. He never rose above the rank of private for the duration of his service. He took part in many of the greatest battles, including the Battle of Gettysburg, where he was wounded near the end of the war. Denair also served as a bodyguard to Pres. Abraham Lincoln during the war. After the war ended, Denair found work with the railroad where he flourished and became superintendent of several large railroad lines. Denair soon found himself in San Francisco in 1880 when he was 33 years old. It was in San Francisco that he met his future wife, Ida May Hiester, who was only 19 at the time. Ida was the daughter of prominent San Francisco publisher and newspaper owner Amos C. Hiester. Denair moved to Flagstaff, Arizona, but continued his long-distance relationship with Ida. In June 1894, John and Ida were wed. In September of the following year, John and Ida welcomed the arrival of their only child, John Jr., born in Needles, California.

In late 1899 or early 1900, John Denair Sr. established the Denair Mercantile Land & Development Company, with an investment of $1 million. His backer and partner at the time was a Needles banker only known as a Mr. Cunningham. Together, they made an initial purchase of 2,900 acres in the Elmwood Colony area. They eventually purchased an additional 4,500 acres between Elmwood Colony and Delhi. Another one of Denair's investments was the purchase of 800 acres north of Elmwood Colony owned by Clara Sperry. He later sold it off in sections.

In 1905, the now 58-year-old John's health was beginning to fail. He retired from the Santa Fe Railway and concentrated on his land development and mining companies. In 1907, at the age of 46, Ida died suddenly, leaving John, now 60, a widower with a 12-year-old son. Three years later, with John traveling all over the state adding to his fortune, his relationship with his son, John Jr., suffered. John Jr.'s uncle and aunt in San Francisco, Eugene and Marguerite Light, adopted him and provided a stable home.

On October 8, 1915, John Denair Sr. died from complications of pneumonia at the Santa Fe Hospital in Los Angeles. John was buried in a family plot in the Woodlawn Memorial Park Cemetery in Colma, California, just south of San Francisco.

Even though the relationship between John Denair Sr. and his son was strained, John Jr. followed in his father's footsteps. John Jr. went to work for the Western Pacific Railroad in its San Francisco ticket office in 1915. In 1917, he enlisted in the 144th Field Artillery and worked as a private in the regimental headquarters, later being promoted to sergeant and sergeant major. In February of the following year, he was promoted again to second lieutenant and assigned as a liaison officer to the headquarters company at Camp Kearney, California. It is uncertain where John Jr. went from there, as few records exist. He died in San Francisco in 1925 at the age of 30. John Jr. never married.

Even though John Denair never made his fortune selling his land to the Santa Fe Railway, his legacy lives on in the town named in his honor. Many people, businesses, families, farms, crops, and animals have come and gone over the years, but as the old saying goes, "In Denair, nothing ends—it just changes."

One

The Early Days

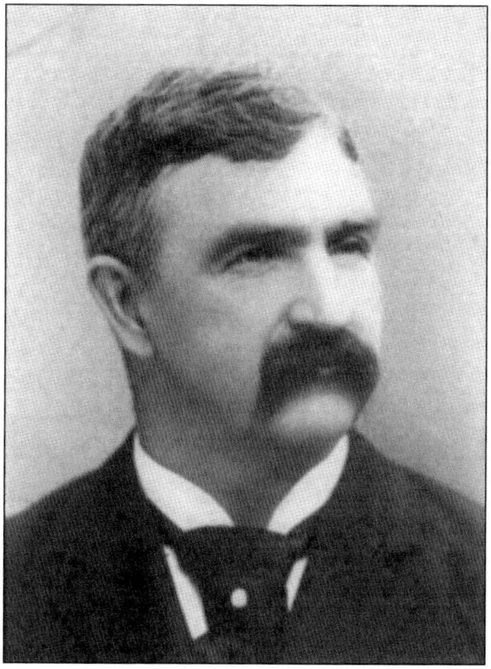 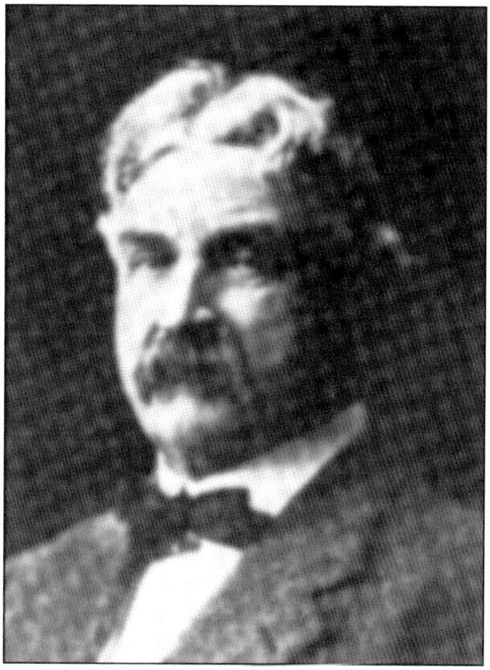

John Denair was born November 10, 1846, in Germantown, Pennsylvania. At the age of 14, he enlisted in the Civil War and took part in many of the greatest battles, including Gettysburg, where he was wounded near the end of the war. John also served as a bodyguard to President Lincoln during the war. After the war ended, John found work with the railroad, where he flourished and became superintendent of several large railroad lines, eventually working his way west to Southern California. Upon retiring from the railroad, he established the Denair Mercantile Land & Development Company and, in 1906, purchased 9,000 acres in the Stanislaus County area, including much of what was then Elmwood Colony. Denair went through several name changes during those early years, including Elmwood, Elmdale, and Elms. On April 24, 1907, the town changed its name for the last time—to Denair, honoring its most prominent landowner. John died on October 5, 1915. His only son, John "Jack" Denair Jr., died at the young age of 30 in 1925. (Left, courtesy of *Out West* magazine; right, courtesy of *Santa Fe* magazine.)

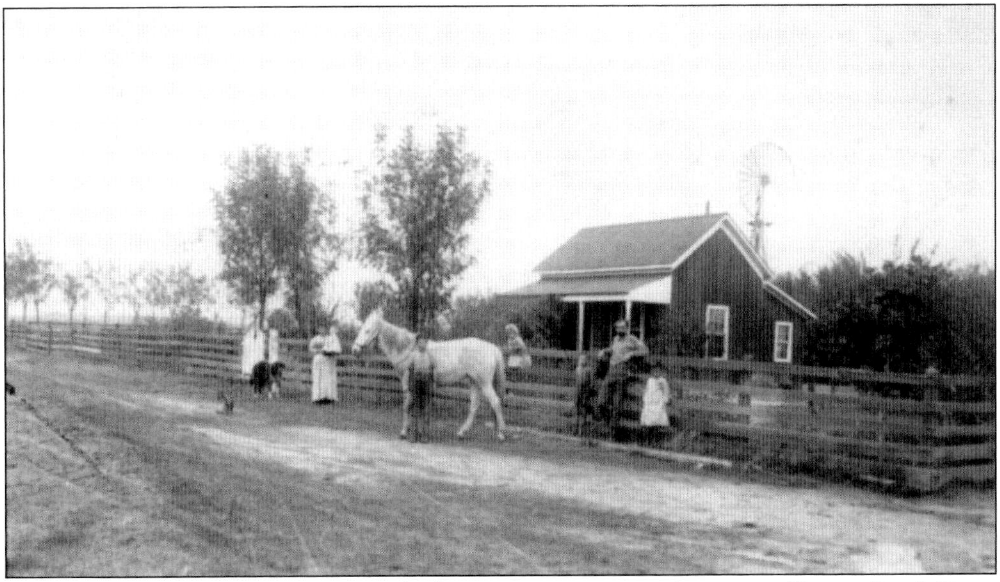

"Big" John Davis settled in the area, which is now Monte Vista Avenue and Lester Road. Davis purchased 327.97 acres in 1871 from Green Baker, who had been deeded the land by the federal government in 1869. Baker deeded the land to Davis for $2.48 per acre. Davis soon built the home shown in the photograph in 1871. Davis purchased an additional 1,120 acres at the cost of $3. In January 1905, Davis sold 2,605.46 acres to Lester, Whitmore, and Dickinson, with Lester getting 622.9 acres, including the home. James N. Lester added a kitchen, dining room, pantry, storage closet, and bathroom among other improvements to the house. (Courtesy of Denair Community Service District.)

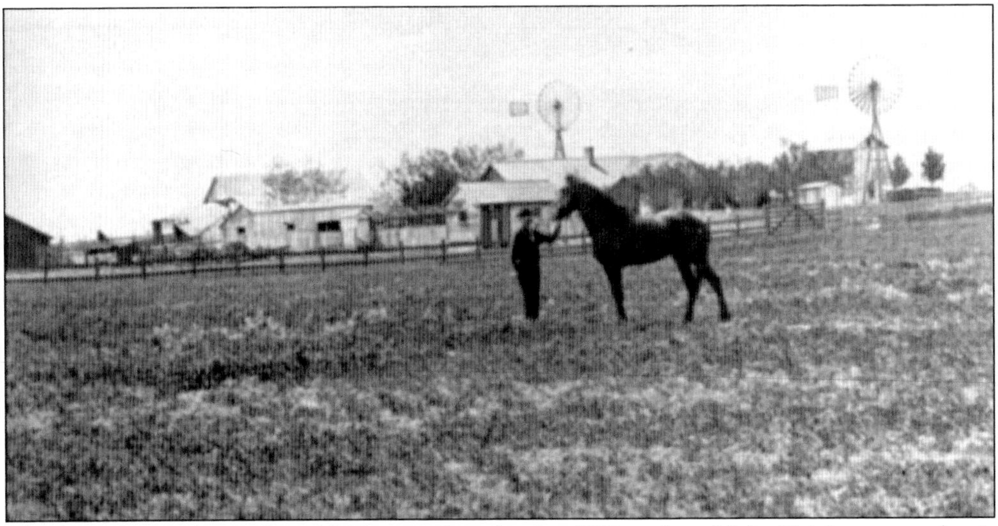

Charles E. Sperry Sr. purchased 966 acres of raw land in 1880 and established his home on what is now Sperry Road, located between Service and Keyes Roads. Sperry and his sons Charles, Louis, and Willard planted and raised grain and stock until irrigation water started flowing through the land. Charles Sr. was the first to move a 10-mule team combine to harvest grain. Soon after 1900, the Sperrys joined other local landowners to subdivide their acreage into 20- and 40-acre farms. The Sperry ranch became a small community of irrigated farms growing alfalfa, beans, grains, fruits, and nuts. (Courtesy of Denair Community Service District.)

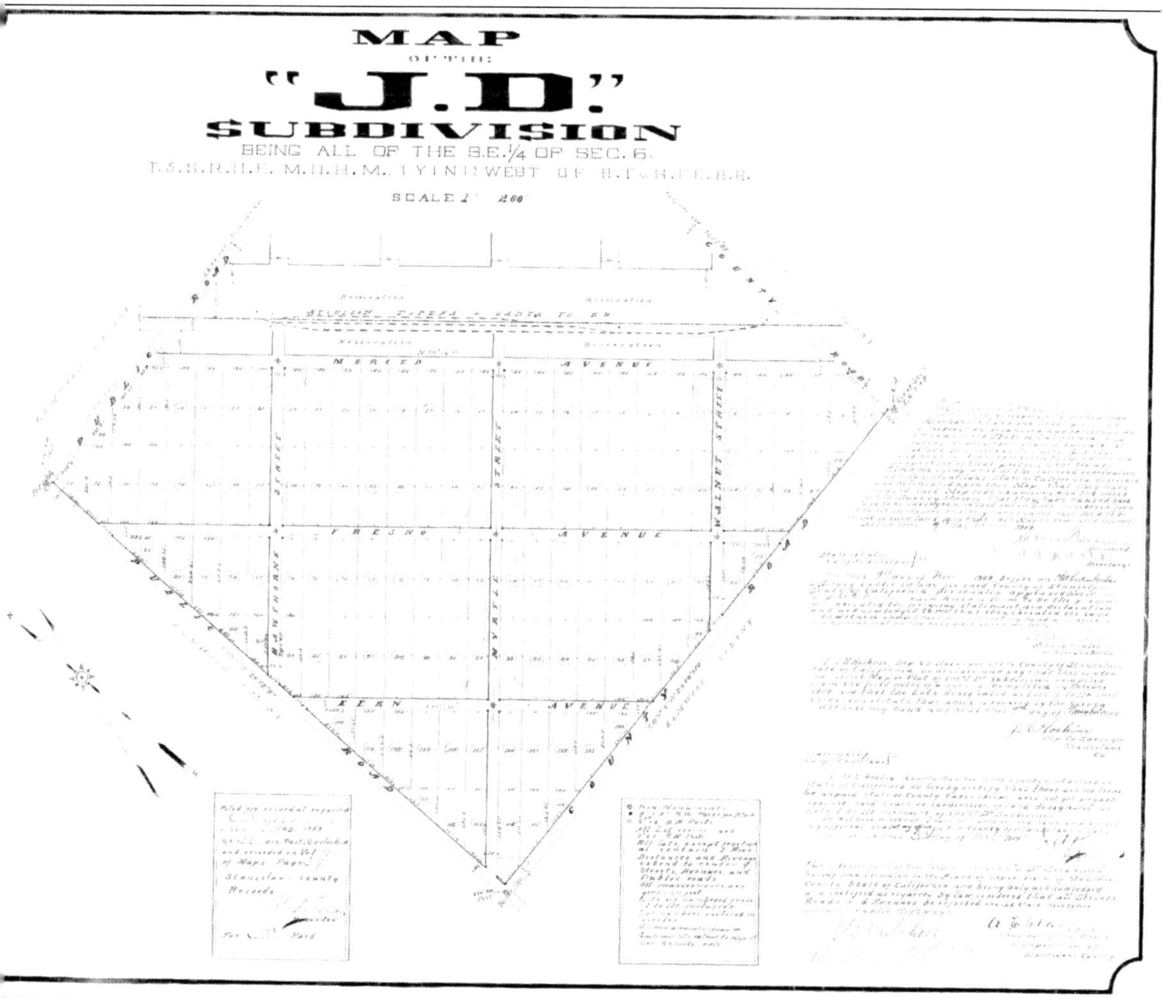

Twelve acres of land were sold to the San Francisco and San Joaquin Railway on July 15, 1896, to provide a right-of-way for the railroad. A townsite was laid out in John Davis's barley fields in 1897 around the railroad land and named Elmwood. A few homes were built around the area in 1902 and 1903. In 1906, land developer John Denair purchased the townsite. After holding the townsite until 1909, Denair decided the lots were too small. He redesigned the street layout, eliminating half of the streets and creating lots about an acre in size, much of which forms the town today. East-west streets were named after tree species, and north-south streets were named after several California counties. (Courtesy of Denair Community Service District.)

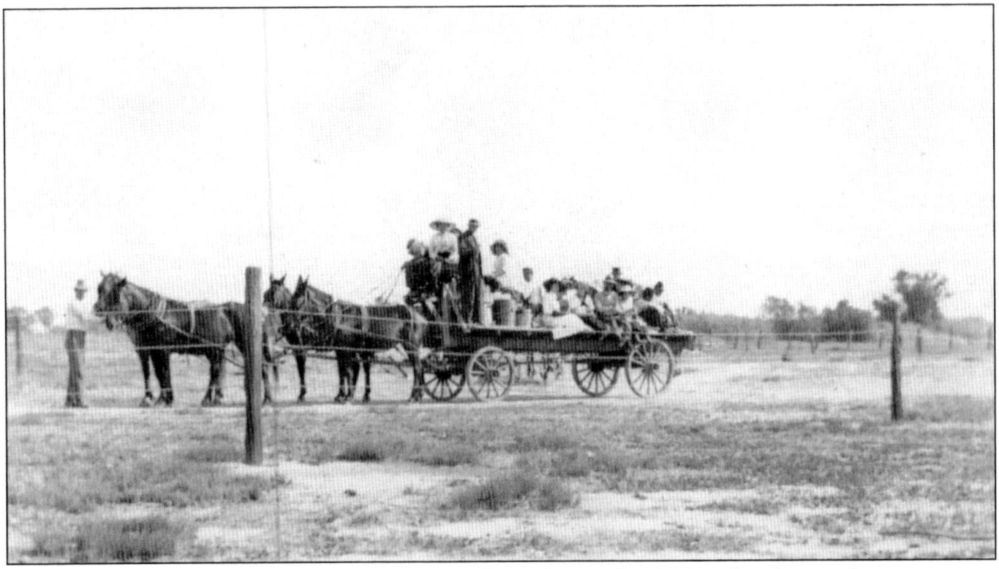

Many families started moving into the area and purchasing land. New families to the area meant new churches, businesses, schools, and family outings. (Courtesy of John Chance.)

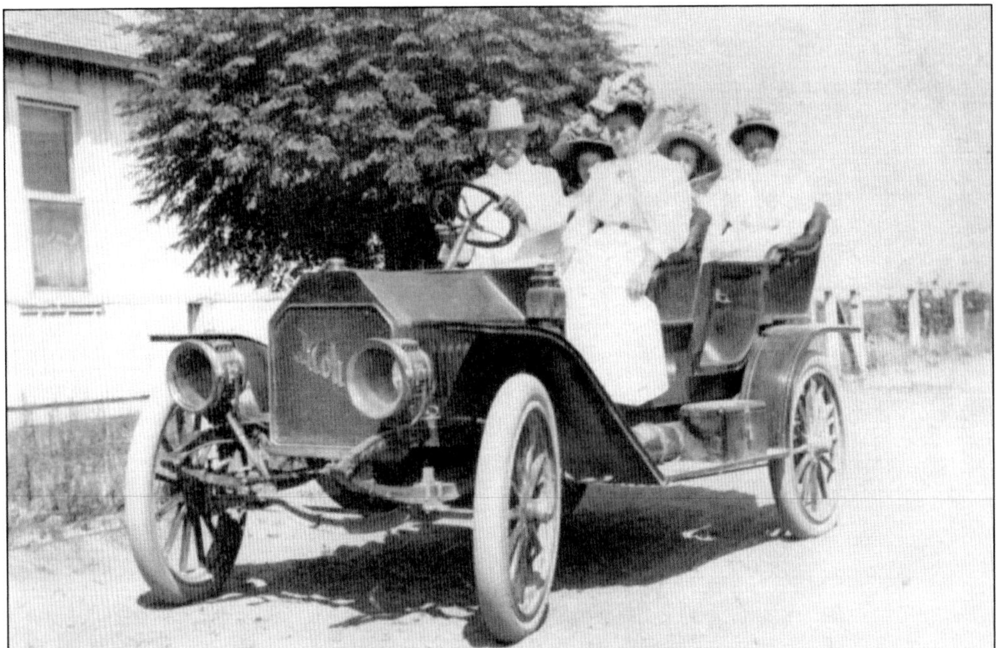

Back in the day, family outings might have included a ride in the family's new car. Pictured here is the Binford family, who lived on Sperry Road, with guests from Whittier visiting. Among the riders are Josephine Binford in the front seat, and in the back, Lena Binford, Lena's daughter, and Christine Hollingsworth. This photograph was taken sometime around 1909–1910. (Courtesy of John Chance.)

Prior to Denair High School opening in 1912, students took the long, hour or more horse ride to Turlock High School every day. Some were lucky enough to have mechanical means of getting to school. This of course came with the usual breakdowns associated with early cars. Here is the Turlock High School physics class on a trip to La Grange in May 1912. Pictured are Ida Mills, Mildred Hollingsworth, Joseph Anderson, and an unidentified helping hand. (Courtesy of John Chance.)

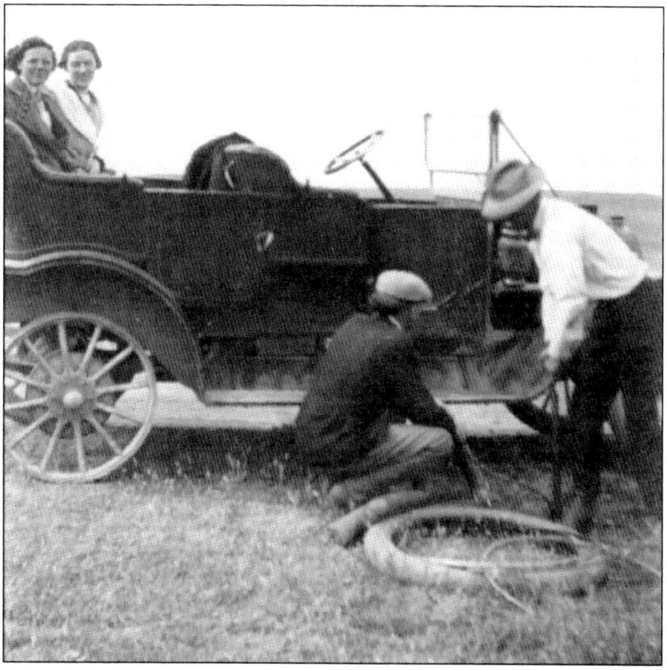

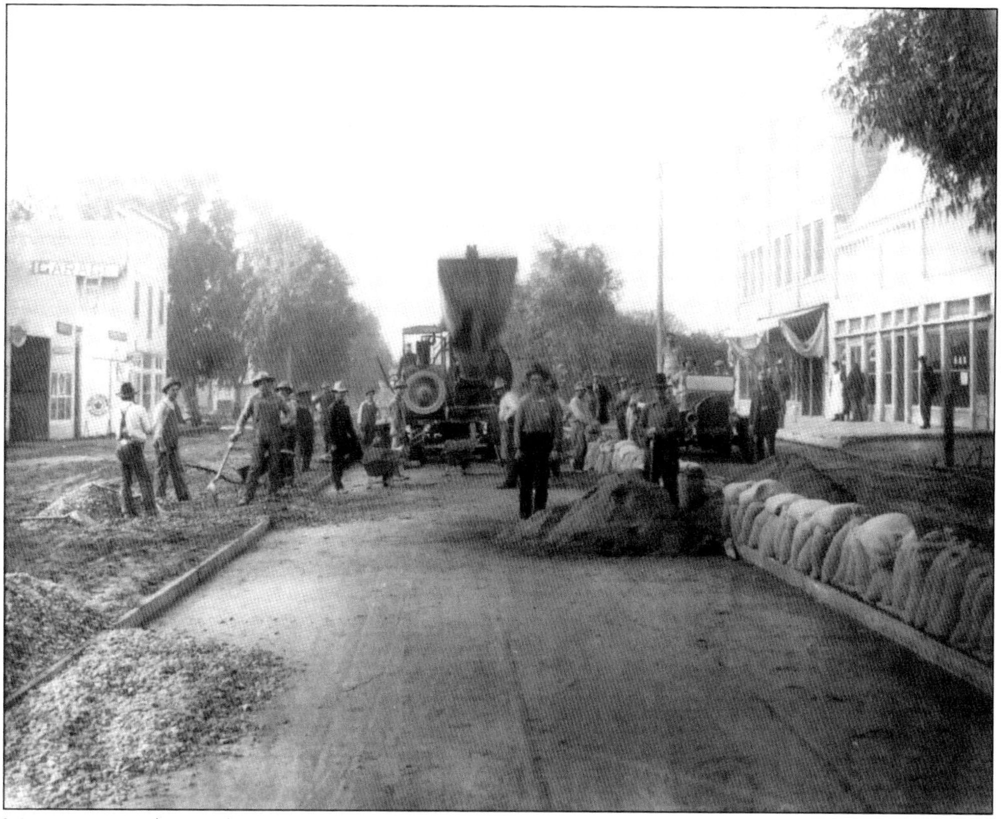

More cars on the road meant the residents needed better roads. Here, workers pave Main Street. On the right is the Bank Building. (Courtesy of Denair Community Service District.)

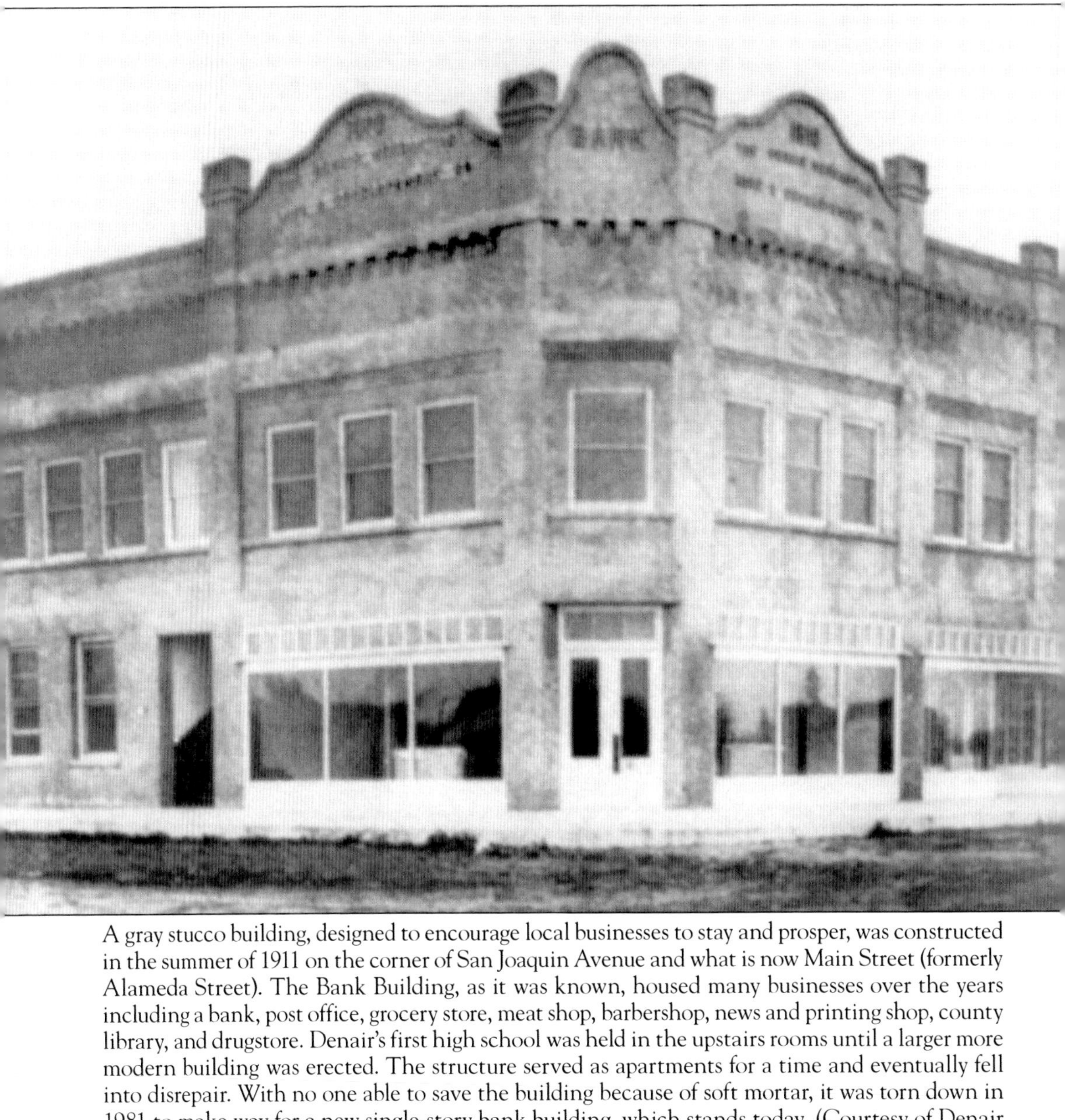

A gray stucco building, designed to encourage local businesses to stay and prosper, was constructed in the summer of 1911 on the corner of San Joaquin Avenue and what is now Main Street (formerly Alameda Street). The Bank Building, as it was known, housed many businesses over the years including a bank, post office, grocery store, meat shop, barbershop, news and printing shop, county library, and drugstore. Denair's first high school was held in the upstairs rooms until a larger more modern building was erected. The structure served as apartments for a time and eventually fell into disrepair. With no one able to save the building because of soft mortar, it was torn down in 1981 to make way for a new single-story bank building, which stands today. (Courtesy of Denair Community Service District.)

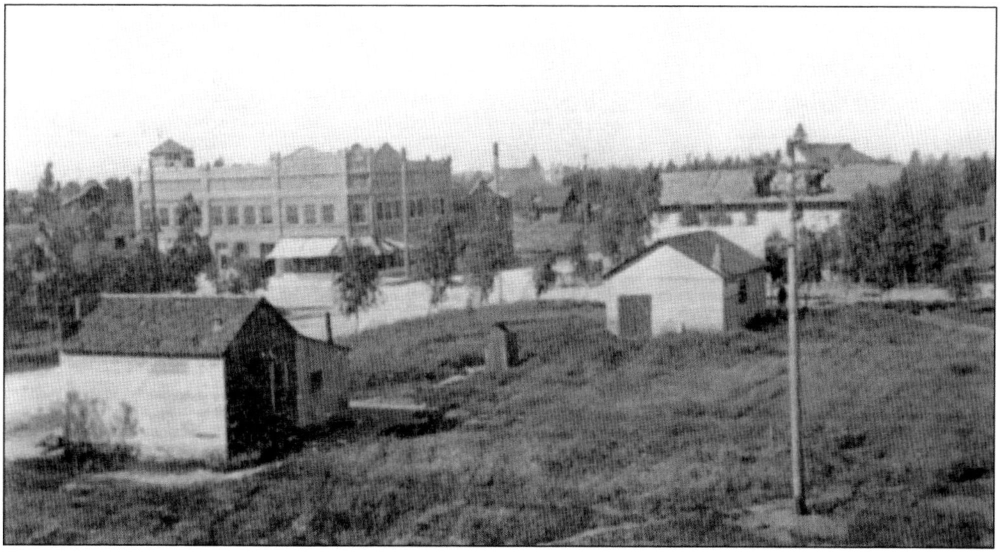

This is a photograph of Main Street, with a view looking northeast toward the Bank Building. (Courtesy of Bryan Tribble.)

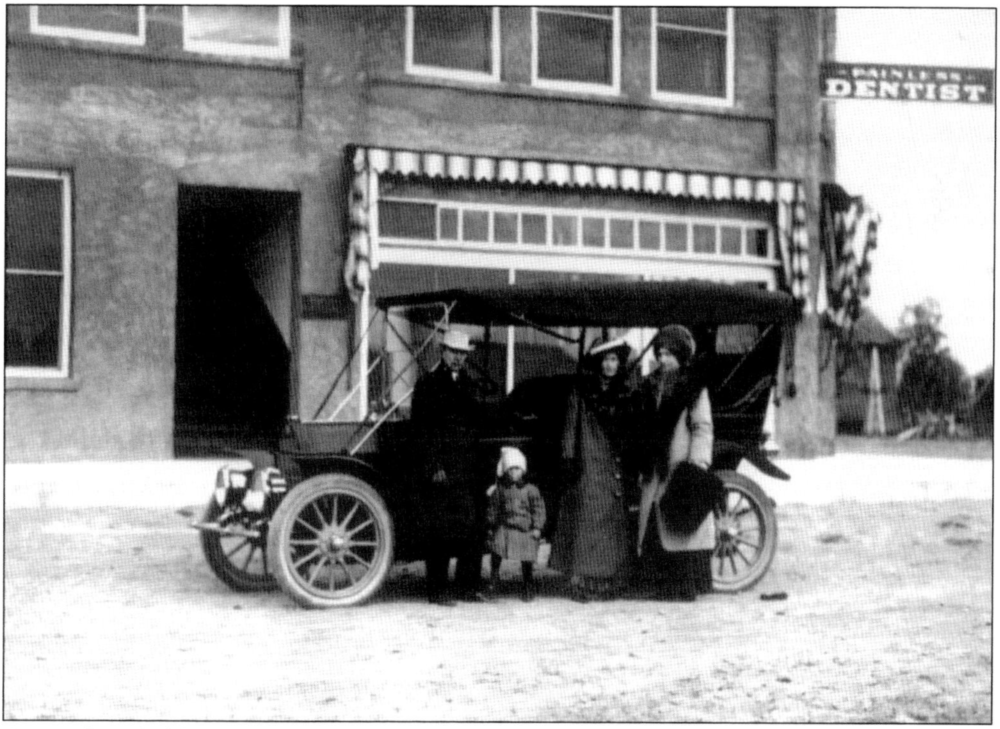

An unidentified family is pictured here in front of the Bank Building. (Courtesy of the Turlock Historical Society.)

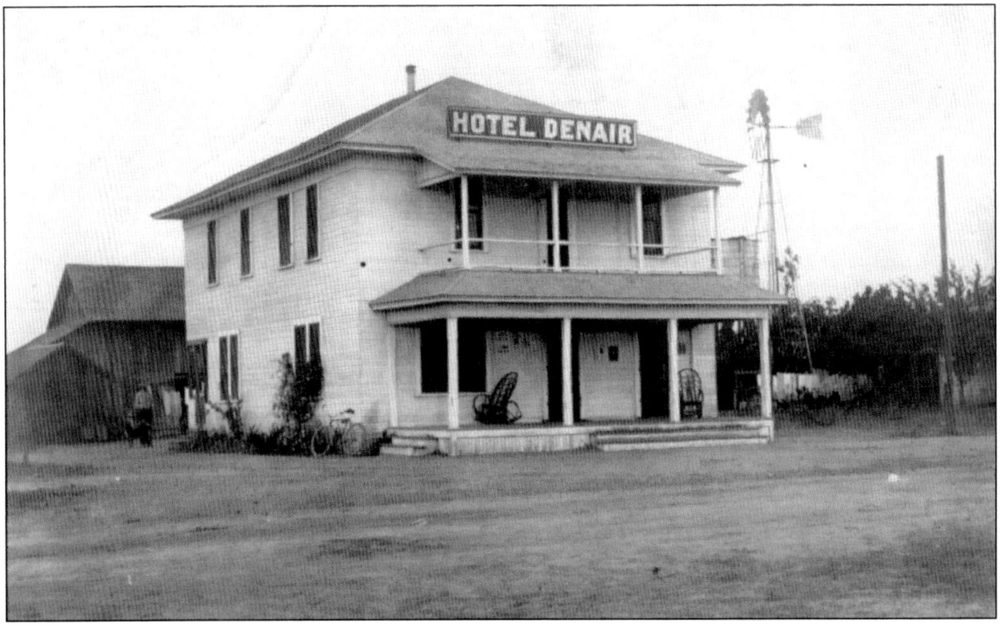

Travelers passing through town by rail, horse and buggy, or car needed a place to stay. The Hotel Denair was built in 1905 by the Whitmore Co. It served as a place for weary travelers to stay for many years. Later, it was sold and turned into a private residence. That home still stands today. (Courtesy of Denair Community Service District.)

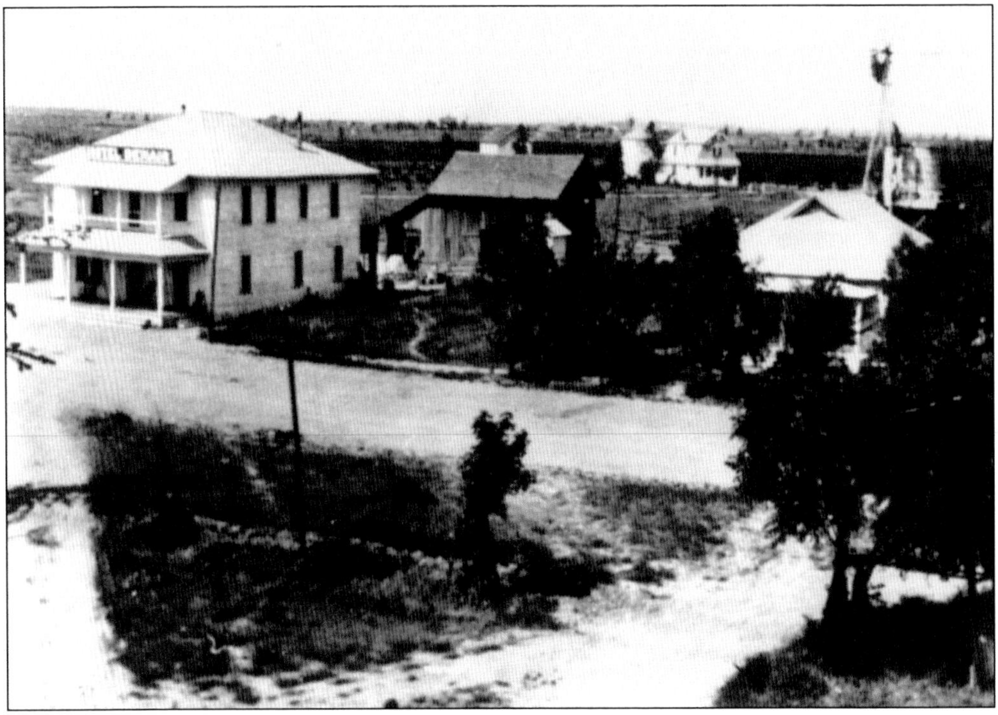

This photograph of an unpaved Santa Fe Avenue was taken from the top of the train depot. This view looks northeast, with the Hotel Denair on the left and several homes in the background. (Courtesy of Denair Community Service District.)

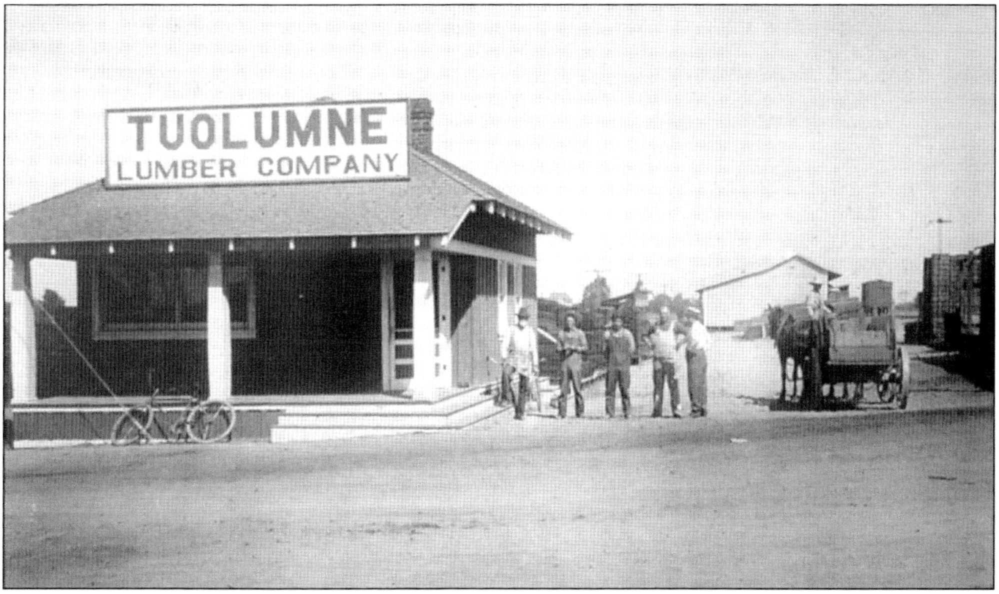

One by one, businesses began opening in the small community. Among those was the Tuolumne Lumber Company, owned by a Mr. Kewin of Modesto and operated by Clark Utterback. The yard sat beside the railroad, allowing for the unloading of boards from distant locations. The growing town desperately needed the lumber. The United Lumber Company later bought the lumberyard and served the community until 1953, when James Silva of Turlock purchased it and changed the name to Denair Lumber Company. Denair Lumber is still in business today, owned by Kelley Bros. Many longtime Denair residents will recognize buildings in the photograph that still stand, with some slight changes. (Courtesy of Denair Lumber Company.)

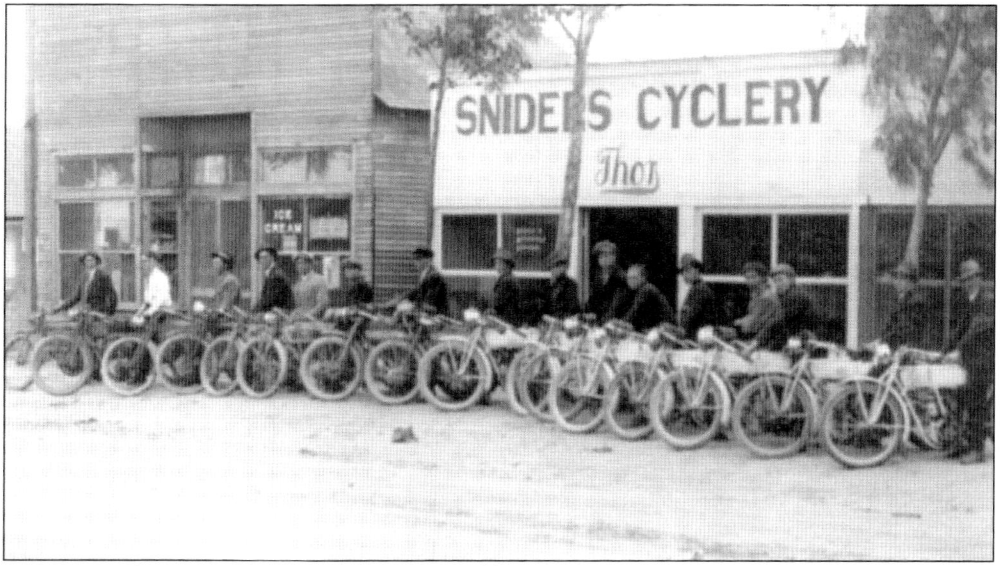

Stewart Snider, a young entrepreneur, opened his own business across the street from the new Bank Building in 1912. Snider's Cyclery served all of the young motorcycle enthusiasts in town. Stories were told of Stewart demonstrating his prowess and startling residents by driving his motorcycle down Alameda Avenue (later Main Street) at 30 miles per hour while looking backward. (Courtesy of Cheryl Cline.)

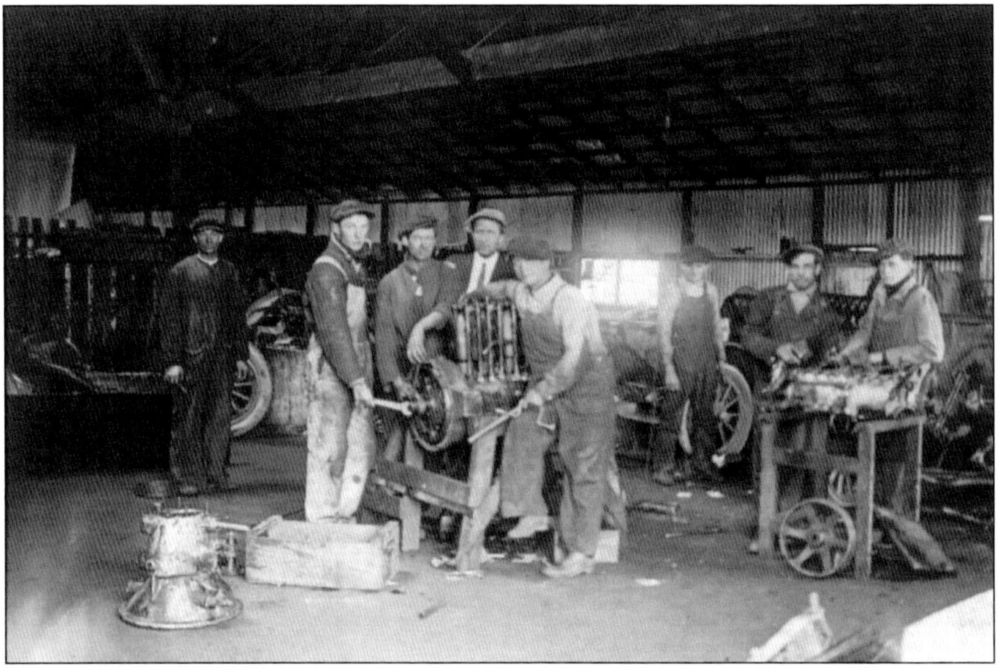

Working hard to repair and rebuild the motorcycles of the day, the boys of Snider's Cyclery stopped for a quick photograph. Below, Stewart Snider poses with one of his motorcycles. (Both, courtesy of Cheryl Cline.)

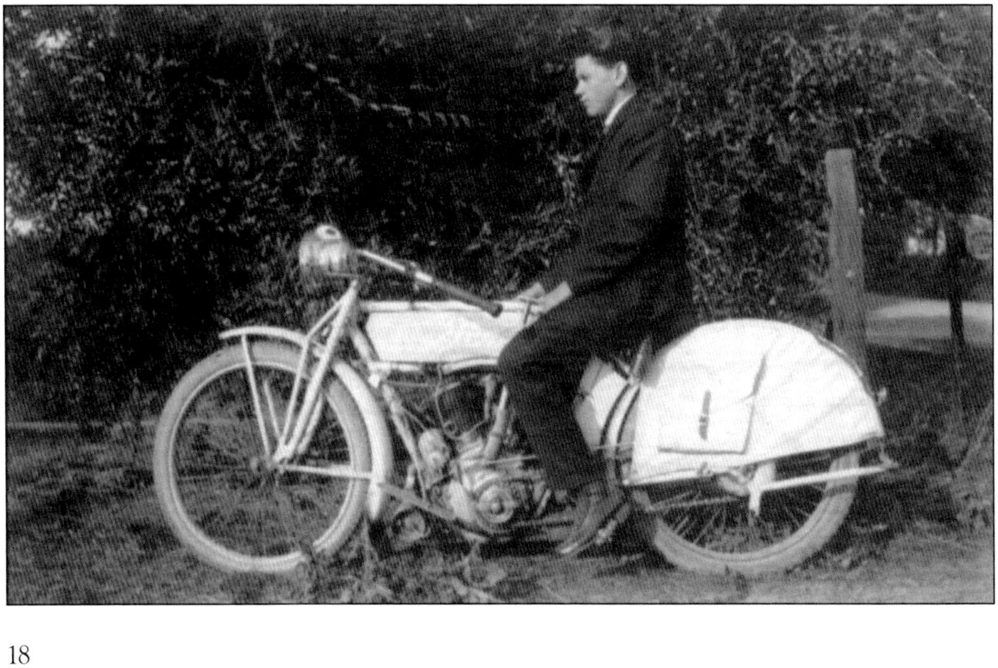

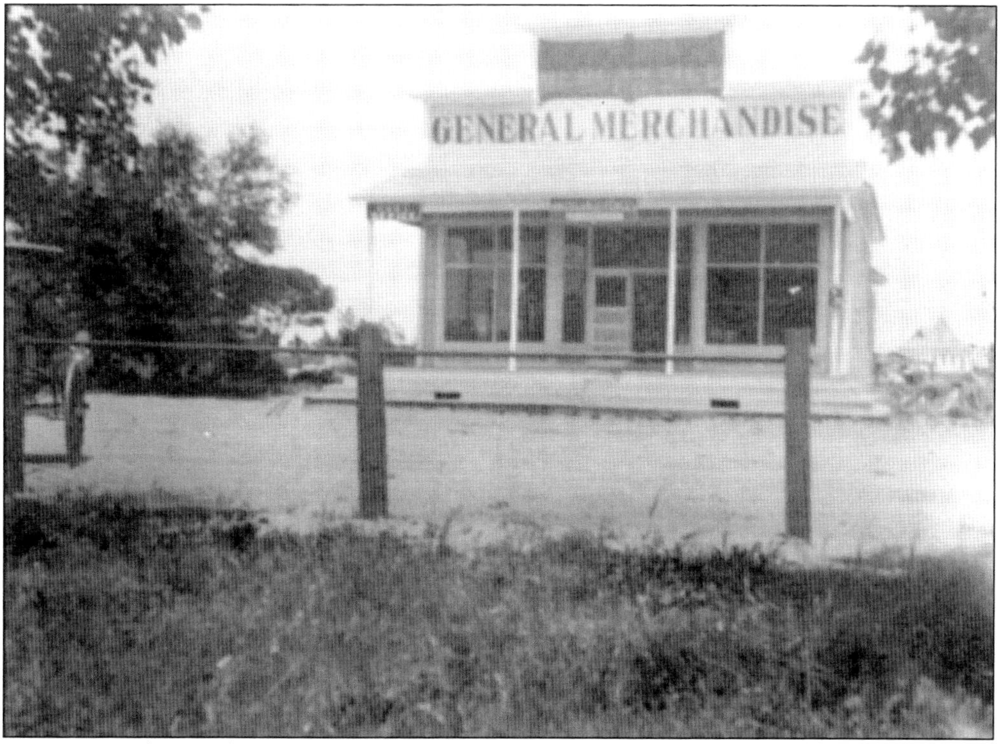

Groceries and general merchandise were a basic need for any growing town. In 1903, Crouch-Warner General Merchandise was established on Santa Fe Avenue. In 1904, Mr. Warner sold his part in the business to Roy Crouch, and the sign over the door was changed to read "Crouch Brothers General Merchandise." (Courtesy of John Chance.)

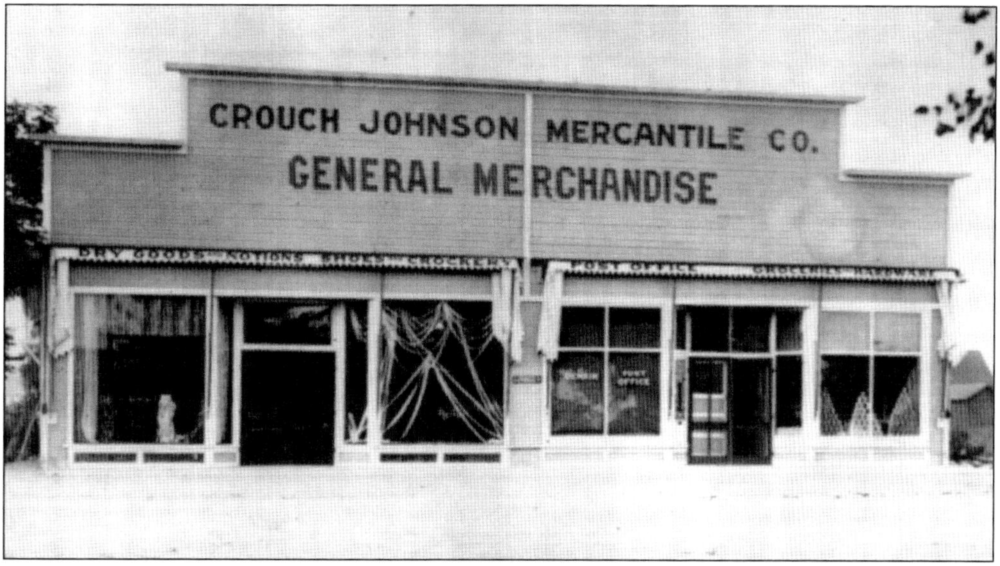

In 1908, the name changed again to Crouch Johnson Mercantile Company, when Norman Johnson, a cousin of the Crouches, came from Missouri and purchased Earl Crouch's portion of the business. That name remained until the business was closed in the early 1930s. (Courtesy of the Turlock Historical Society.)

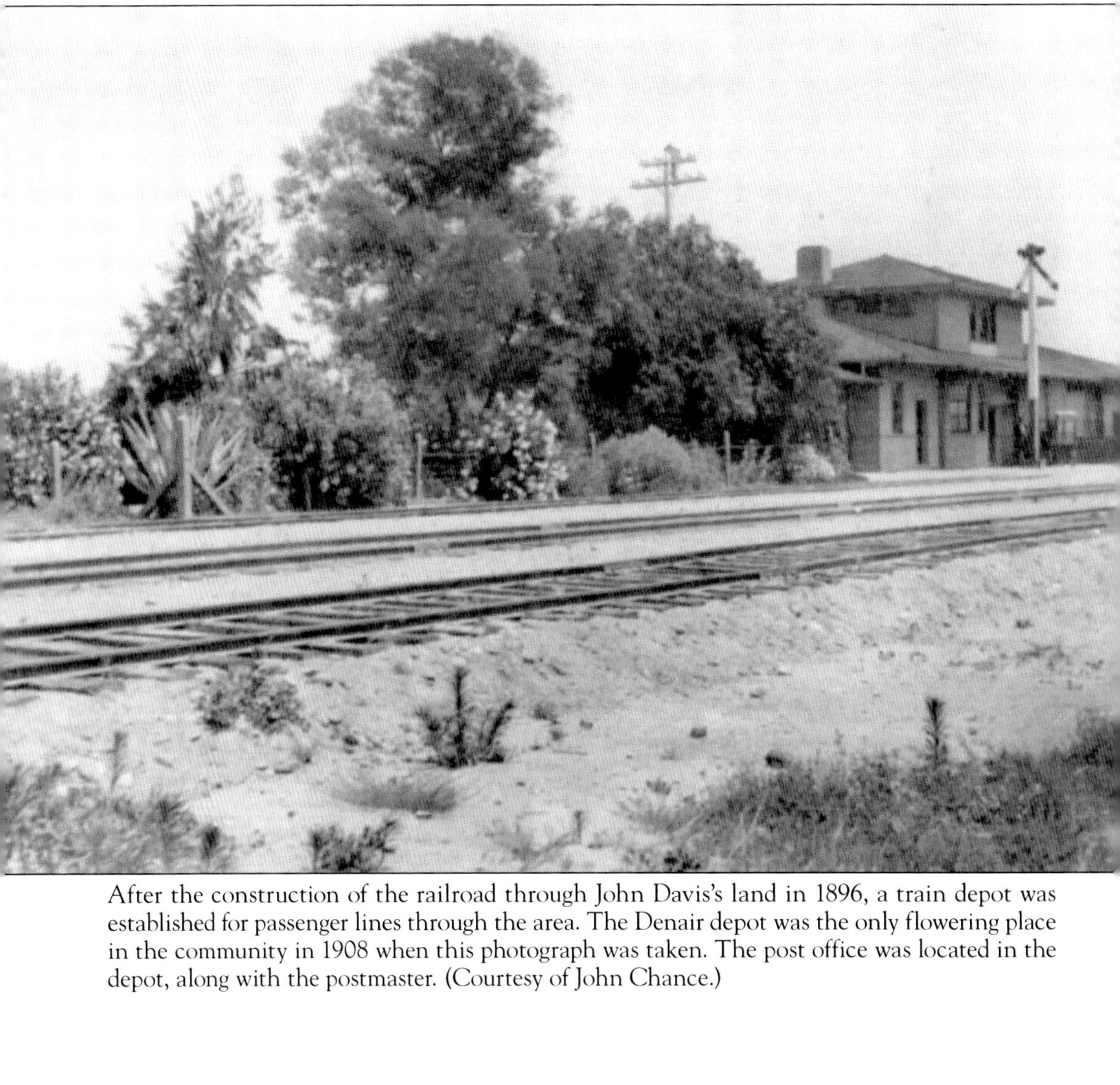

After the construction of the railroad through John Davis's land in 1896, a train depot was established for passenger lines through the area. The Denair depot was the only flowering place in the community in 1908 when this photograph was taken. The post office was located in the depot, along with the postmaster. (Courtesy of John Chance.)

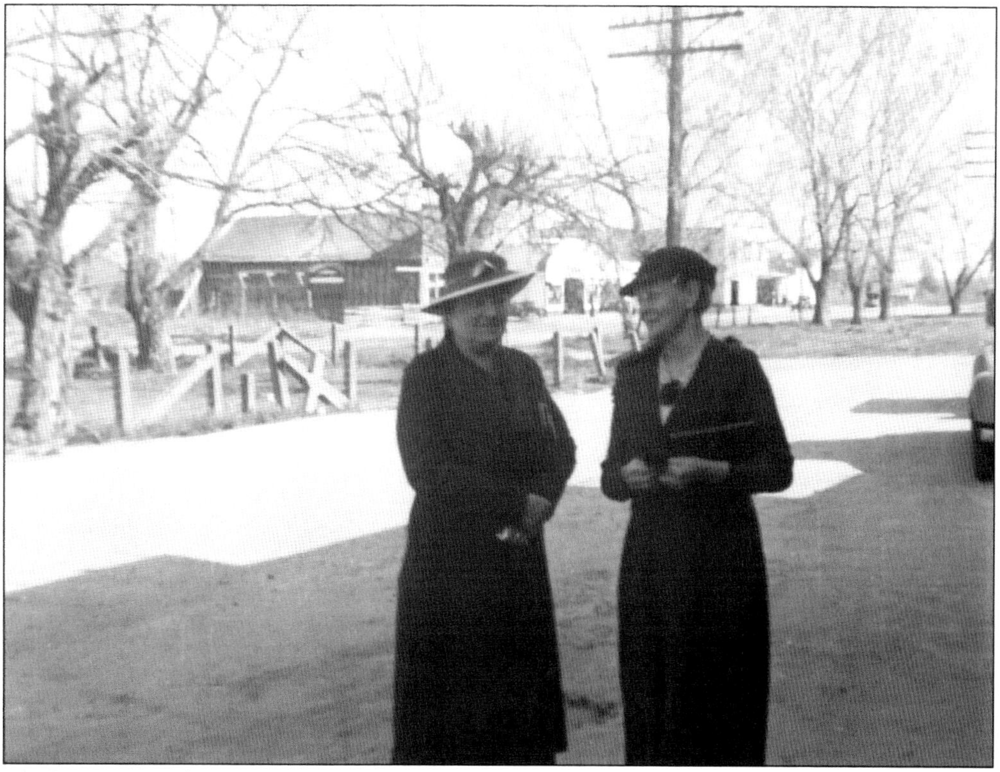

The Denair train depot was well used by local residents to drop off and/or collect relatives and friends traveling to and from the area. In the background of this photograph are several buildings along Santa Fe Avenue at Main Street, some of which still stand today. (Courtesy of John Chance.)

Not only was the railroad used for passenger trains, it was also more commonly used to ship fresh fruit, vegetables, nuts, grains, and other commodities out of the area. In the background of this photograph is what was known as the "Warehouse." This building served as the hub of shipment for many local crops for years until it burned down one foggy night in the late 1940s. (Courtesy of John Chance.)

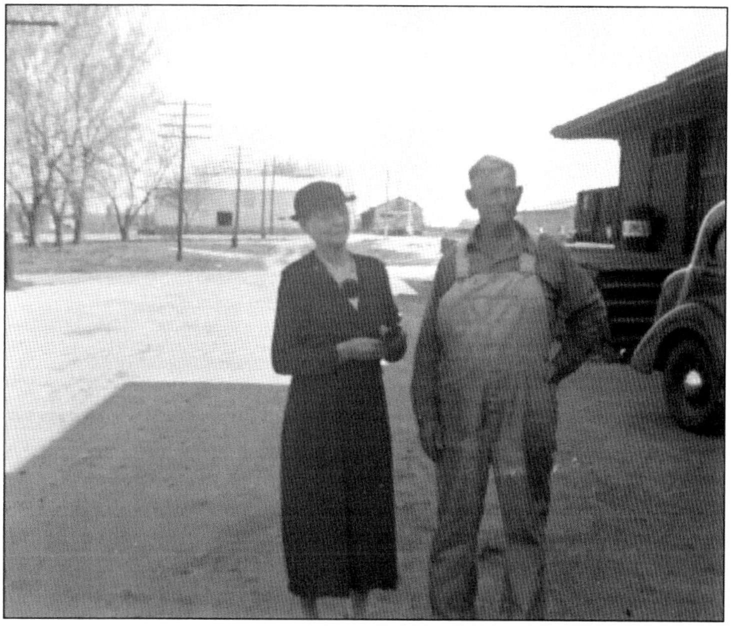

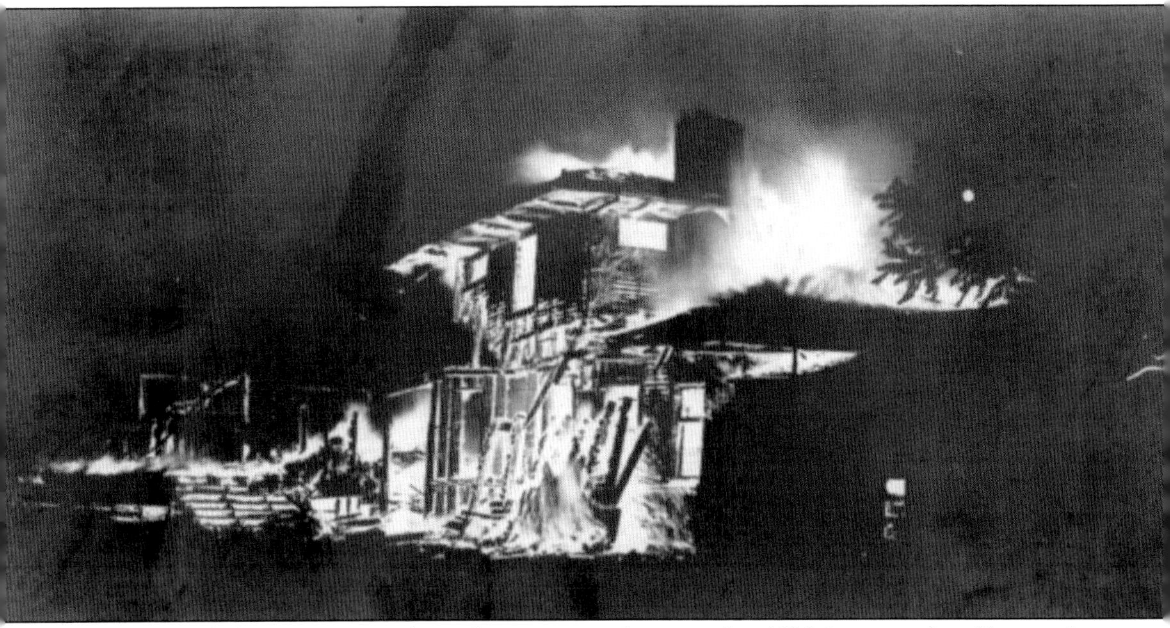

Fire struck the Denair train depot, burning it to the ground in 1928. It was replaced by another structure. (Courtesy of John Chance.)

Two

Farming, the Lifeblood of the Central Valley

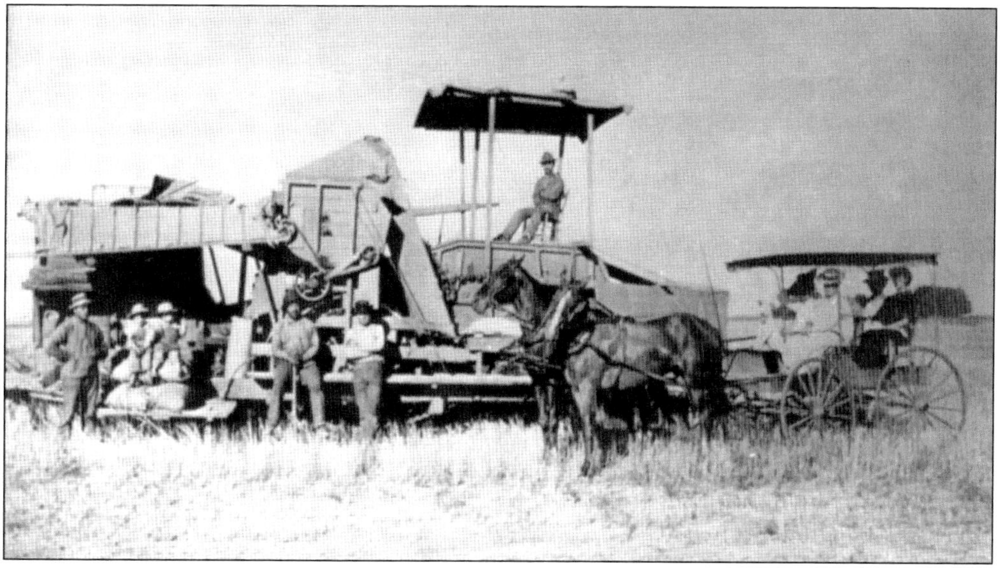

Prior to irrigation waters flowing through the valley, farmers in the area grew grains, barley, and wheat for the most part. Pictured here is one of the first power balers used in the area. Taken in 1909, this photograph shows, from left to right, Jim Roberts, Charles and George Sperry, Charles A. Sperry, an unidentified farmhand, and Ernest Coffinberry (the man in the cab); in the buggy are Mrs. Will Sperry and Lois Sperry (front) and Myra Sperry and Sadie Roberts (backseat). (Courtesy of Denair Community Service District.)

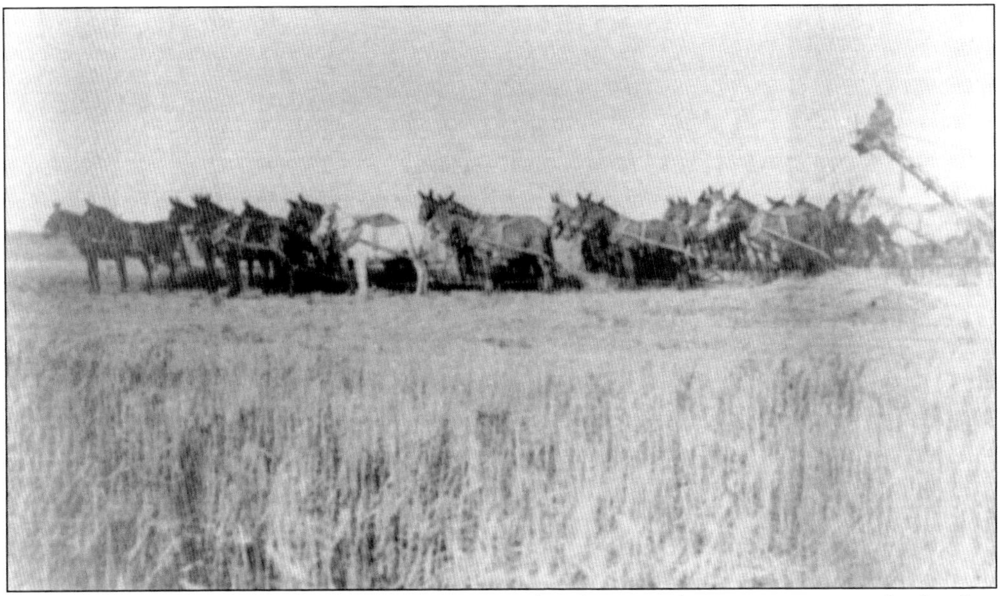

Pulled by teams of mules and horses, these giant threshing machines move across the land to harvest the grains. (Courtesy of Denair Community Service District.)

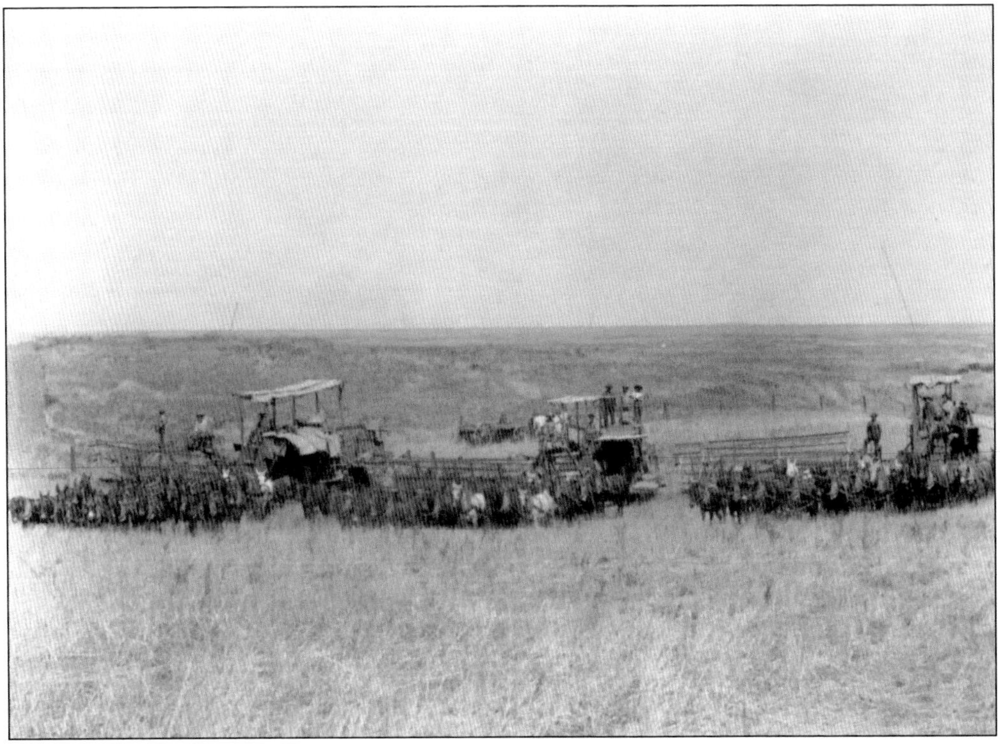

Landowners with large properties often had several crews to harvest the grain. Here, three combines are pictured, each with four to five men and a team of twenty horses and mules. (Courtesy of California State University, Stanislaus.)

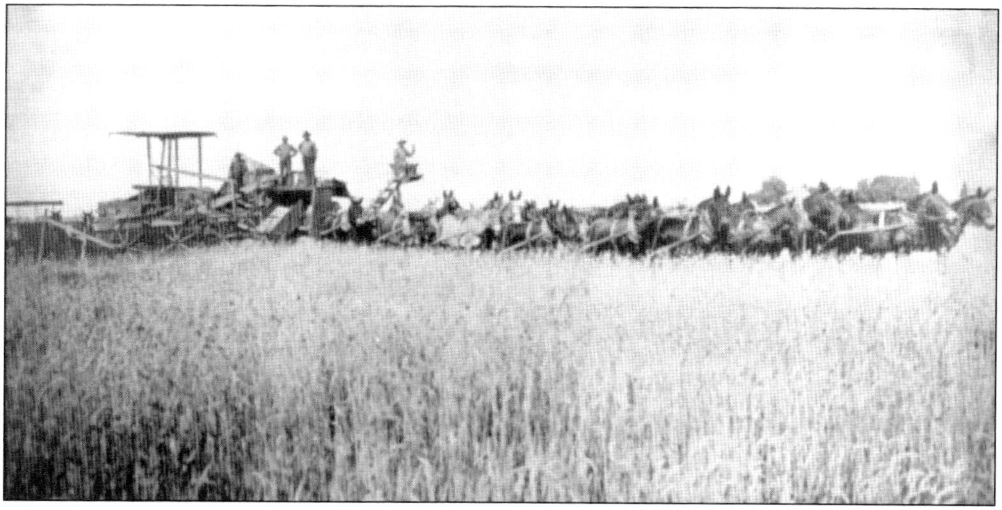

These large combines and teams harvested and gathered the grain in sacks before sending them off to the market. Pictured here is a combine harvester on the Sperry ranch, located northeast of Denair. (Courtesy of Denair Community Service District.)

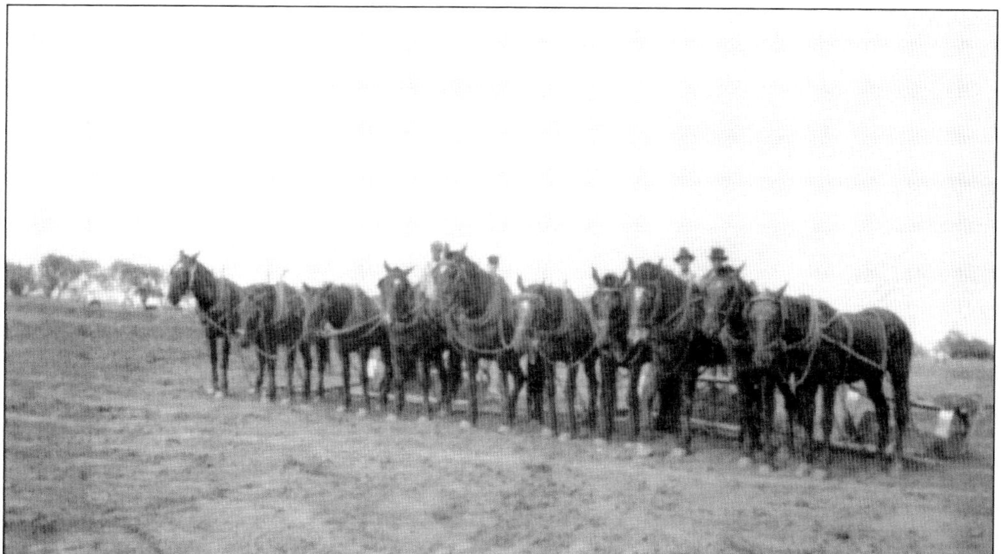

In this c. 1910 photograph, horses pull fresno scrapers. This is the equipment used to build the first canals in the area and level the land. (Courtesy of John Chance.)

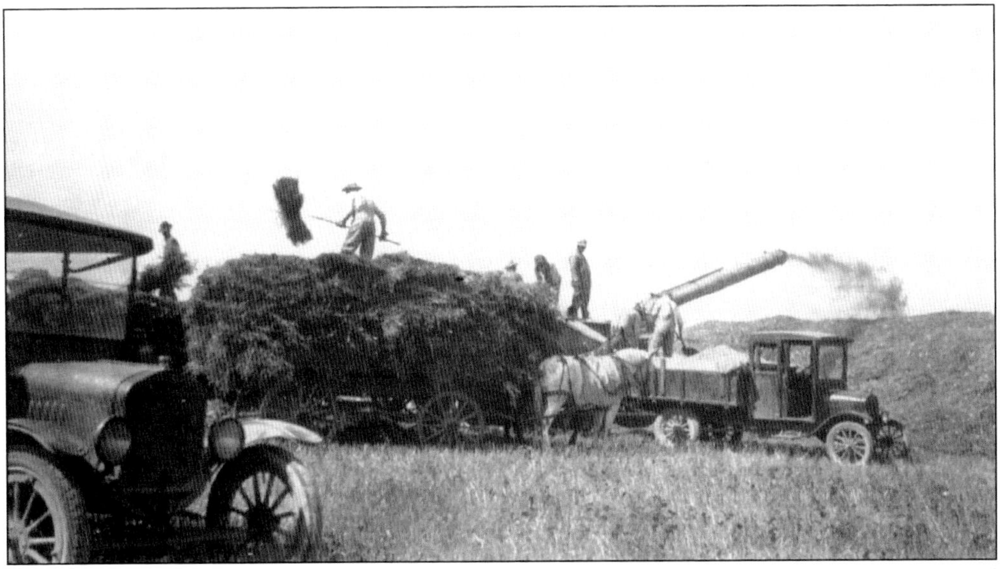

The early 20th century saw many people harvesting wheat or grains in the Denair area. Pictured here, a worker uses a pitchfork to load the harvester from a wagon. (Courtesy of John Chance.)

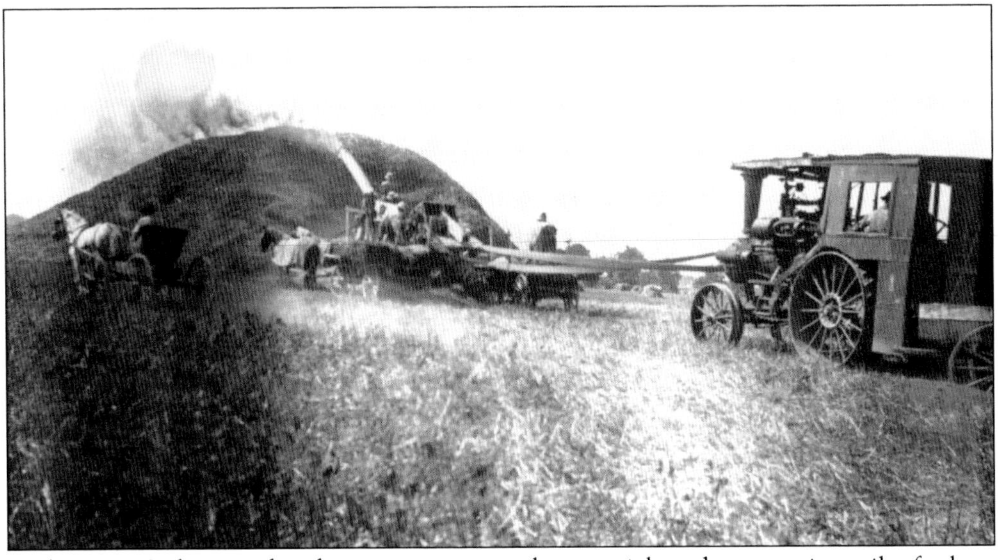

In this c. 1910 photograph, a harvester separates the materials and creates giant piles for later pickup. (Courtesy of John Chance.)

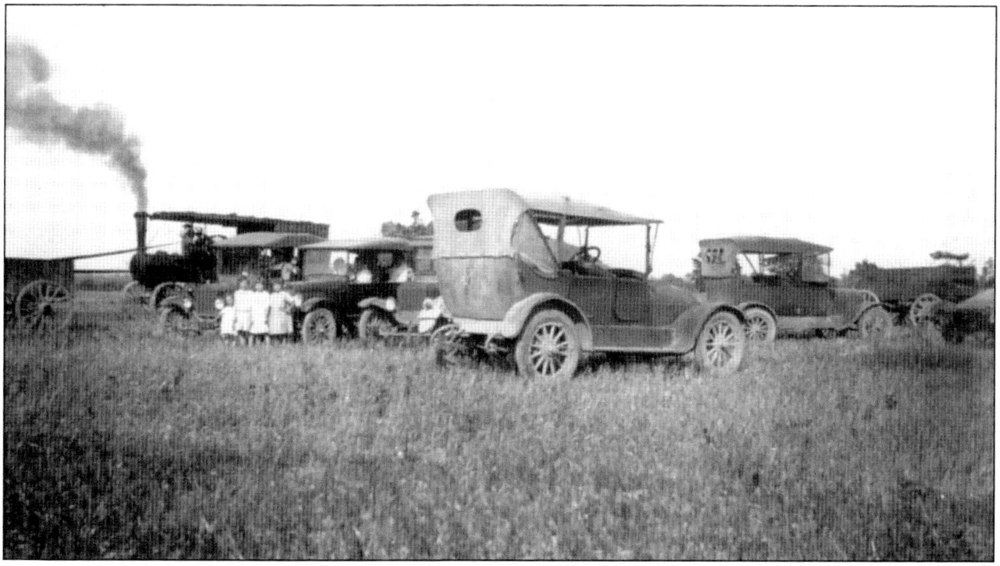

At lunchtime, the wives would bring food to the fields for the workers, often giving the children a chance to see what their fathers and brothers were doing. Notice the children posing in front of the car. This photograph was taken around 1910. (Courtesy of John Chance.)

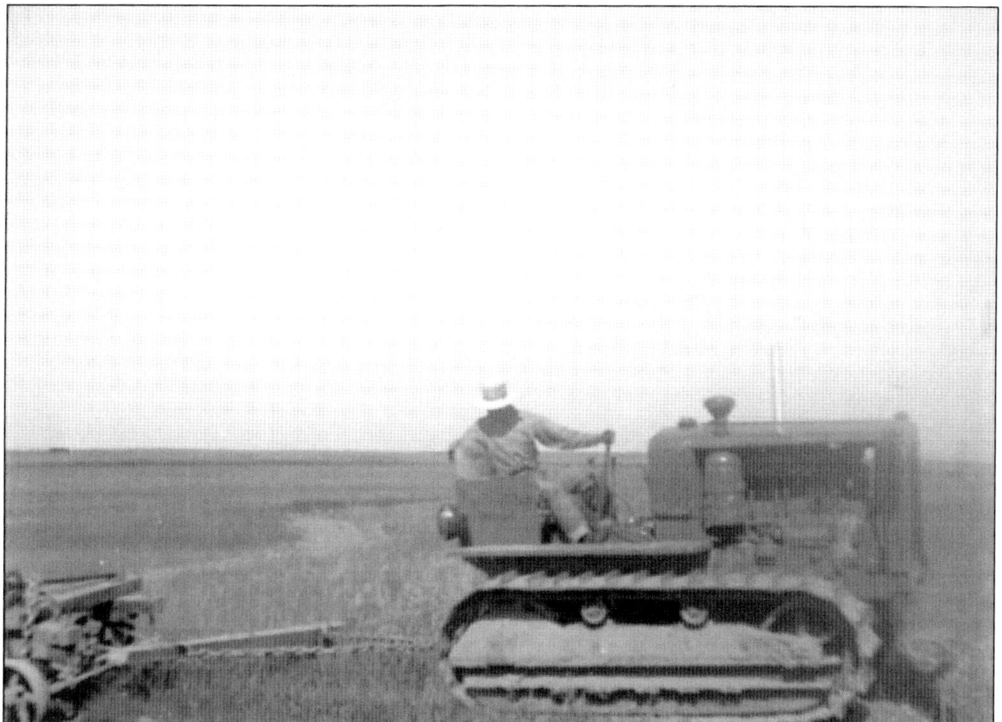

In this photograph, Oliver Chance works leased land near Montpelier. Chance was the son of John Robert Chance and Mabel Leona Wood. Born in New Providence, Iowa, on July 2, 1899, Chance lived in Denair most of his life, passing on June 25, 1963. (Courtesy of John Chance.)

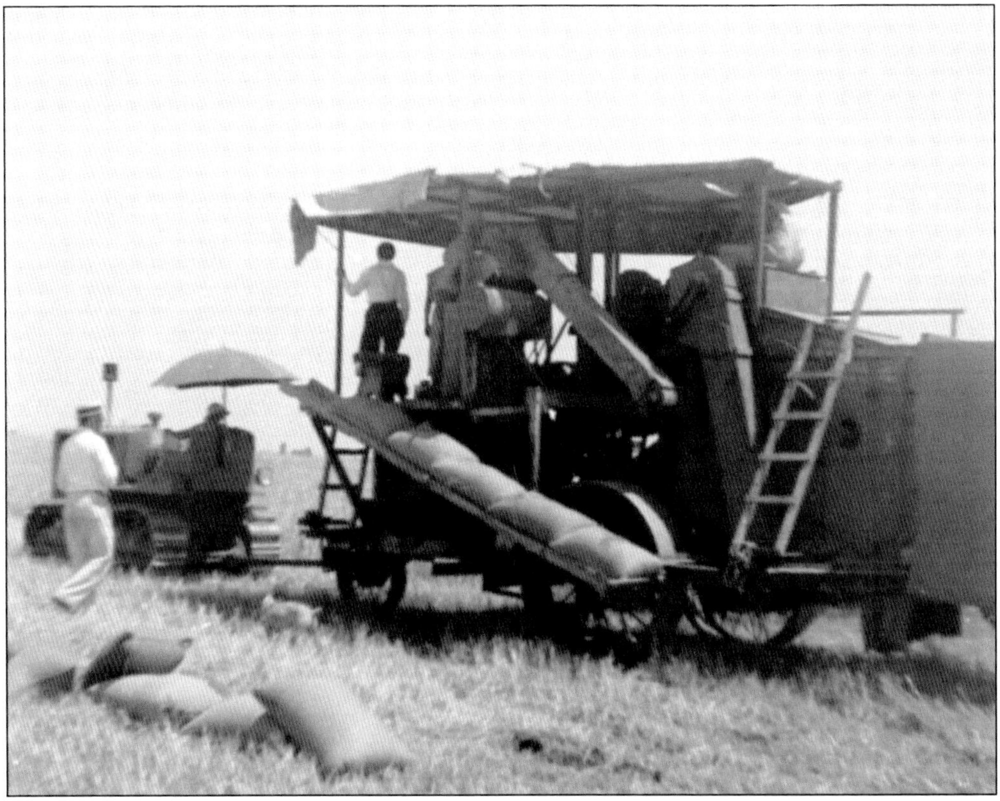

The harvesting of grain became more mechanized in the later years. In this c. 1930 photograph, grain sacks come off a conveyor after being filled on the harvester. (Courtesy of John Chance.)

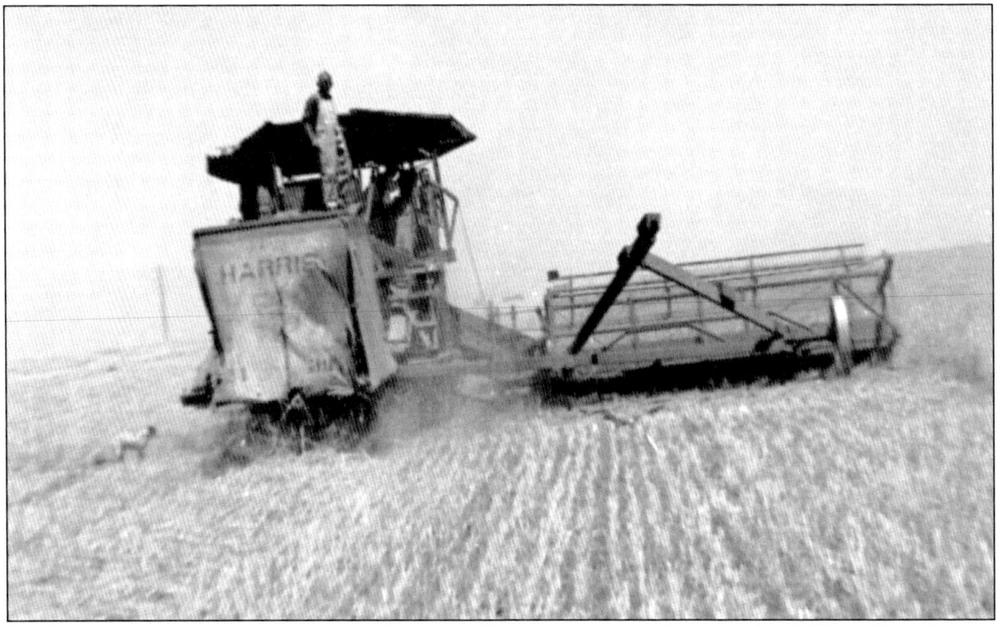

Eventually, no more horses were needed to pull the harvesters through the fields. John Chance Sr. rides atop a harvester, watching the progress. (Courtesy of John Chance.)

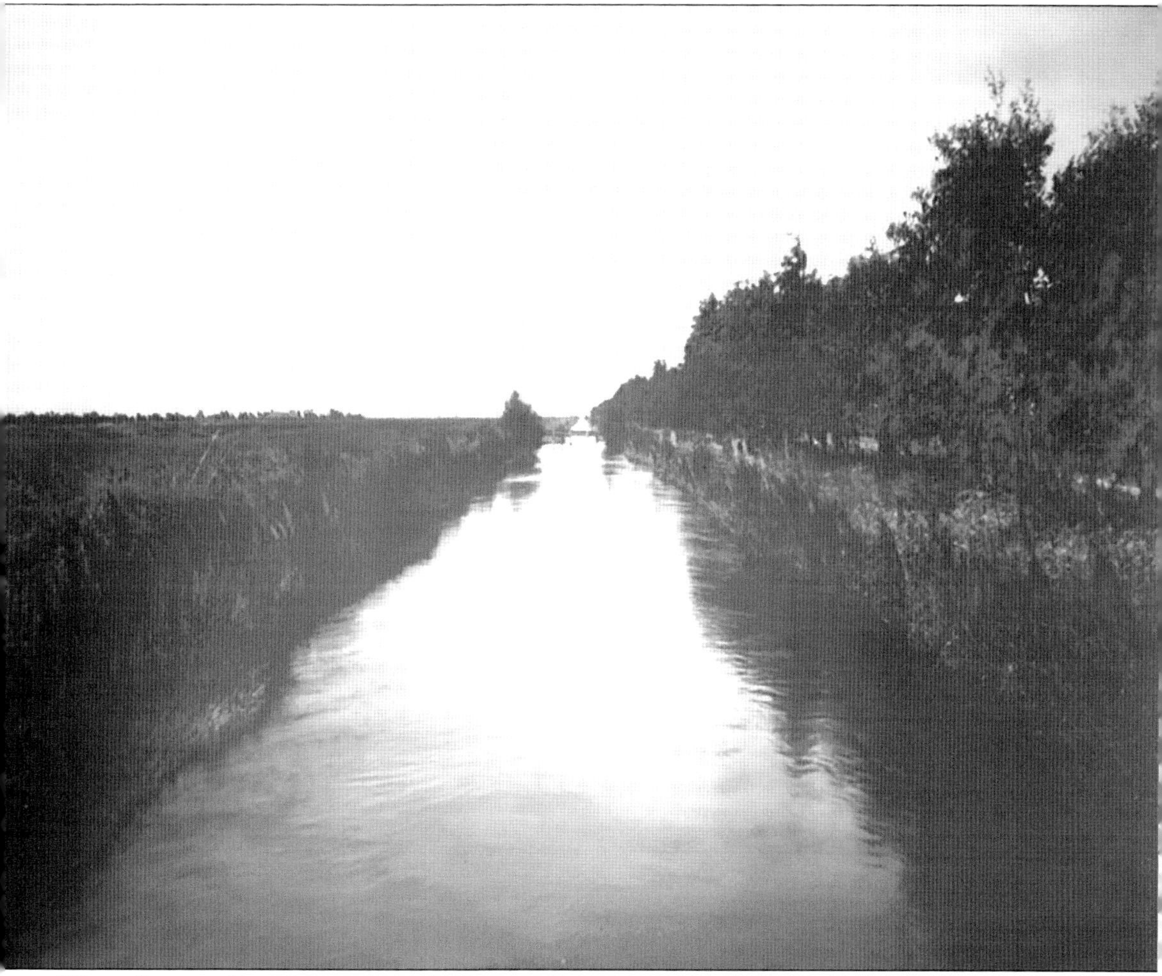

Water flowing through canals in the area meant easier access to water. Other crops such as alfalfa, grapes, and melons and orchards of almonds and fruits soon replaced the vast fields of wheat and barley. This is an early photograph of a canal in the Denair/Turlock area. (Courtesy of John Chance.)

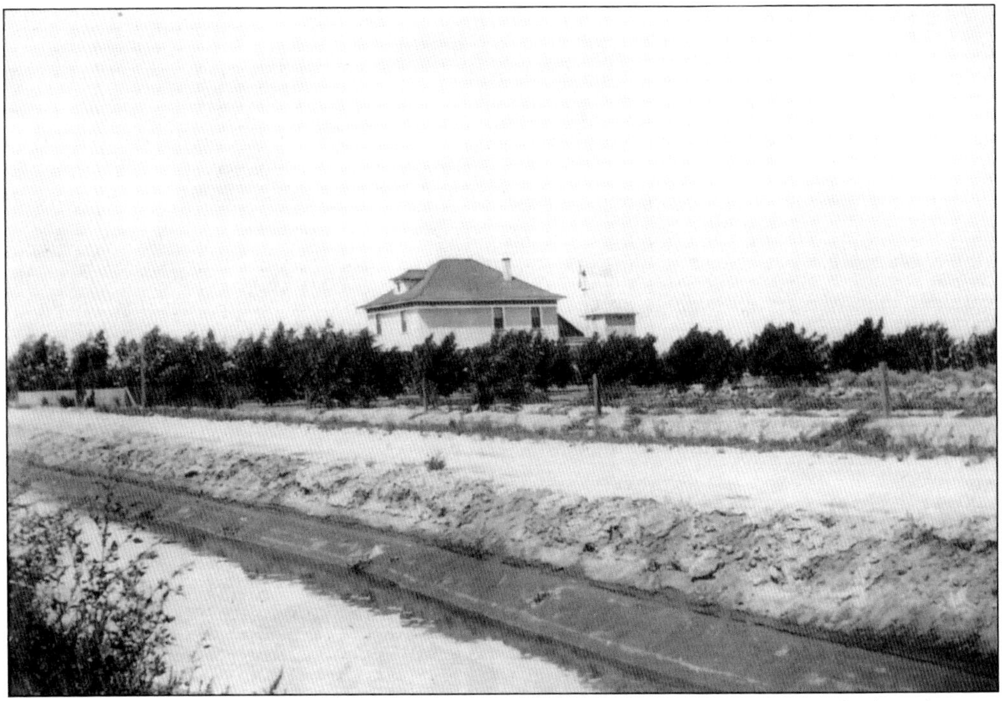

Canals full of water started flowing beside streets and fields. Pictured here is a new ditch with water flowing in front of the Witmer home along Sperry Road. (Courtesy of the Witmer family.)

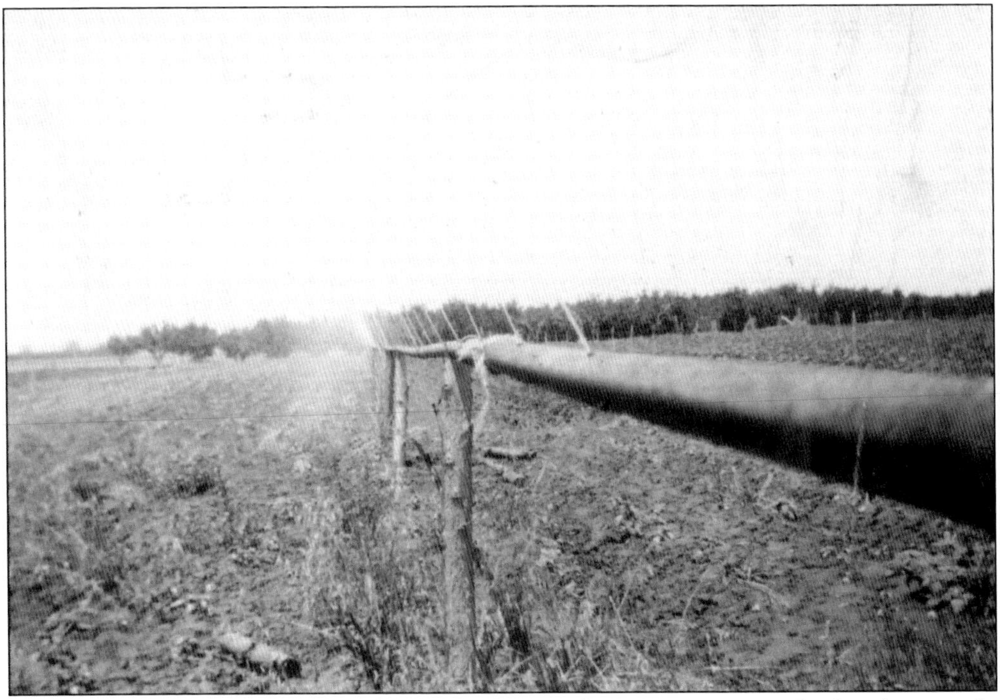

Irrigation waters meant different and innovative ways to bring water to crops. In this photograph, water flows and sprays crops through an improvised sprinkler system. (Courtesy of Alma Jean Mills Coleman.)

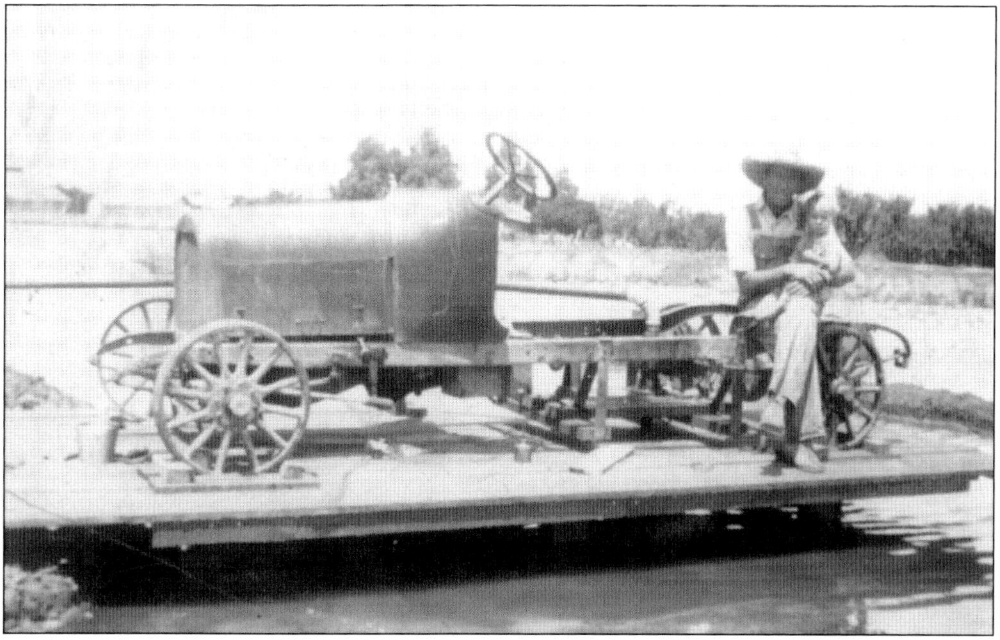

Mechanical means were often used to pump water from canals into ditches and fields. Bill Mills sits with his son Bill on an improvised water pumping station near their home on Downy Road. (Courtesy of Alma Jean Mills Coleman.)

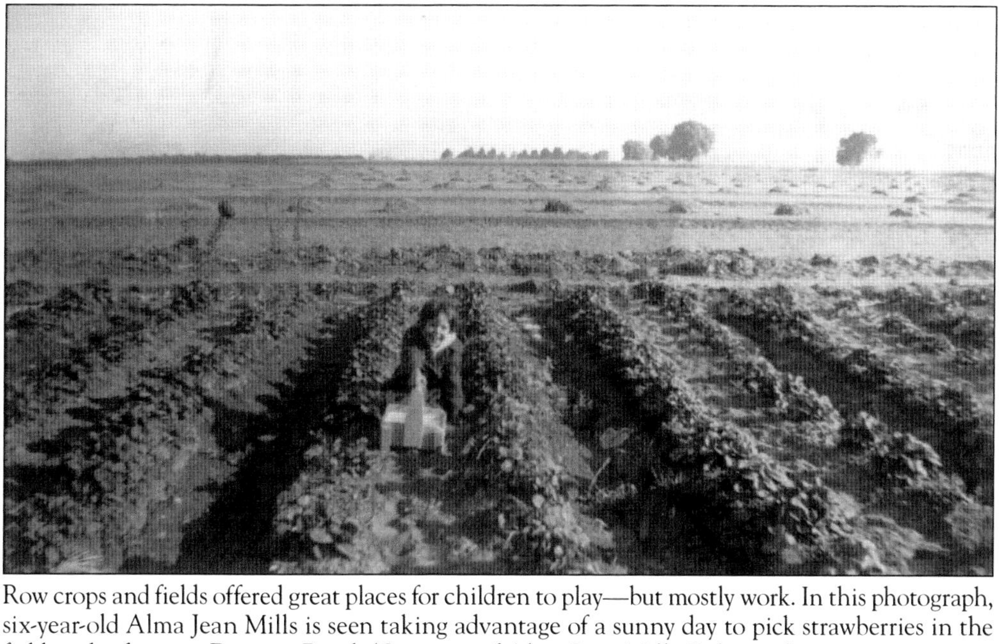

Row crops and fields offered great places for children to play—but mostly work. In this photograph, six-year-old Alma Jean Mills is seen taking advantage of a sunny day to pick strawberries in the field at the farm on Downey Road. (Courtesy of Alma Jean Mills Coleman.)

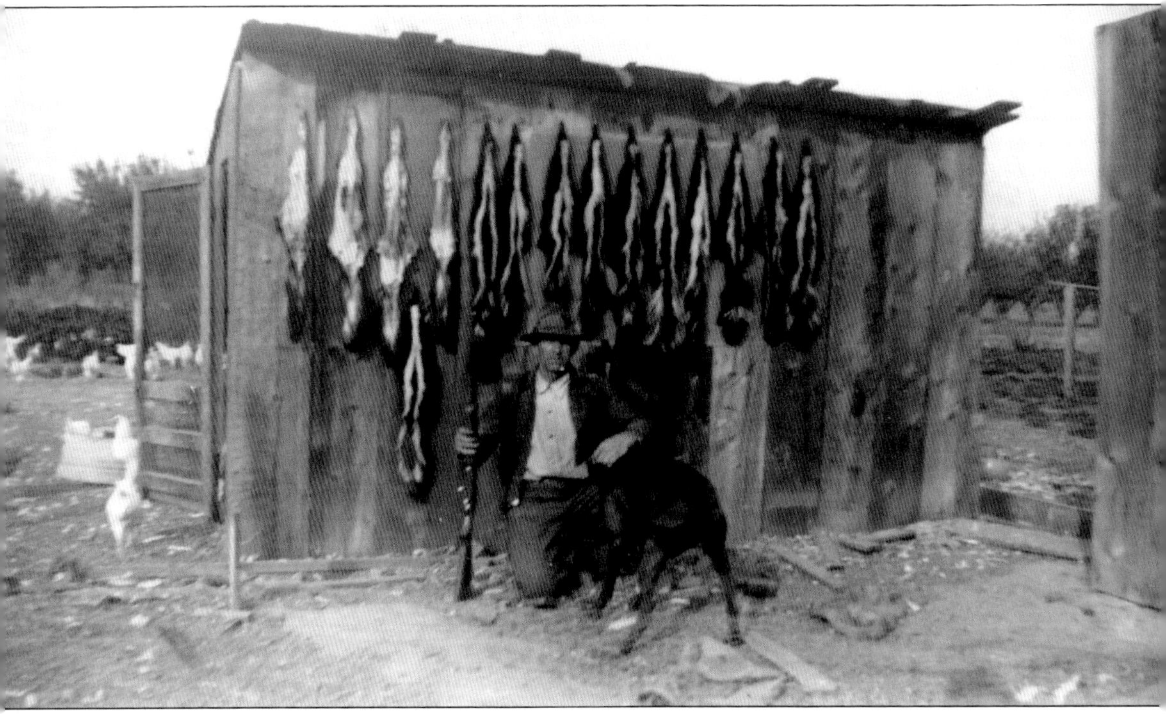

Milo Steeley and dog Mickey show off their falltime harvest of skunks from the Denair area. Hunting under culverts at sunrise was the best time to catch the stinky critters. (Courtesy of Alma Jean Mills Coleman.)

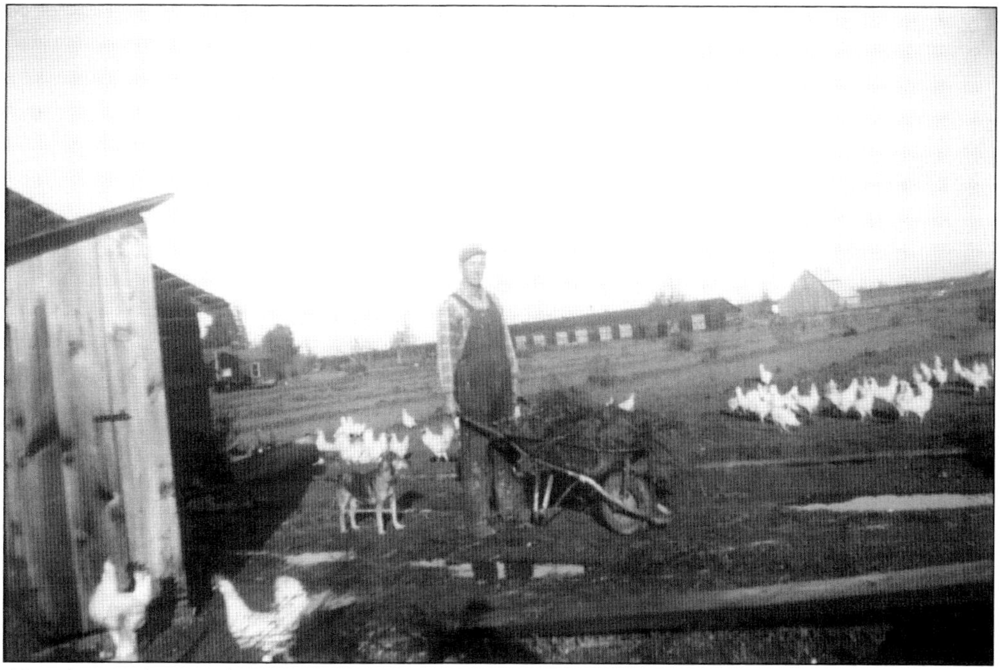

Abundance of water also meant more livestock and, of course, chickens for eggs, food, and income. Here, William "Bill" Mills tends to his flock of hens. Eggs gathered were sold in Denair. (Courtesy of Alma Jean Mills Coleman.)

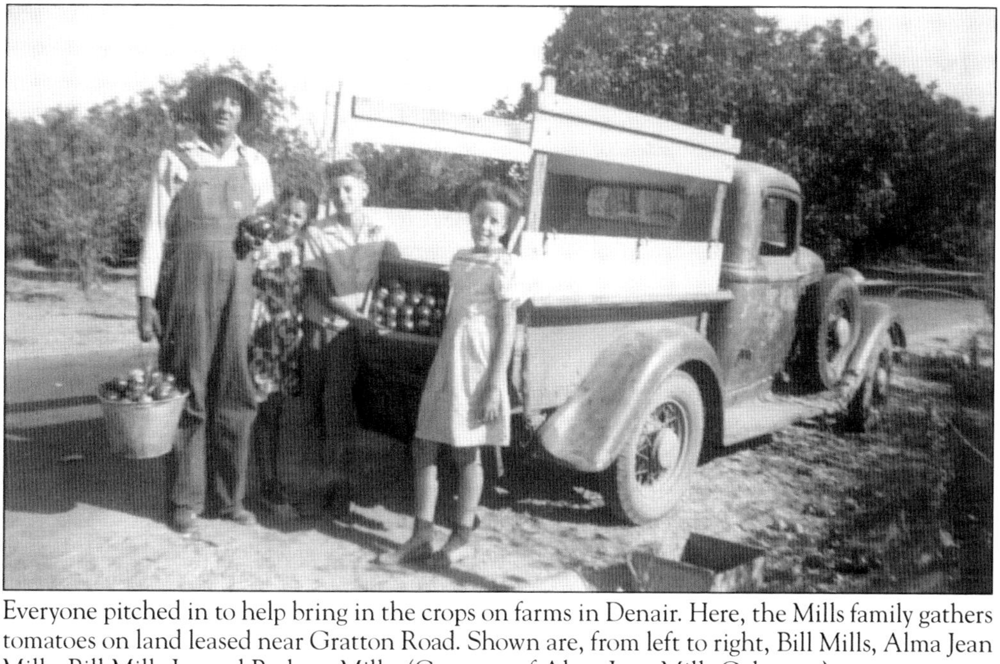

Everyone pitched in to help bring in the crops on farms in Denair. Here, the Mills family gathers tomatoes on land leased near Gratton Road. Shown are, from left to right, Bill Mills, Alma Jean Mills, Bill Mills Jr., and Barbara Mills. (Courtesy of Alma Jean Mills Coleman.)

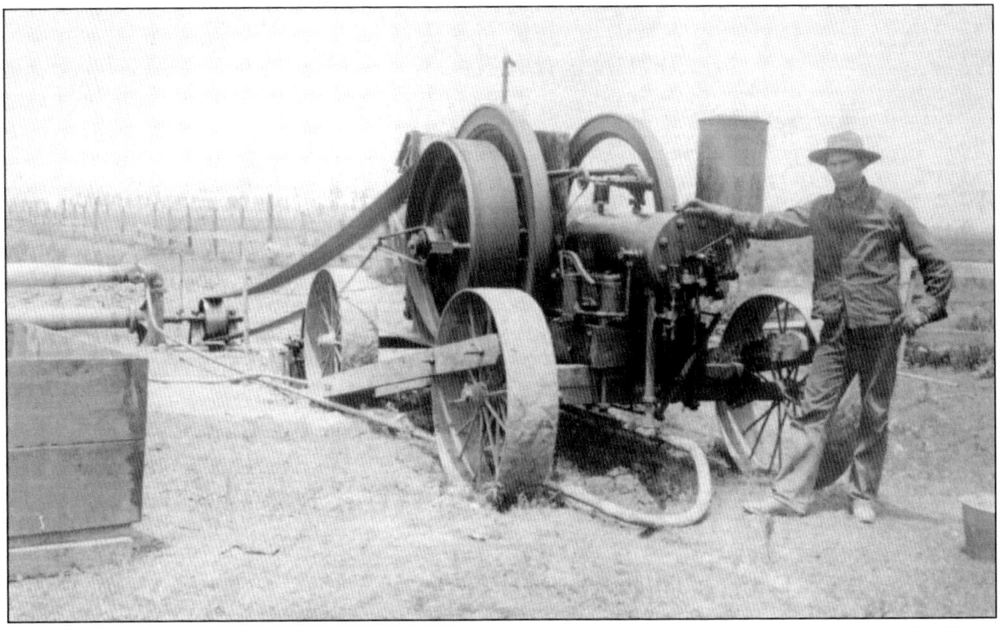

As time progressed, the innovative ways to pump water from canals progressed as well. Here, George Lambert stands beside his pumping machine. (Courtesy of Cheryl Cline.)

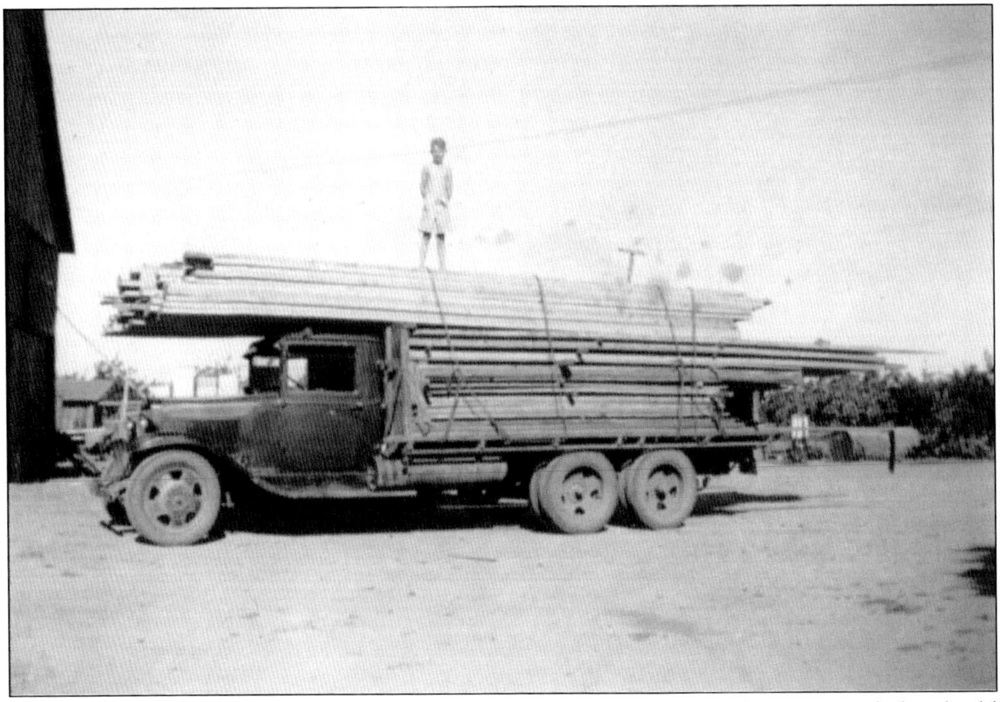

Of course, farming crops was not the only industry in the area. Lumber was needed to build homes and barns. The Snider Lumber Company was established in the late 1930s on Keyes Road, providing the local residents with lumber and supplies for over 20 years until the family moved the operation to Turlock. In this image, Paul Snider stands on top of a loaded truck ready for delivery. (Courtesy of Cheryl Cline.)

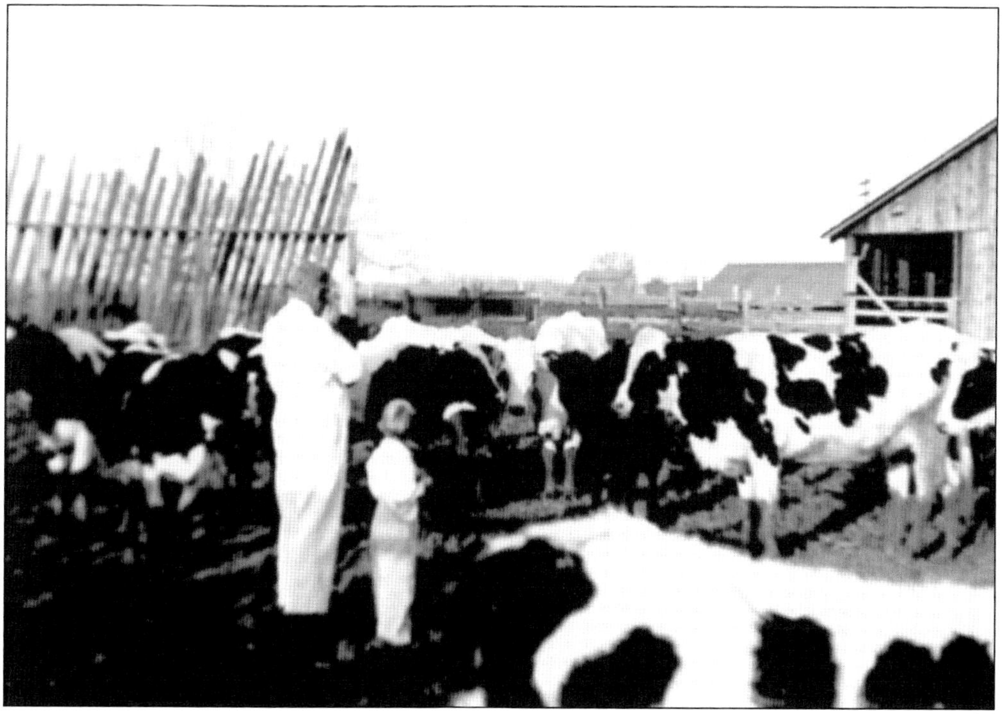

Water also meant farmers could raise livestock for food. Here, John Chance and son John Jr. tend to Holstein cows on the farm. (Courtesy of John Chance.)

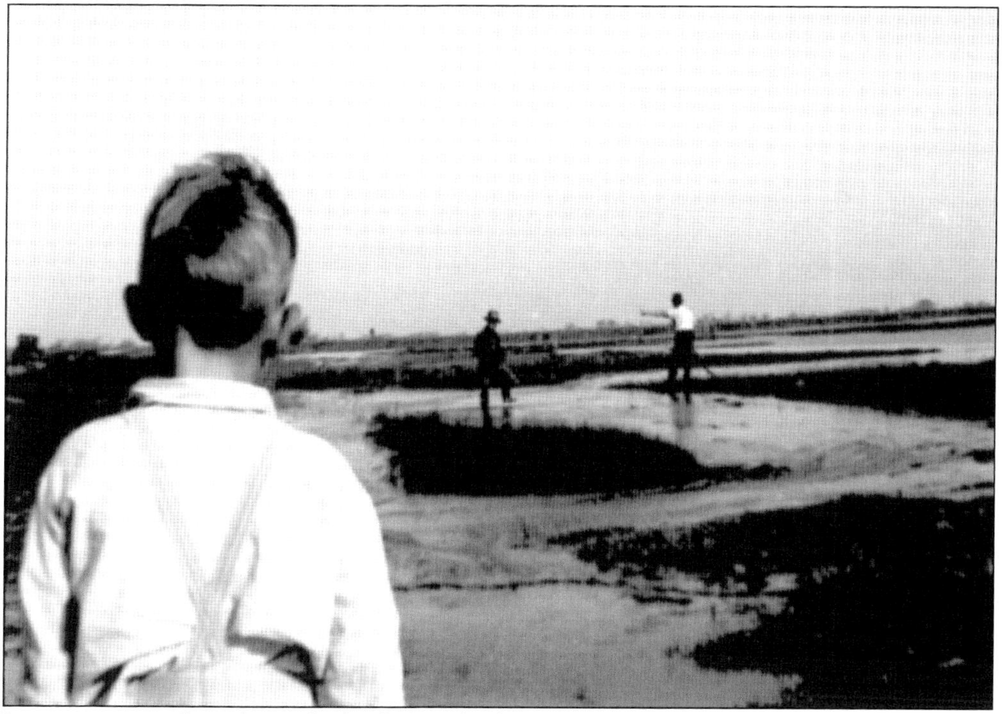

Irrigation waters flowed over the land, though often not where they were intended to go. Pictured is John Chance Jr. as he watches workers direct water in the field. (Courtesy of John Chance.)

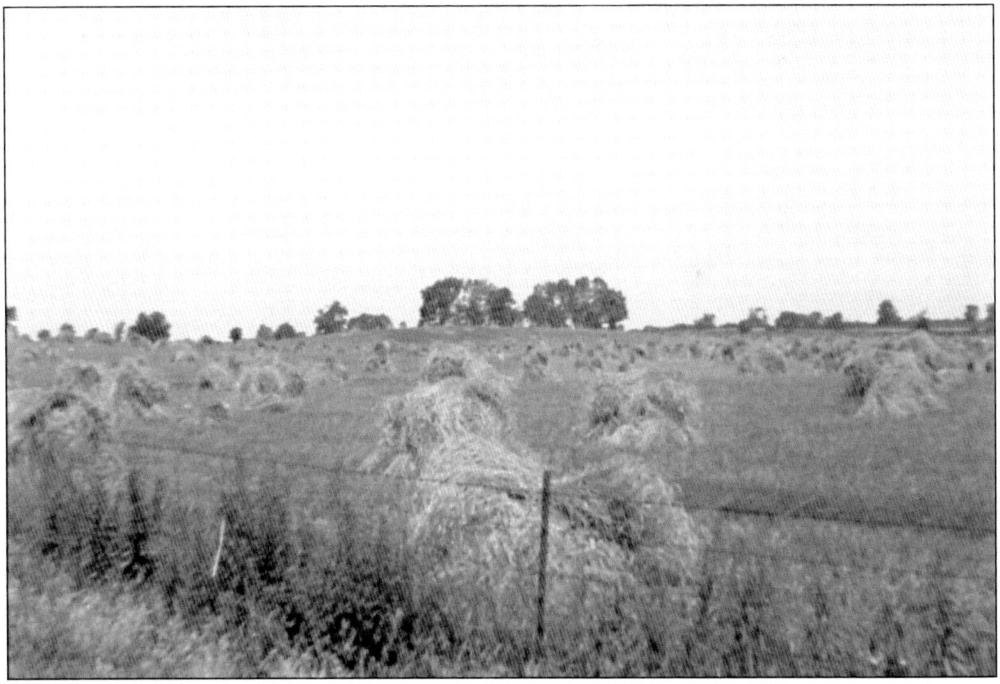

Bountiful harvests of hay were produced to feed the livestock. Farming in those days was difficult at best. Having a good team of mules to help out made life just a little easier. Below, John Chance and John Chance Jr. use a fresno scraper to level the land while pulled by their trusty mule team. (Both, courtesy of John Chance.)

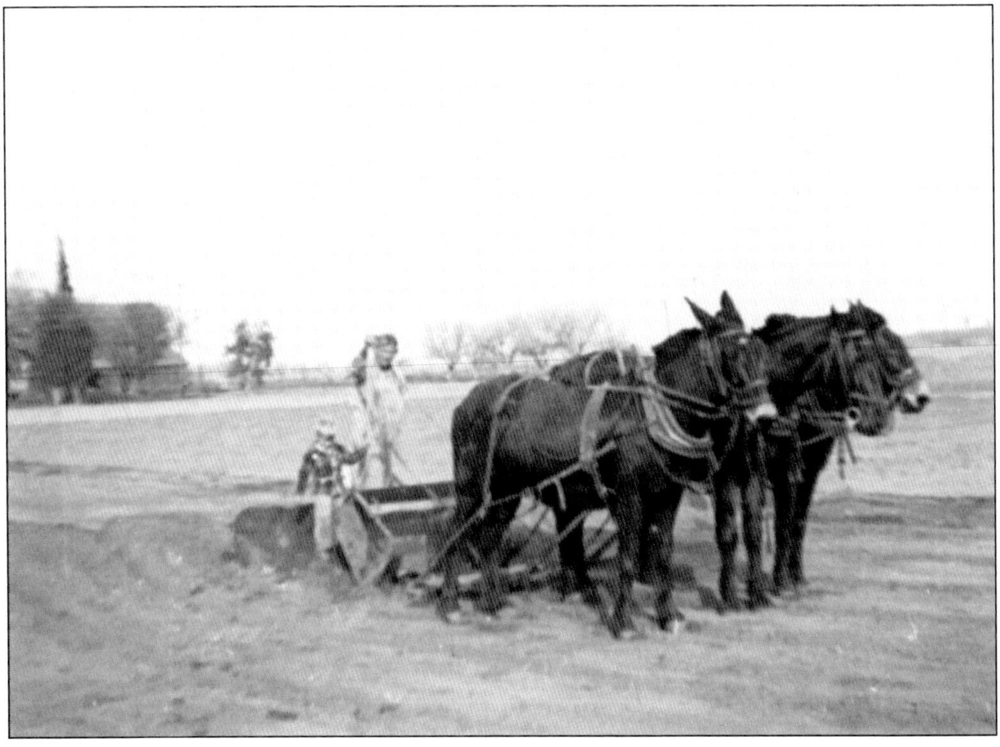

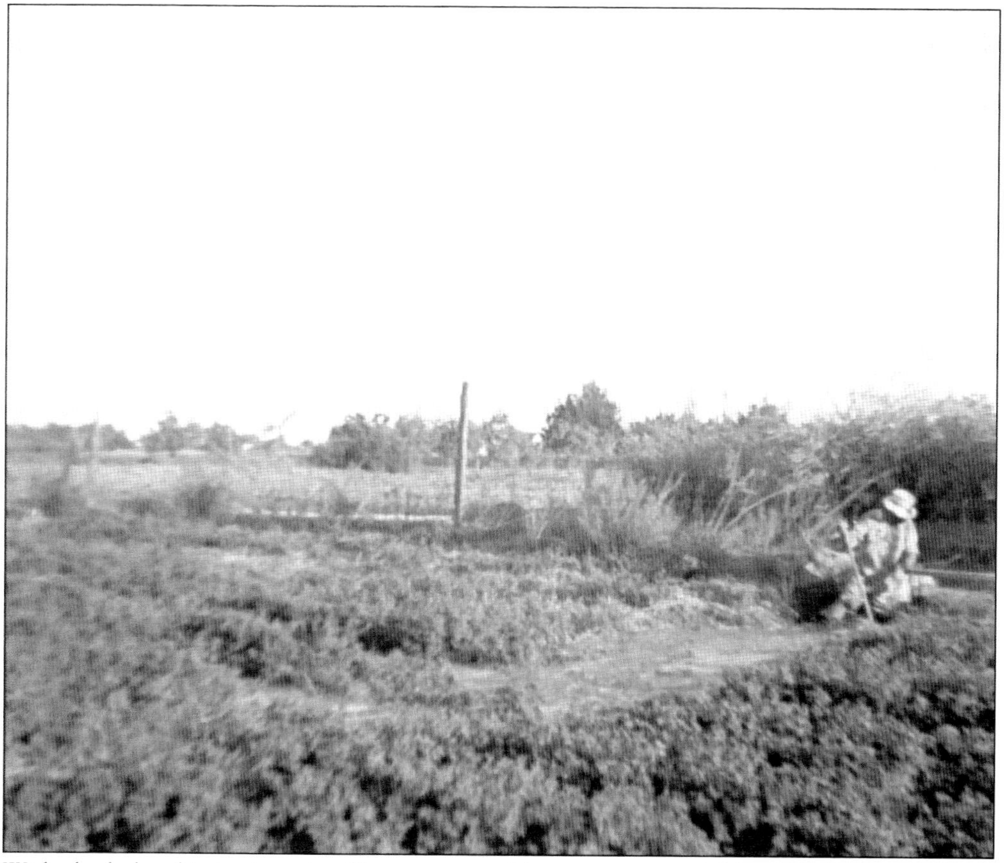

With the help of irrigation, the Chances were able to grow great fields of alfalfa. (Courtesy of John Chance.)

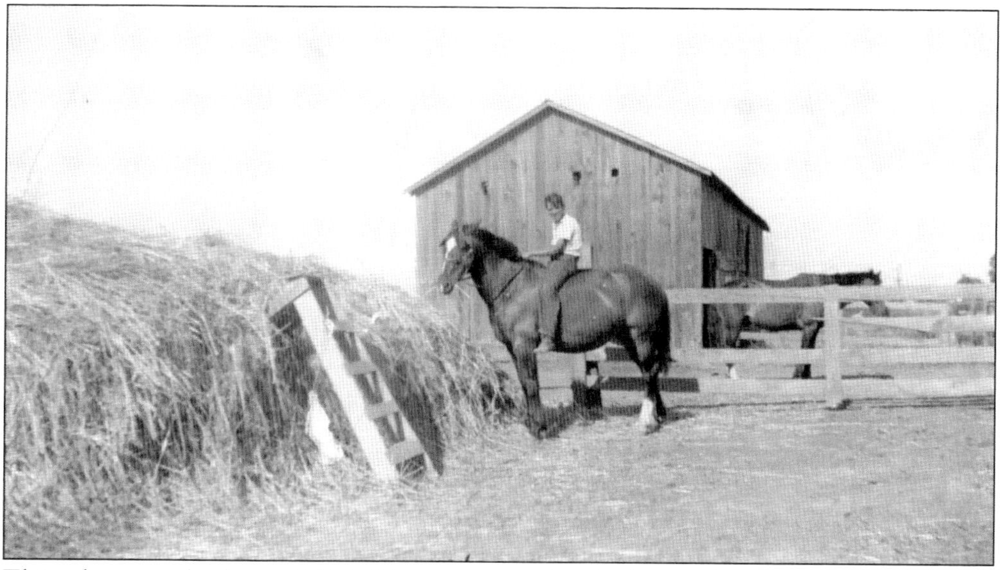

This photograph shows Bill Mills Jr. atop a family horse. (Courtesy of Alma Jean Mills Coleman.)

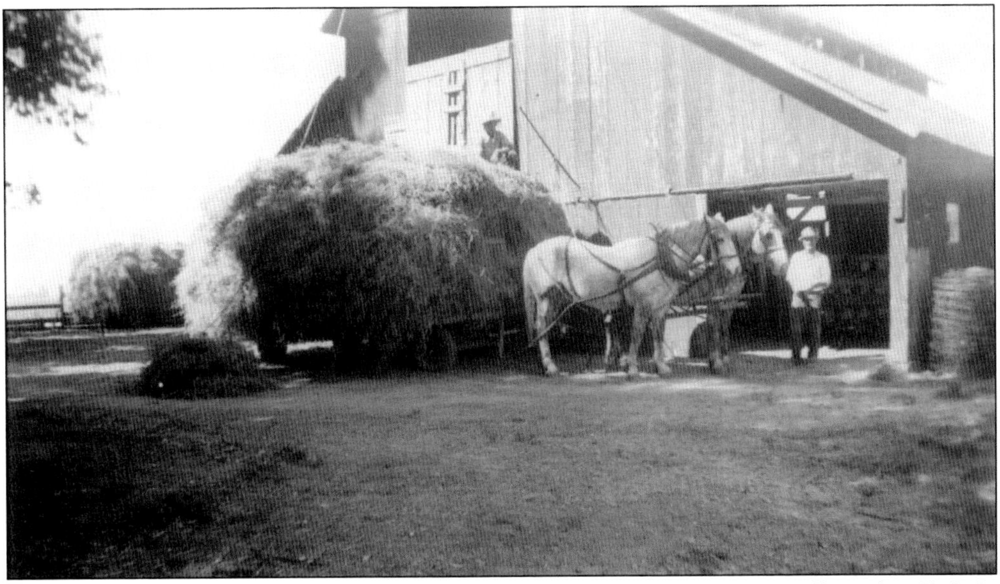

Horses made hauling any crops from the fields easier. In this image, horses Belle and Nelle help Lester Domecq and Alva Haile haul hay in 1942. (Courtesy of Louis Domecq.)

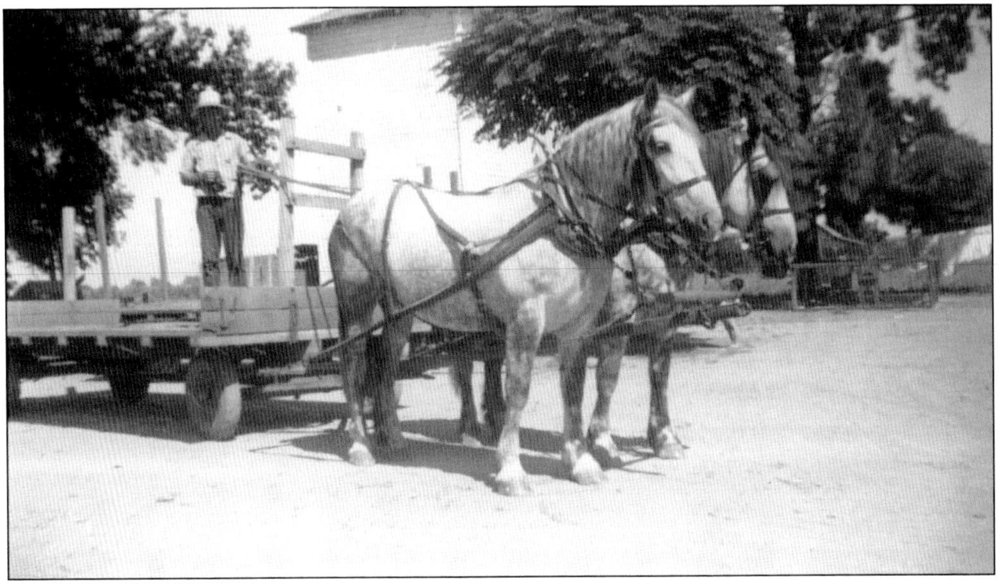

Belle and Nelle helped on the Domecq farm for many years, until tractors and other machines took their place. (Courtesy of Louis Domecq.)

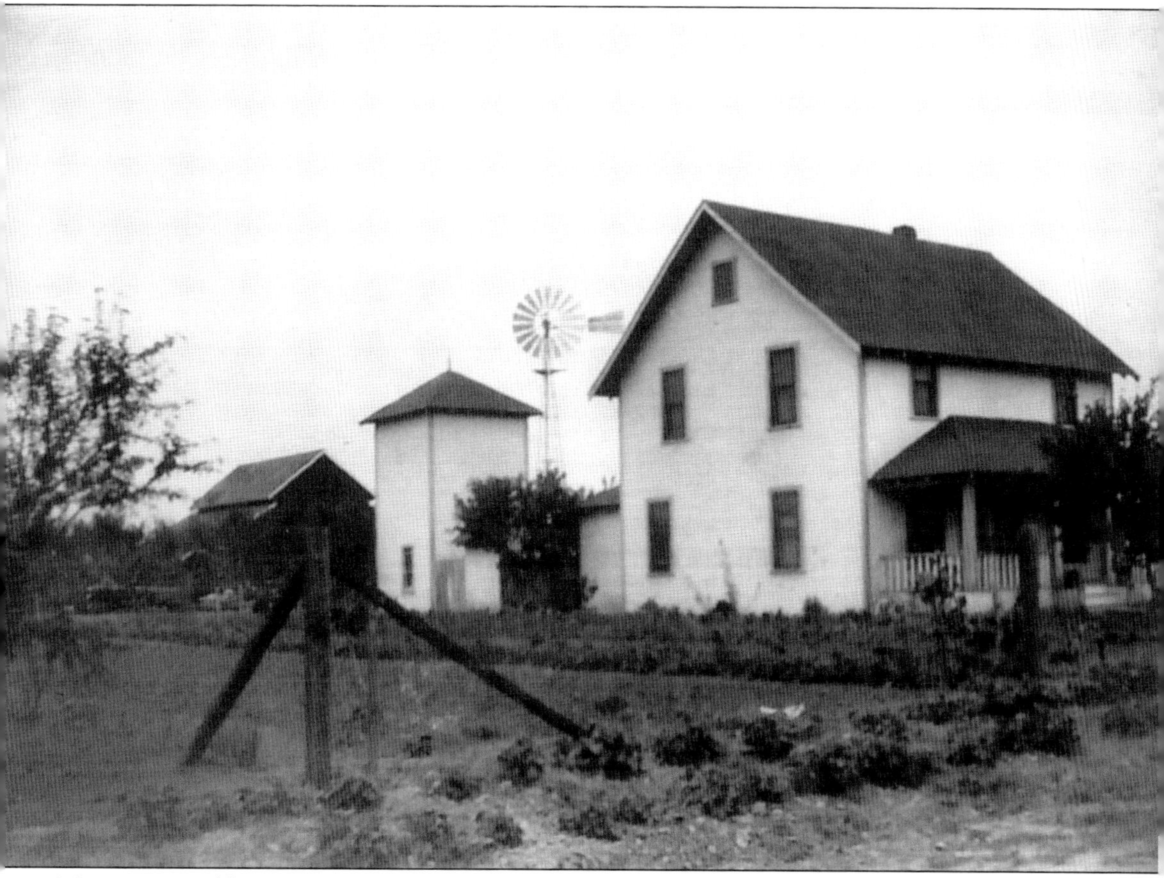

More crops and livestock meant farmers needed a way to keep their property safe and predators out. Fences started dotting the landscape to protect the farms investment. Shown here is the Witmer home, located along Sperry Road. (Courtesy of the Witmer family.)

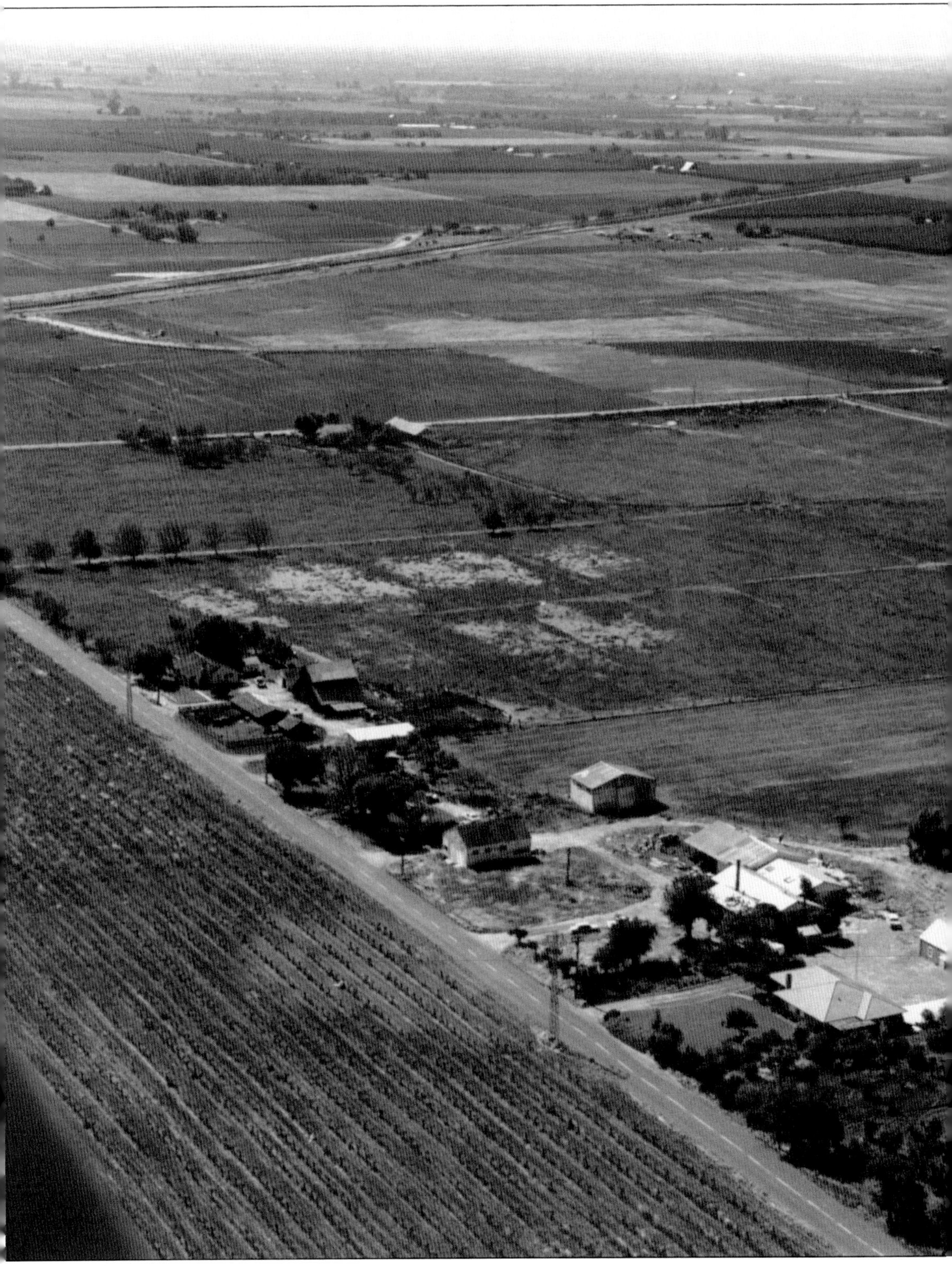

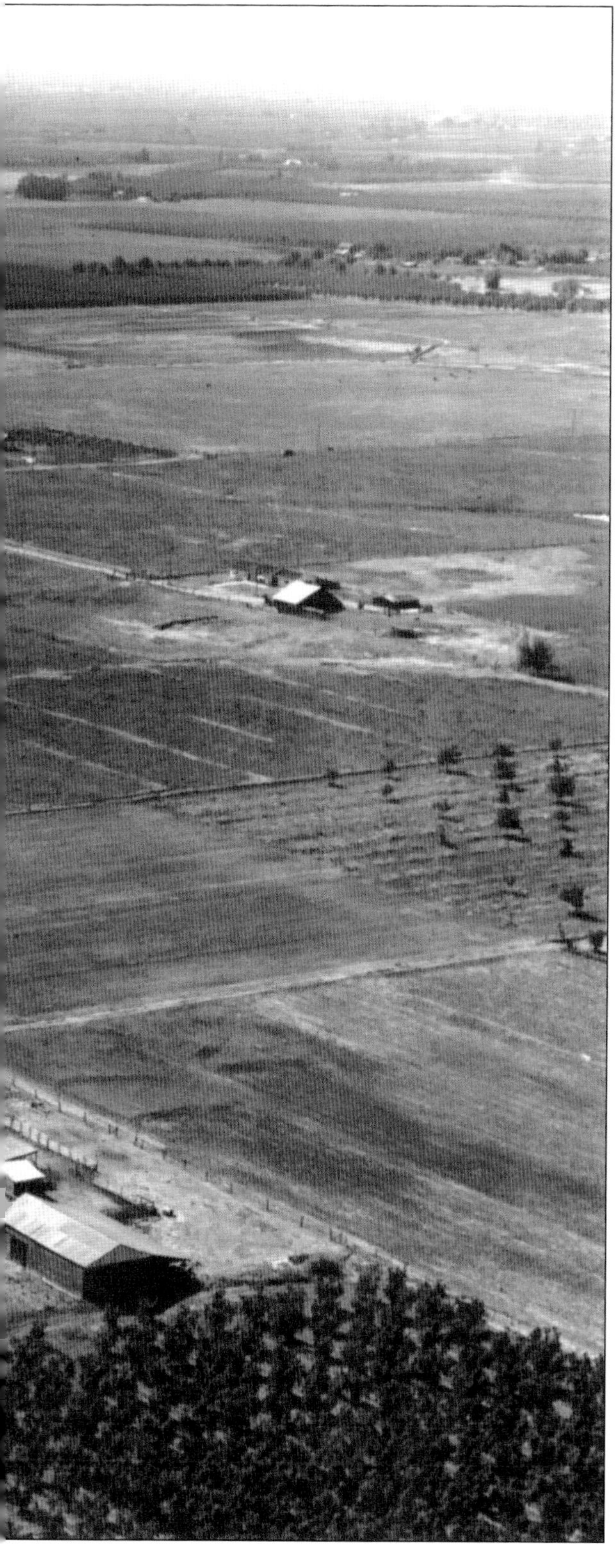

As time progressed, the number of farms grew, making the checkerboard pattern of land as seen in this 1965 aerial view of the Snider ranch on Keyes Road. (Courtesy of Cheryl Cline.)

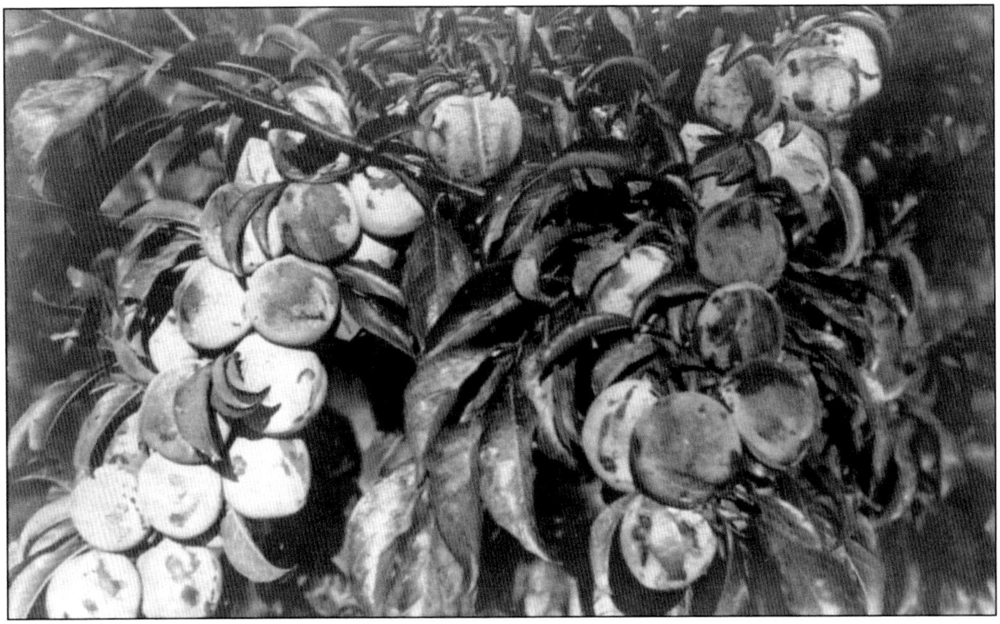

This is a great example of early orchard crops grown in the Denair area. In this photograph, taken by Harry Hollingsworth in 1911, one can see the abundance of Satsuma plums on the tree. (Courtesy of John Chance.)

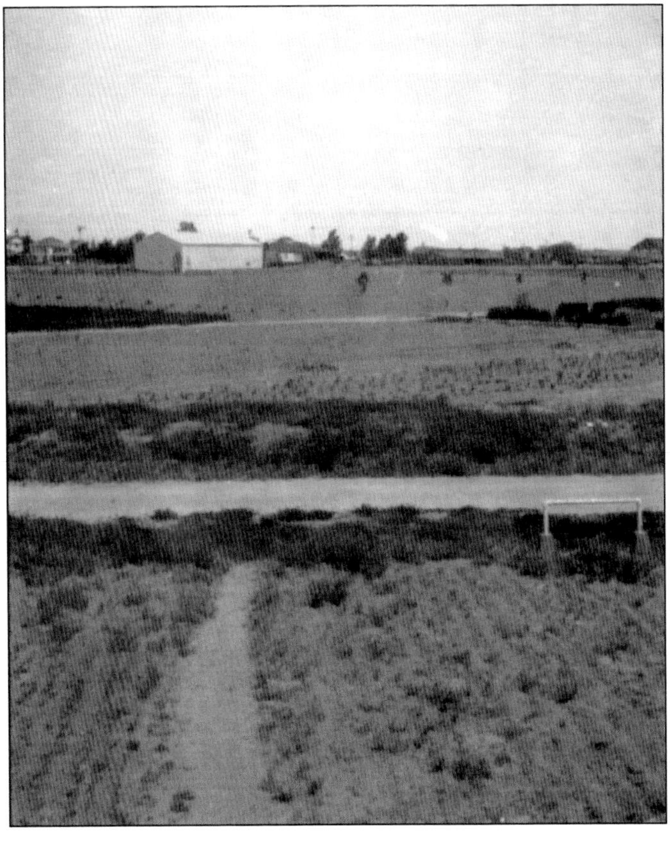

The face of the Denair area has changed much over the years. This view looking east was captured from the Hollingsworth home on Lester Road. The view today is very different, with homes on the opposite side of Lester Road and the Denair Schools behind that. (Courtesy of John Chance.)

Three

Denair Schools

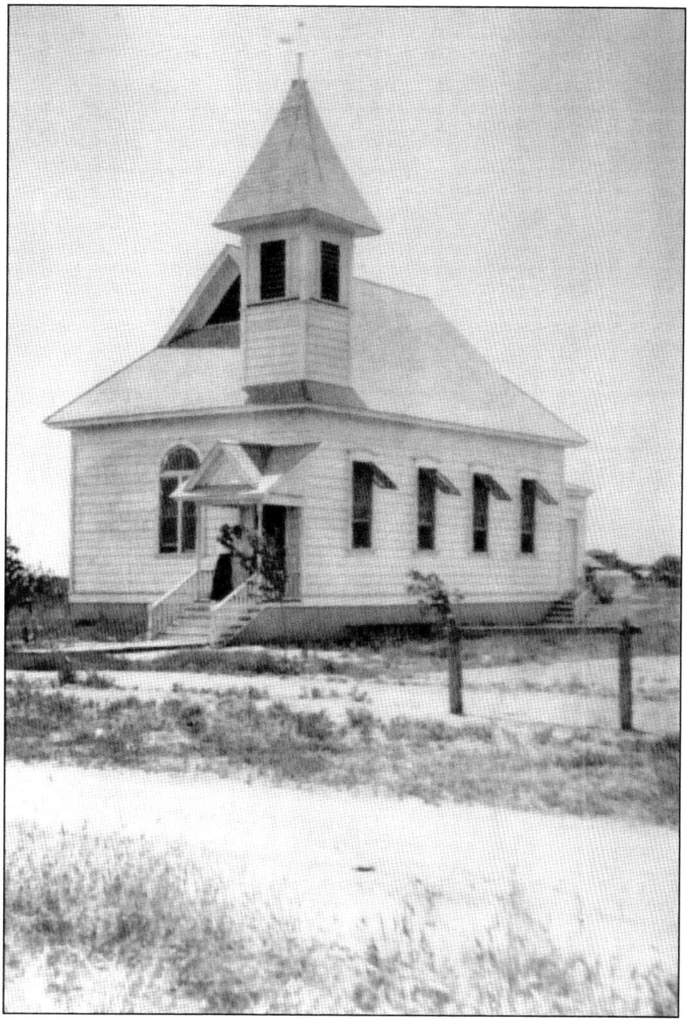

On April 10, 1902, John Davis deeded 15 lots in the newly formed town to the Elmdale School District. On the property, the one-room schoolhouse shown here was built, with Arletta Scott as the first teacher. There were five students that first year—Harry, Hazel, and Leslie De La Mater and Jack and Mary Pickford. The Christian Church used the schoolhouse on Sundays. (Courtesy of the Turlock Historical Society.)

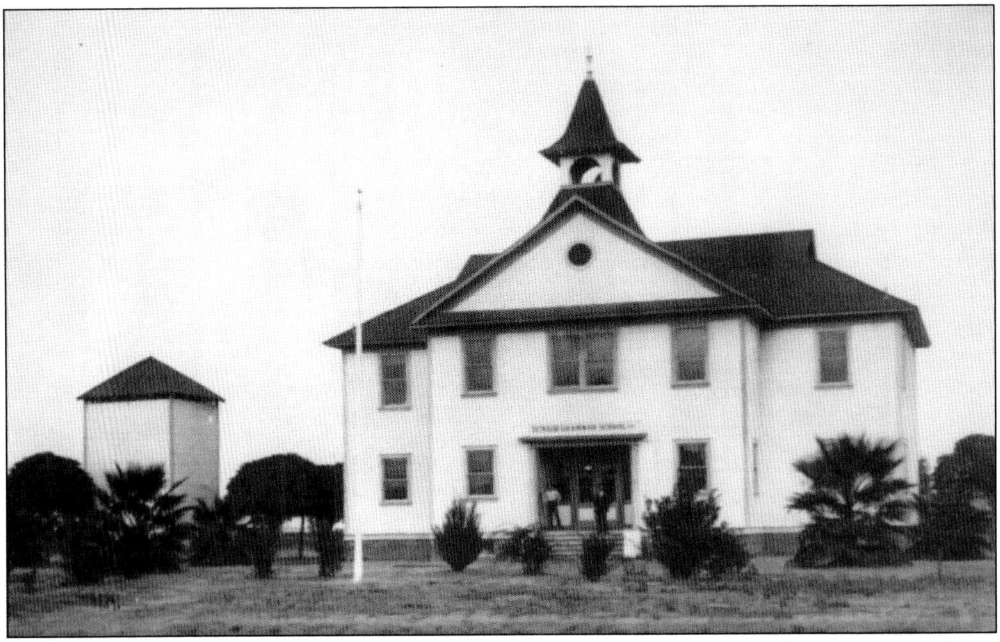

A two-story frame building was constructed five years later across the street to house more students. Denair resident Jacob Witmer was hired as contractor. On February 18, 1907, the new building was occupied for the first time. The new schoolhouse meant more students and more teachers—two teachers in fact, Elsie Cottle and Leta Haworth. (Courtesy of Denair Unified School District.)

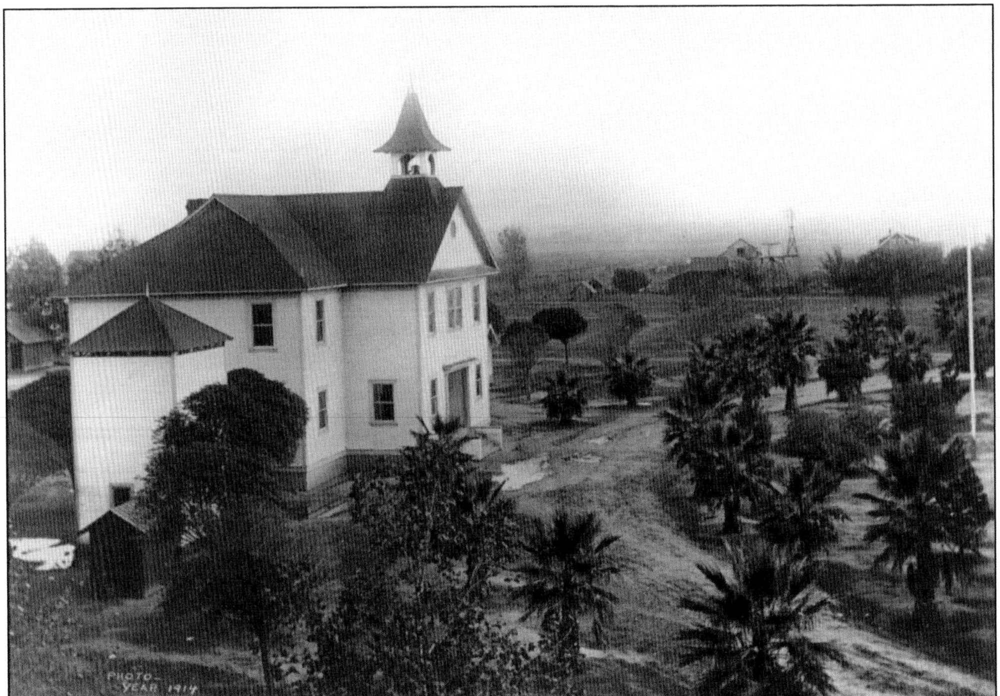

Elsie Cottle and Leta Haworth carried the desks from the one-room schoolhouse to the new building one-by-one. (Courtesy of Denair Community Service District.)

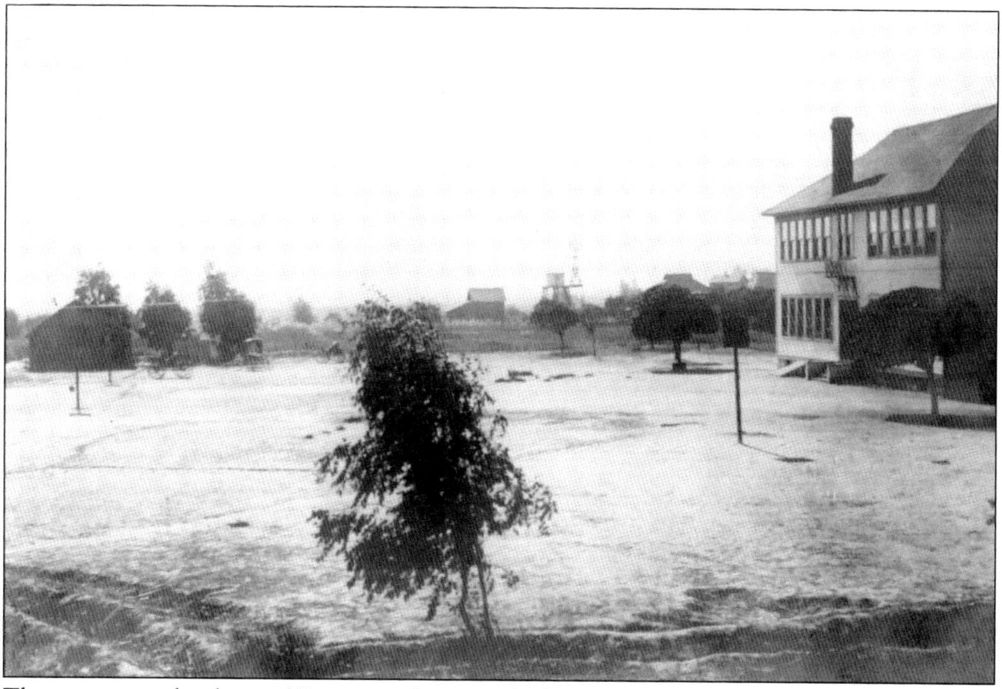

The two-story school served Denair students until it burned to the ground in 1916. For two years, students used the old one-room schoolhouse, the Denair Friends Church, and temporary buildings until a new school was constructed. (Courtesy of John Chance.)

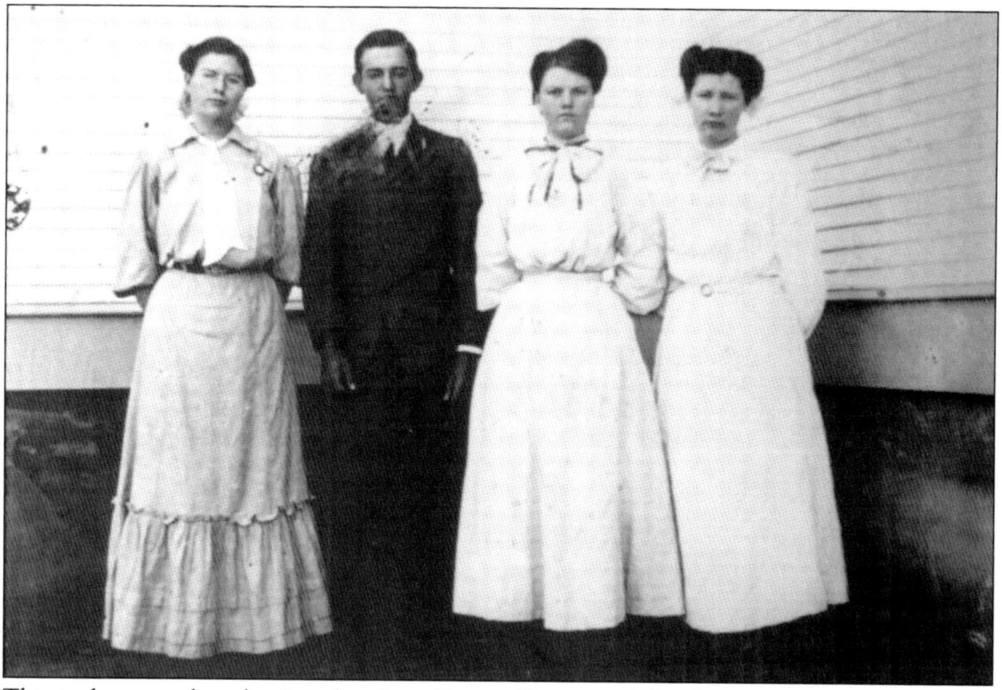

This is the second graduating class from Denair Grammar School, in 1907. Pictured, from left to right, are Thora Newport, Benjamin Binford, Ethel Kriser, and Zela Snider. (Courtesy of the Turlock Historical Society.)

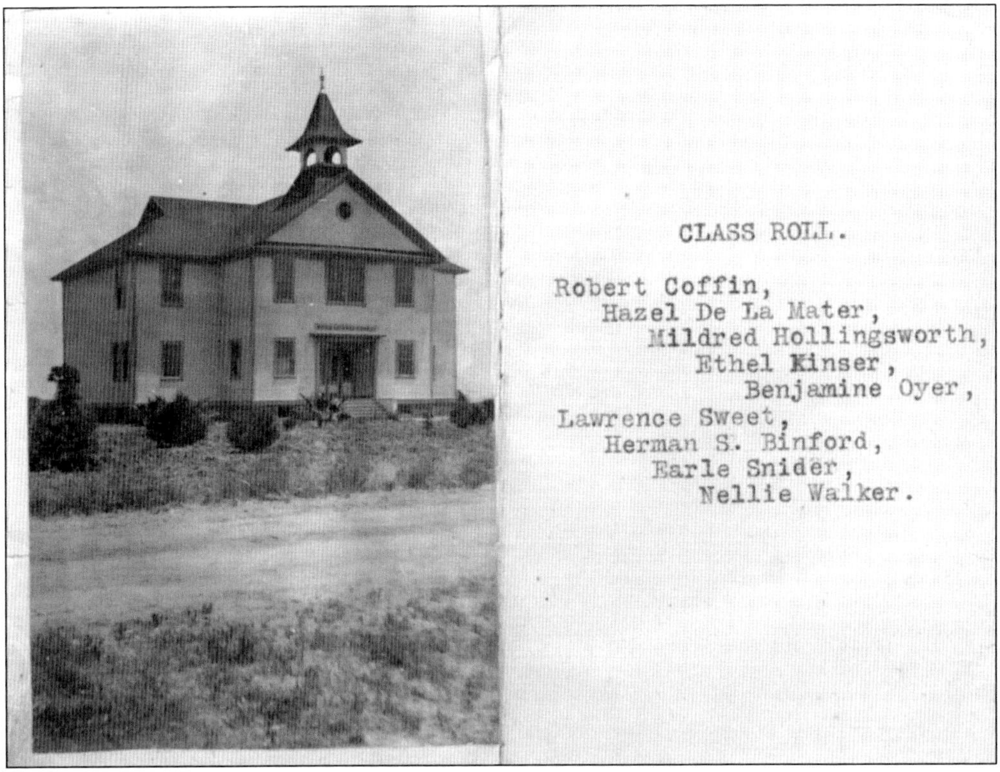

CLASS ROLL.

Robert Coffin,
Hazel De La Mater,
Mildred Hollingsworth,
Ethel Kinser,
Benjamine Oyer,
Lawrence Sweet,
Herman S. Binford,
Earle Snider,
Nellie Walker.

The following year, in 1908, the graduating class grew. Nine students graduated this time. Above is their graduation announcement, and below is a photograph of the graduating class of 1908. (Above, courtesy of Denair Unified School District; below, courtesy of California State University, Stanislaus.)

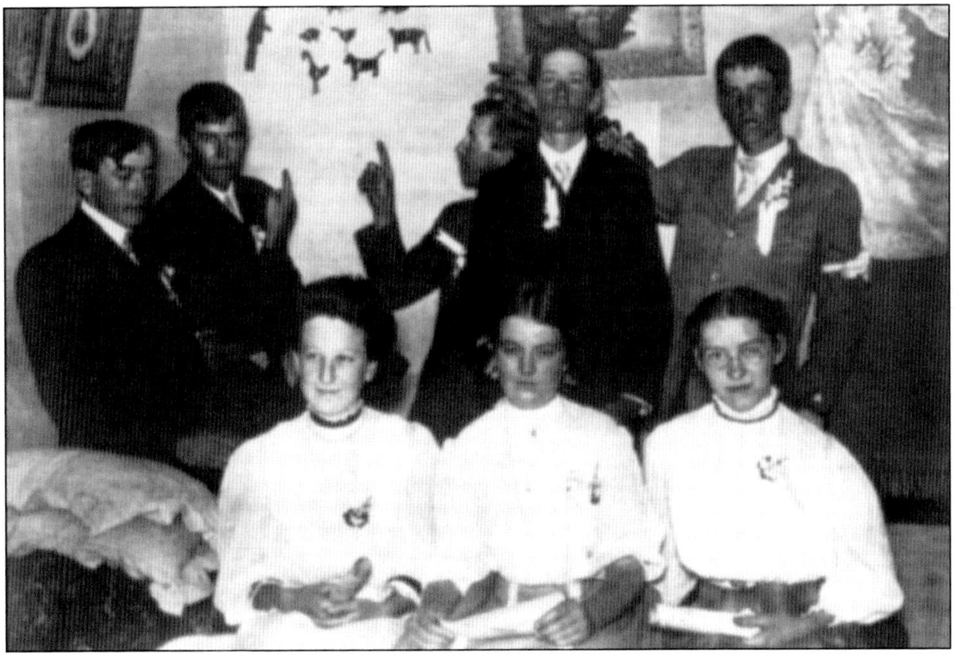

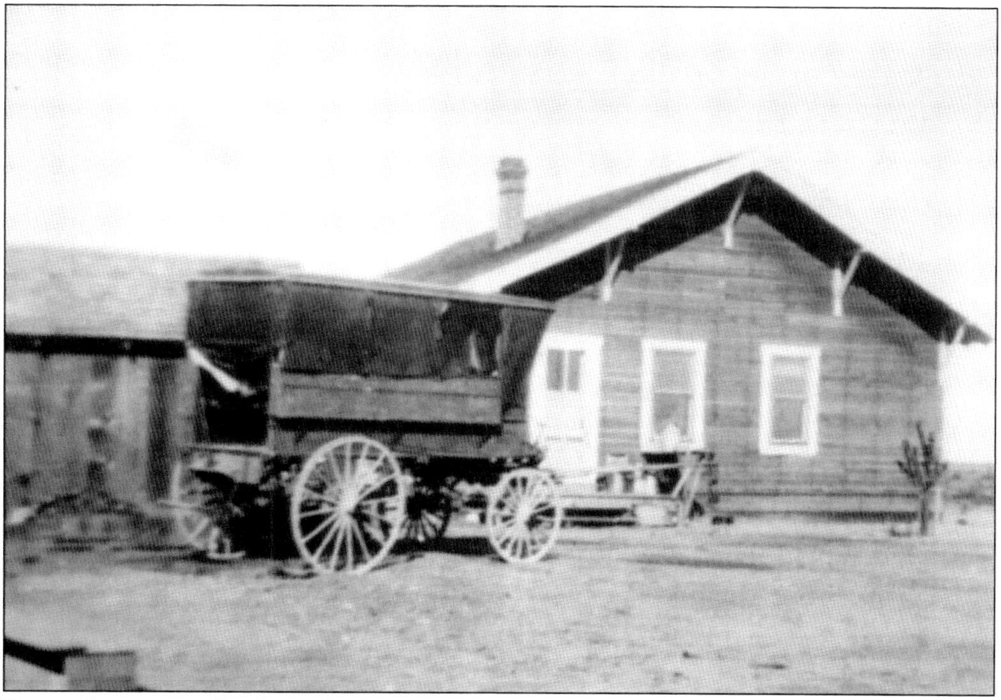

Denair Grammar School soon had its first kid hack, a horse-drawn vehicle used to take children to and from school, driven by U. Cole. The children traveling from a further distance to the school welcomed the transportation. (Courtesy of the Turlock Historical Society.)

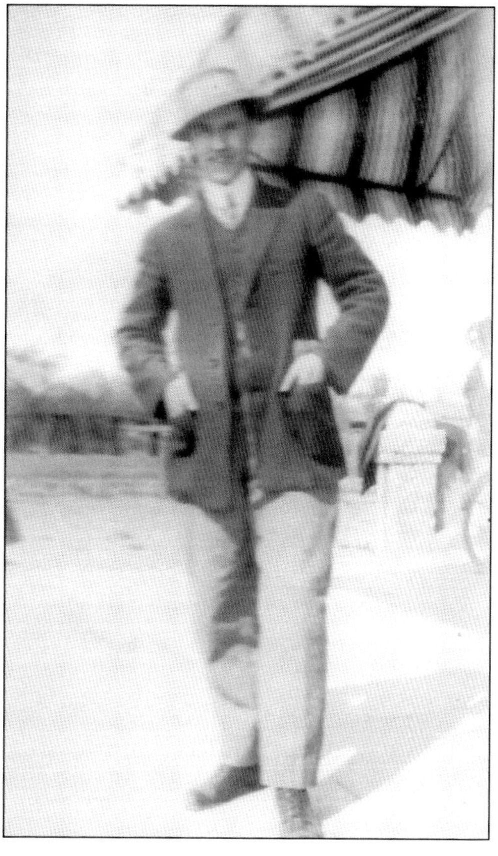

A Mr. Hurt is believed to have been the principal of Denair Grammar School from about 1910 to 1912. (Courtesy of the Witmer family.)

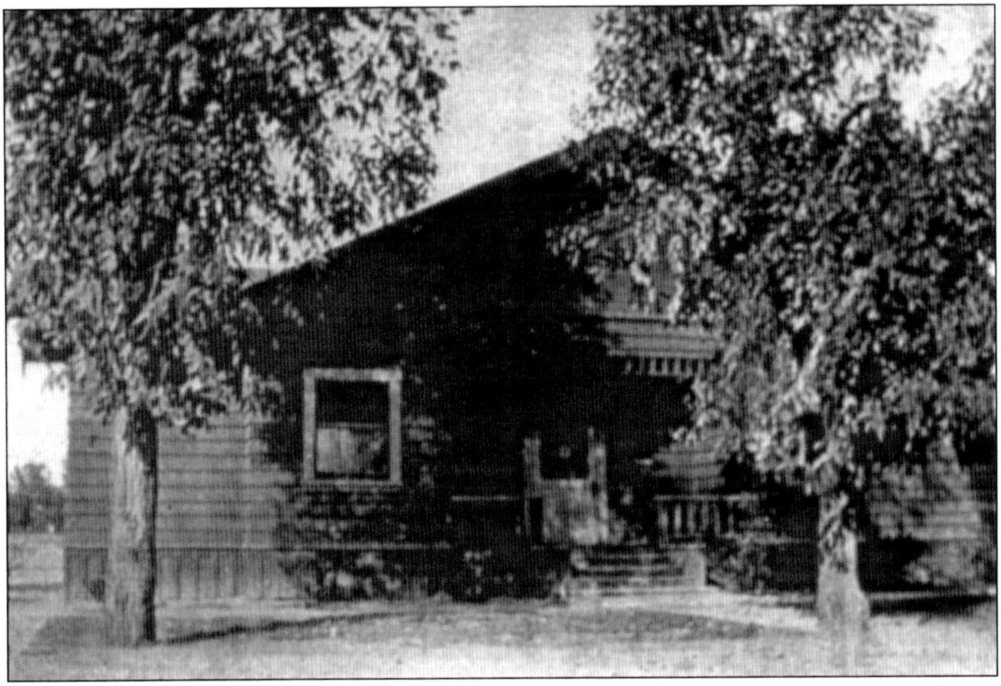

In 1912, the one-room "Little Red Schoolhouse" was built on the Denair Community Park site. It was constructed to house first-grade classes. Pearl Brown was the first teacher. (Courtesy of Denair Unified School District.)

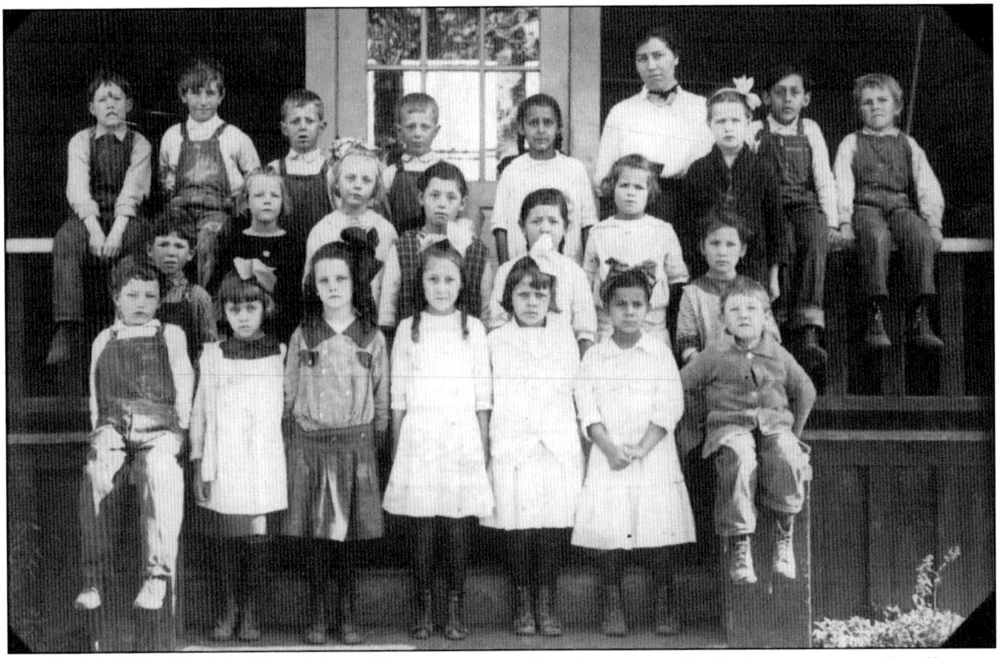

Many first-grade students learned reading, writing, and arithmetic in the little one-room schoolhouse. Here, first graders pose for a class photograph in 1916. Included in this class are twins Chet and Let Domecq (top row, third and fourth from left). (Courtesy of Louis Domecq.)

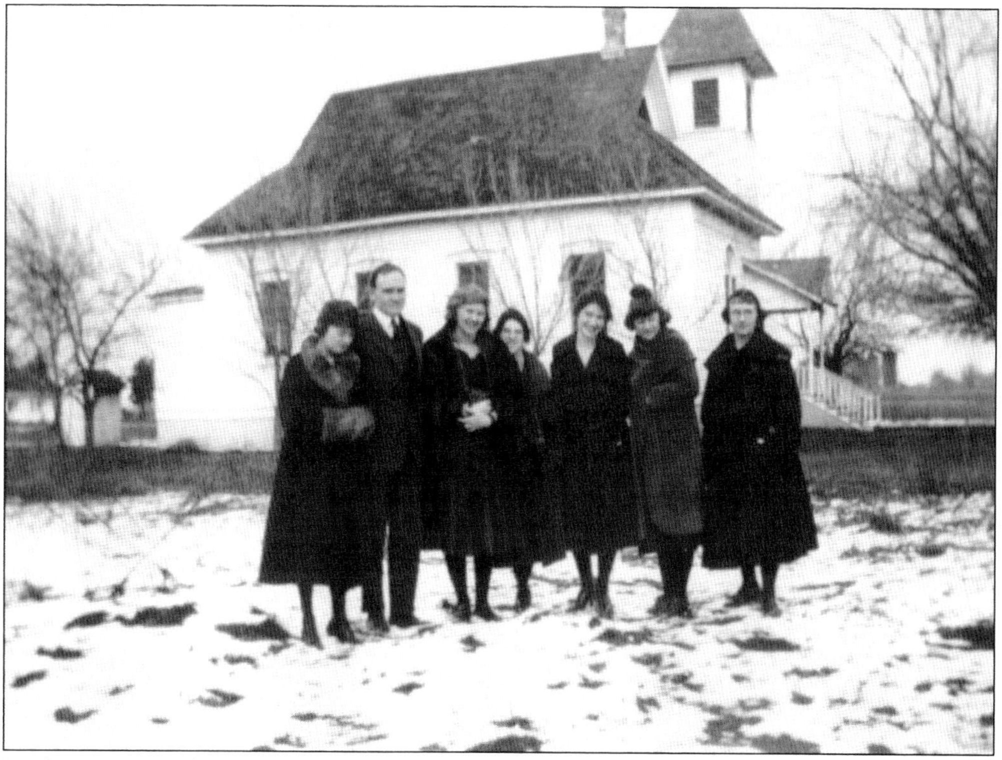

In these images, the Denair Grammar School faculty enjoys a very rare snowy day in Denair around 1922. Pictured above are, from left to right, Helen Smith, R. Simons, Mary Kidder, Hazel Frazer, Christine Hollingsworth, Gertrude Mitchel, and Eva Bergren. (Both, courtesy of John Chance.)

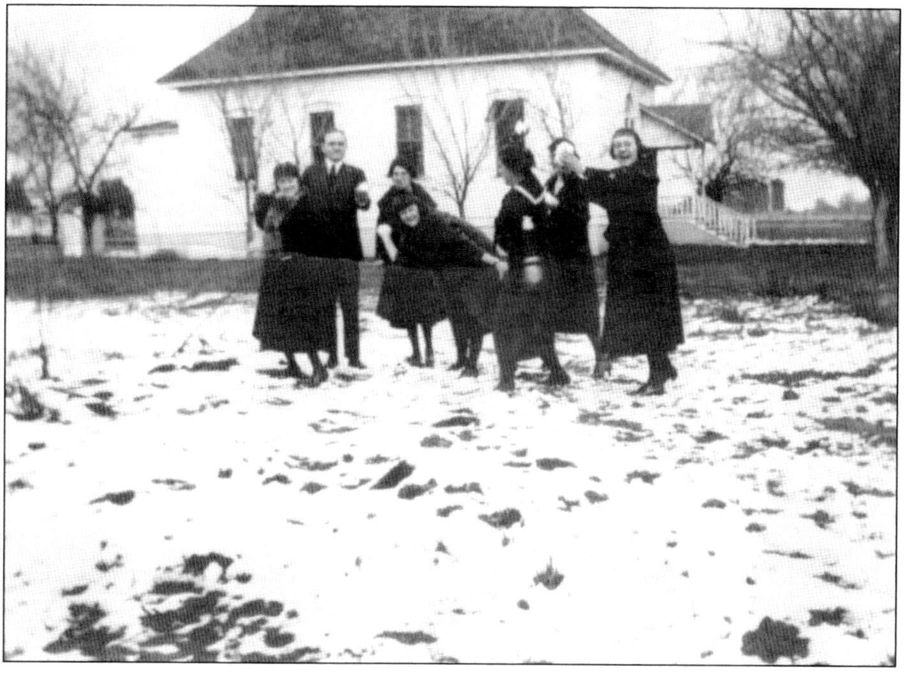

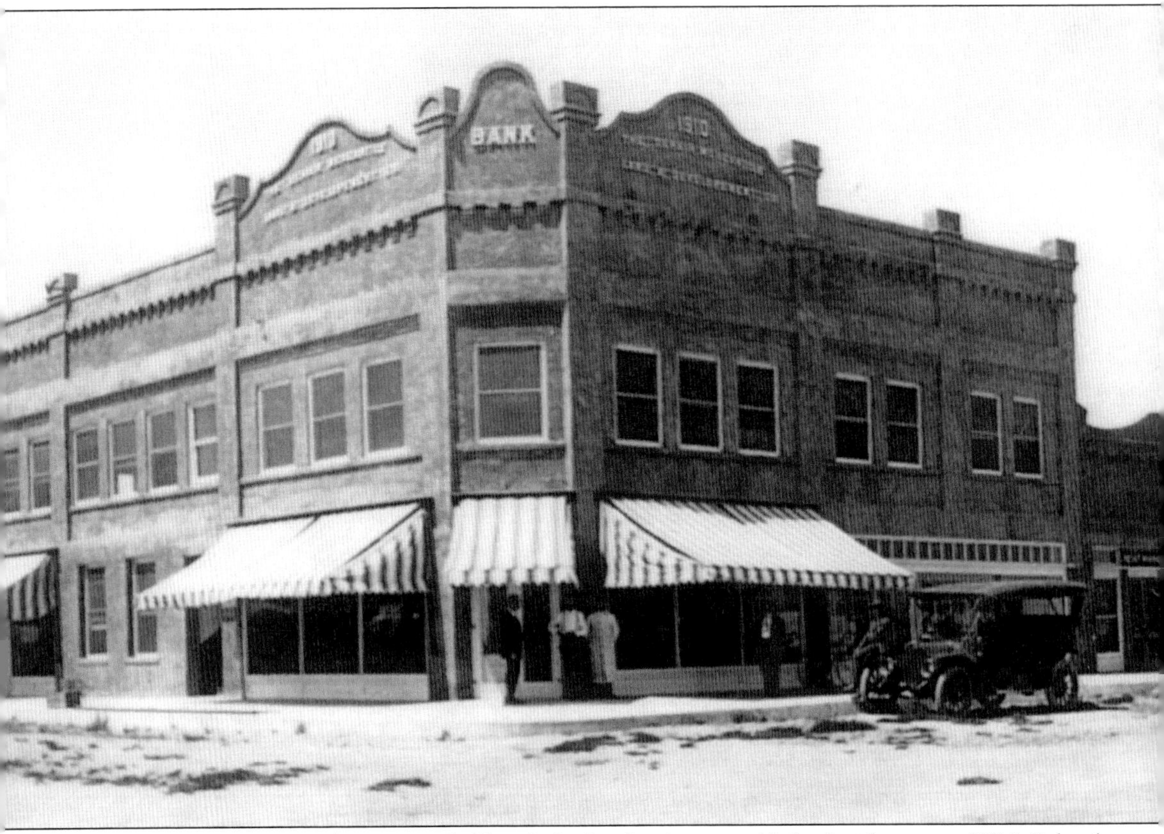

On June 20, 1912, an election was held and a high school was established with a vote of 28-5. School started in the second story of the Bank Building in August of that year. There were 26 students enrolled with two faculty members the first year. (Courtesy of Denair Unified School District.)

At right is Lee C. Newby, the first principal of the newly formed Denair High School. The assets of the high school were $475. Cost of operation was $3,395.38, and the library had 26 volumes valued at $62 total. Below is Maude Starbuck, the second faculty member hired for the first year at Denair High School. Newby and Starbuck were the only two teachers that year. (Right, courtesy of the Witmer family; below, courtesy of John Chance.)

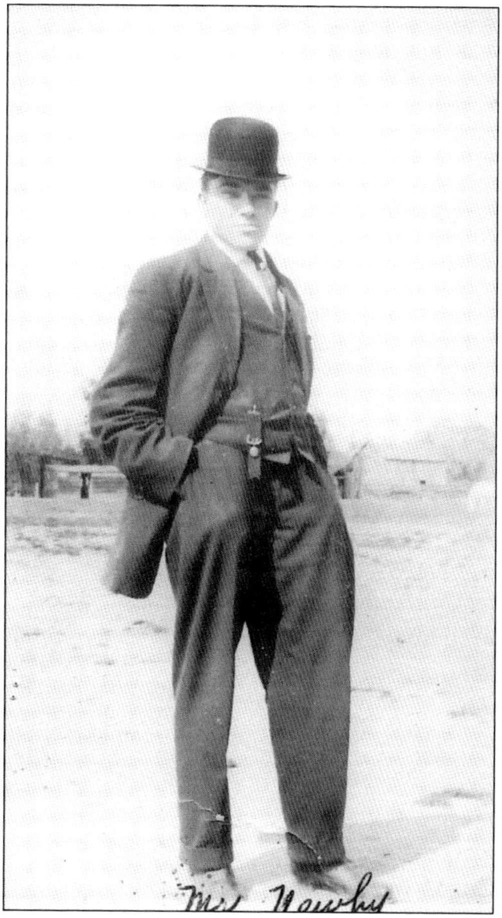

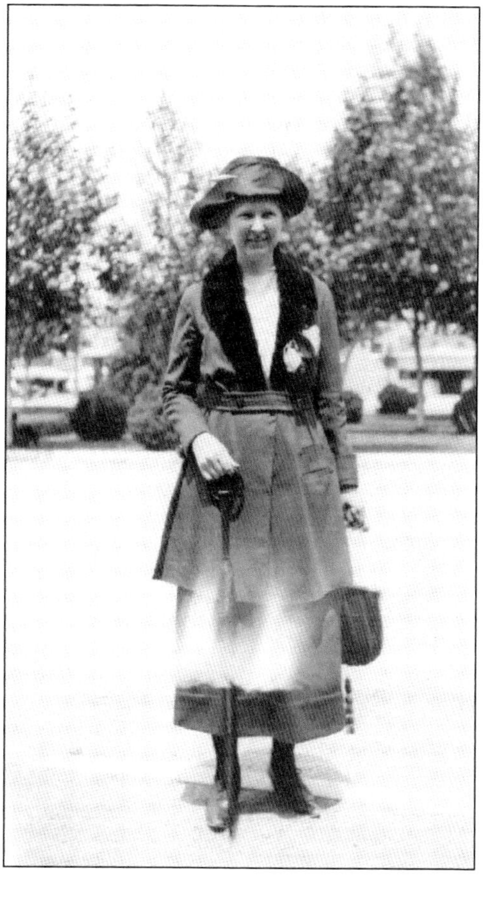

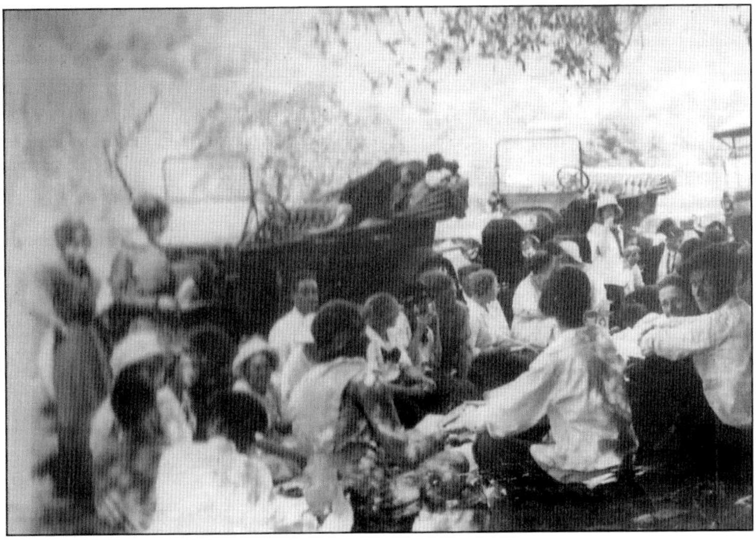

School was not always about hard work; sometimes, the students needed a day outside. This photograph of the high school picnic was taken around 1915. (Courtesy of the Witmer family.)

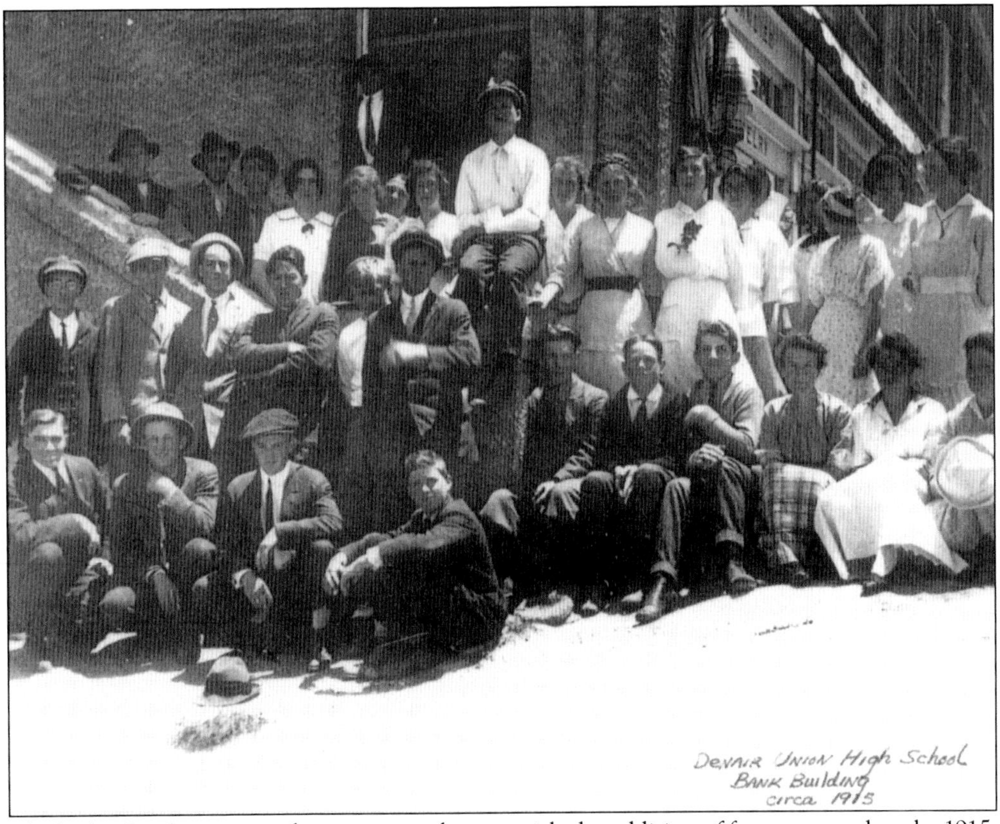

The high school grew over the next several years, with the addition of four new teachers by 1915. The 1915 graduating class consisted of three girls and one boy. Here, the Denair High School student body of 1915 poses on the back steps of the Bank Building. (Courtesy of the Turlock Historical Society.)

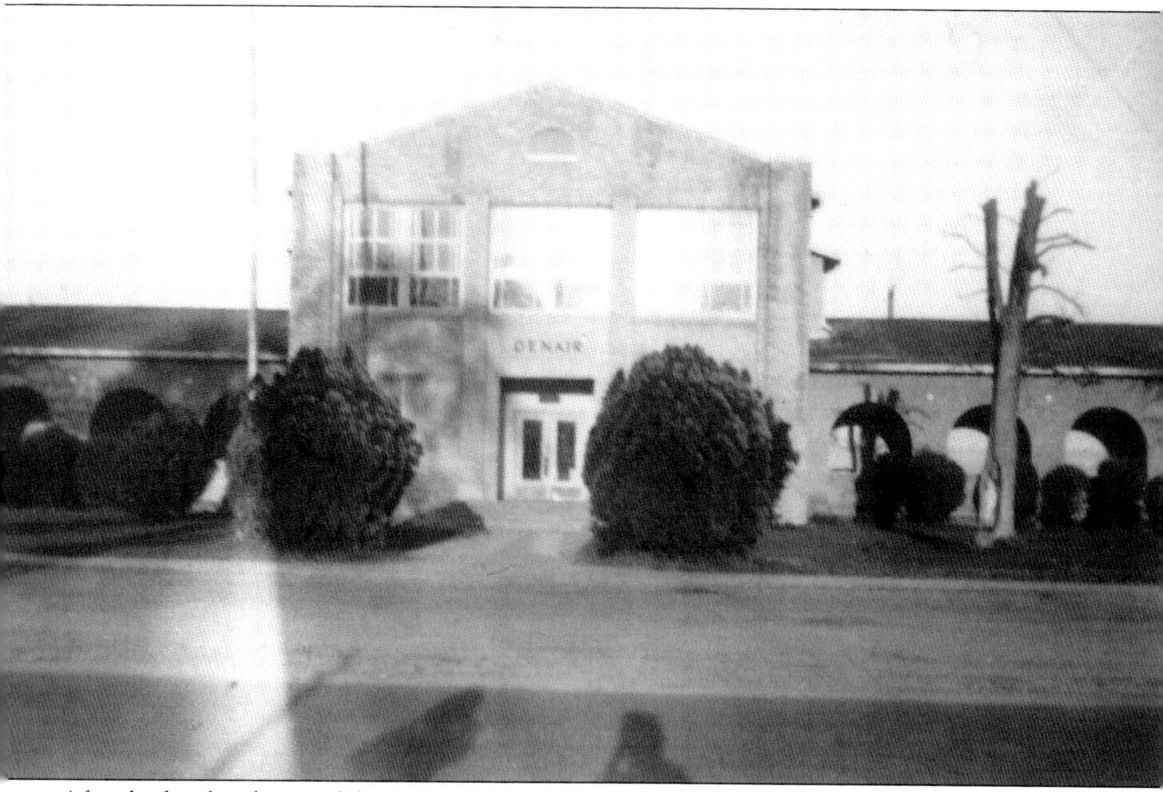

After the fire that destroyed the two-story schoolhouse, it was determined that a new school would have to be built. In February 1917, a $28,000 bond measure was passed for the construction of a new grammar school. There were 280 votes cast, with 211 votes in favor. A new brick grammar school was built slightly south of the site of the burned-down two-story structure at the corner of Gratton and Zeering Roads and was first occupied in 1918. (Courtesy of Carol Royster.)

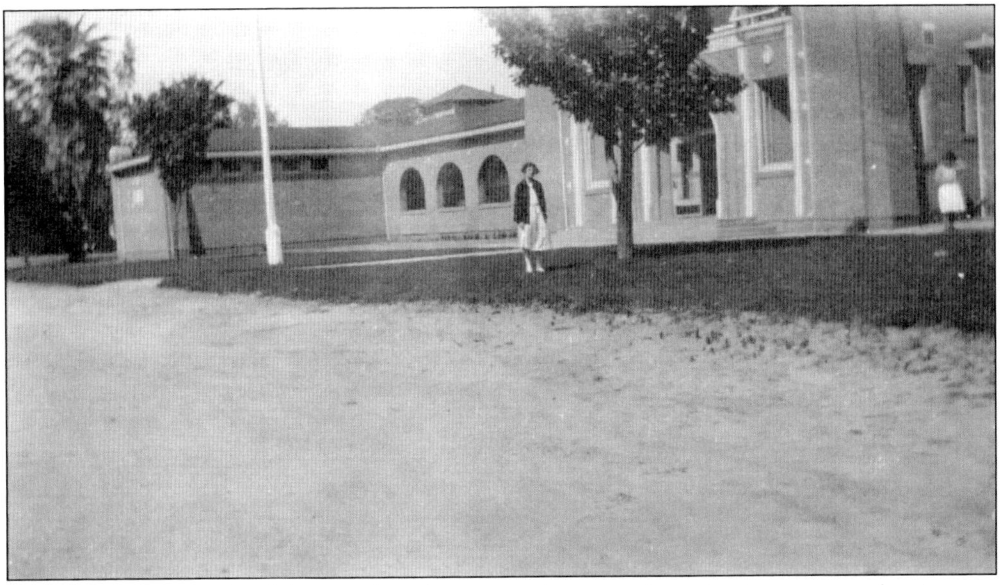

The new grammar school housed five classrooms, library, offices, bathrooms, teachers' room, cafeteria, and auditorium. Here, teacher Hazel Frazier stands in front of the school around 1922. (Courtesy of John Chance.)

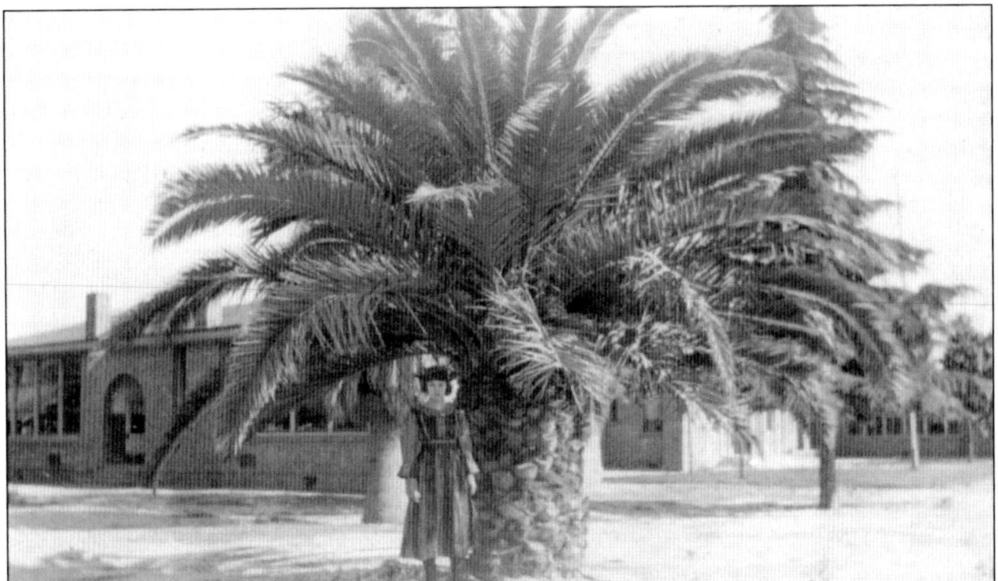

Florence Von Wedell, born in 1899, poses in front of one of the palms on the campus of the grammar school. (Courtesy of John Chance.)

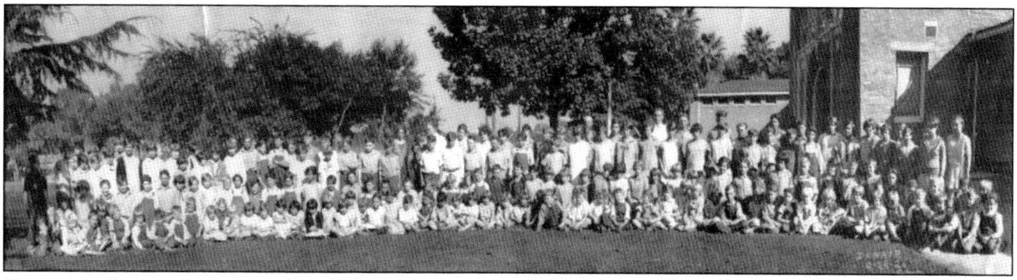

By 1926, the student population had grown at Denair Grammar School substantially. Here are all of the school attendees from that year. (Courtesy of Cheryl Cline.)

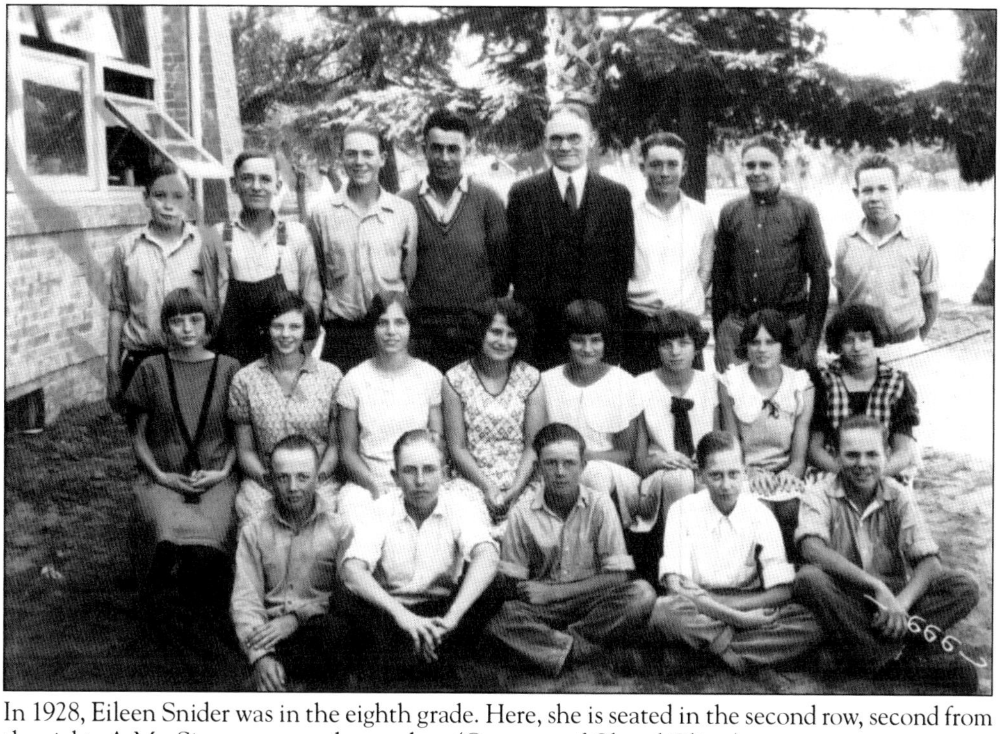

In 1928, Eileen Snider was in the eighth grade. Here, she is seated in the second row, second from the right. A Mr. Simmons was the teacher. (Courtesy of Cheryl Cline.)

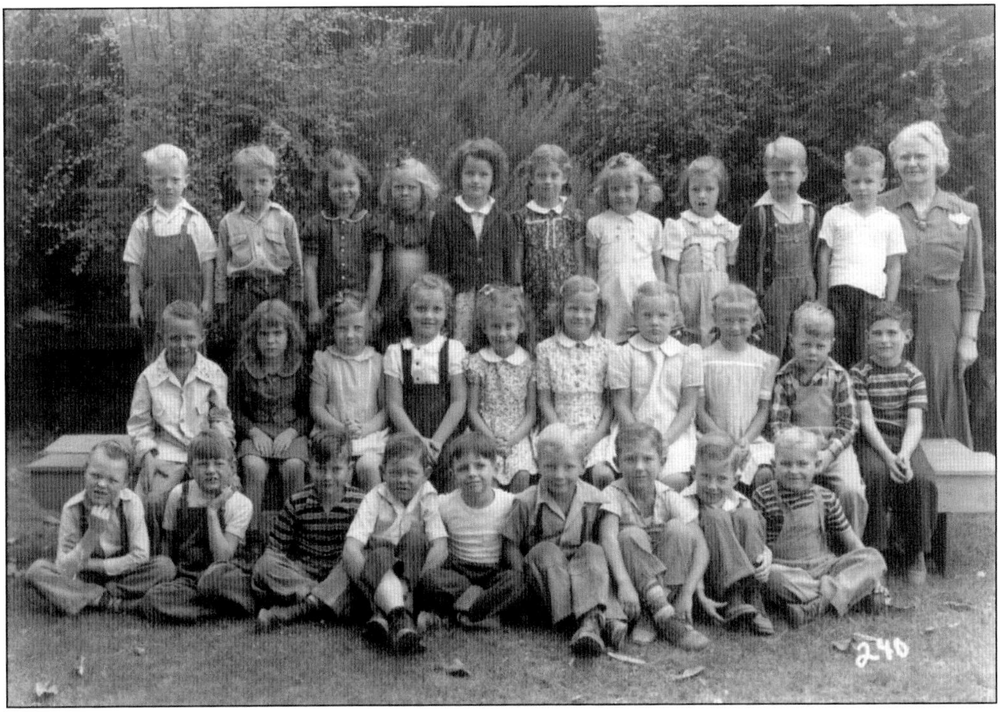

Mary De La Mater taught first grade at Denair Grammar School for many years, from the mid-1920s until the 1950s. She moved to Denair in 1919 and married Leslie De La Mater shortly after. She taught her classes in the little red schoolhouse. Many Denair residents from that time remember her fondly. Here, she is with her first grade class in 1944. (Courtesy of Joyce Morrissey.)

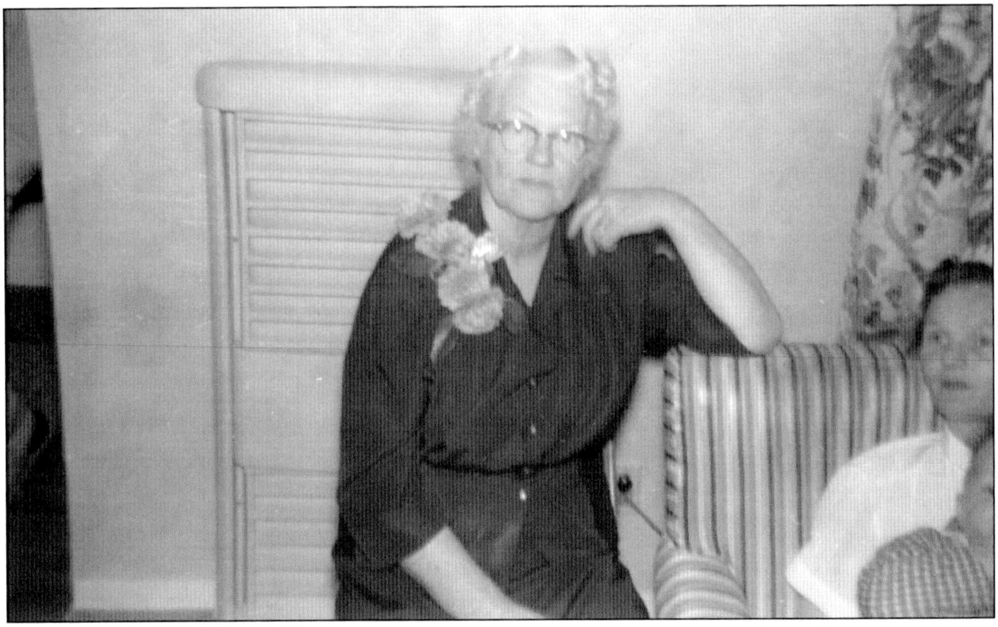

Mary De La Mater retired from Denair Grammar School sometime in the 1950s. To celebrate her retirement, the school organized a *This Is Your Life*–style party for her, held in the grammar school auditorium. (Courtesy of Cheryl Cline.)

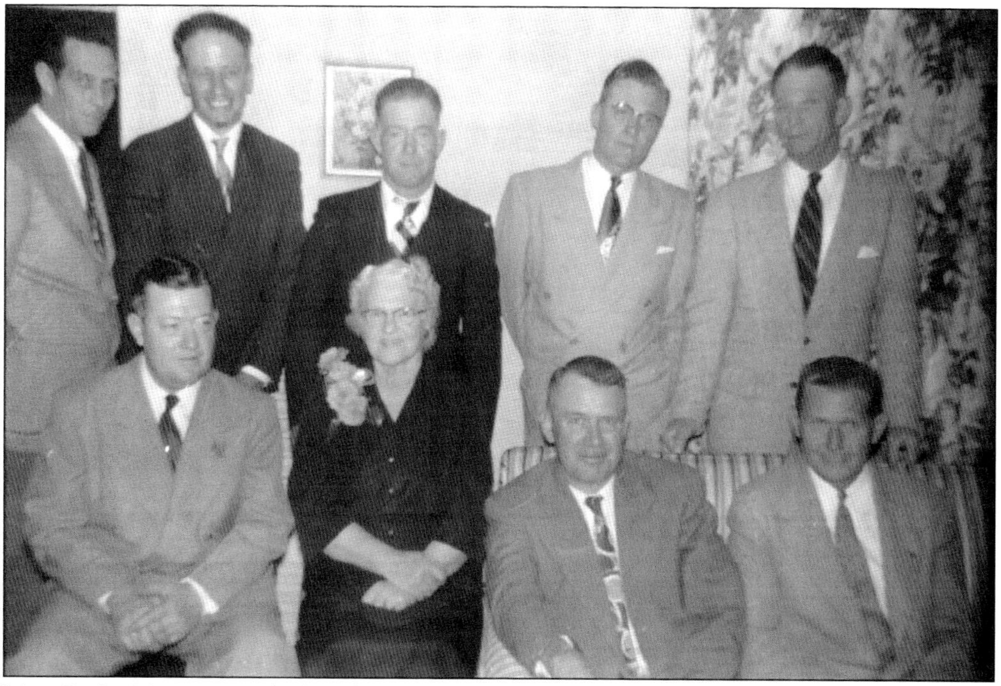

Mary De La Mater sits with the school board of directors at the time. Pictured, from left to right, are (first row) Harold Markley, Mary De La Mater, Leland Hake, and La Verne Johnson; (second row) Bob Fowle, Bob Domecq, Harold Holveck, George Witmer, and Kenneth Fraser. (Courtesy of Cheryl Cline.)

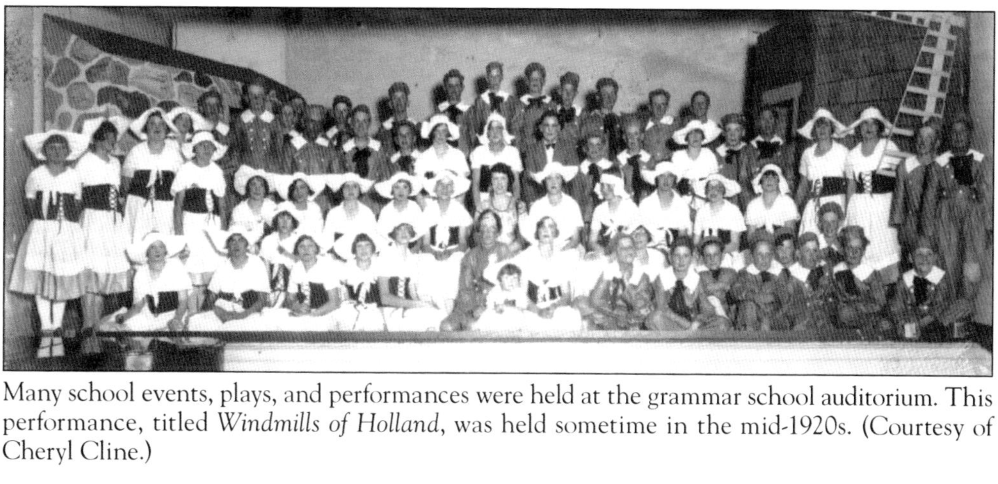

Many school events, plays, and performances were held at the grammar school auditorium. This performance, titled *Windmills of Holland*, was held sometime in the mid-1920s. (Courtesy of Cheryl Cline.)

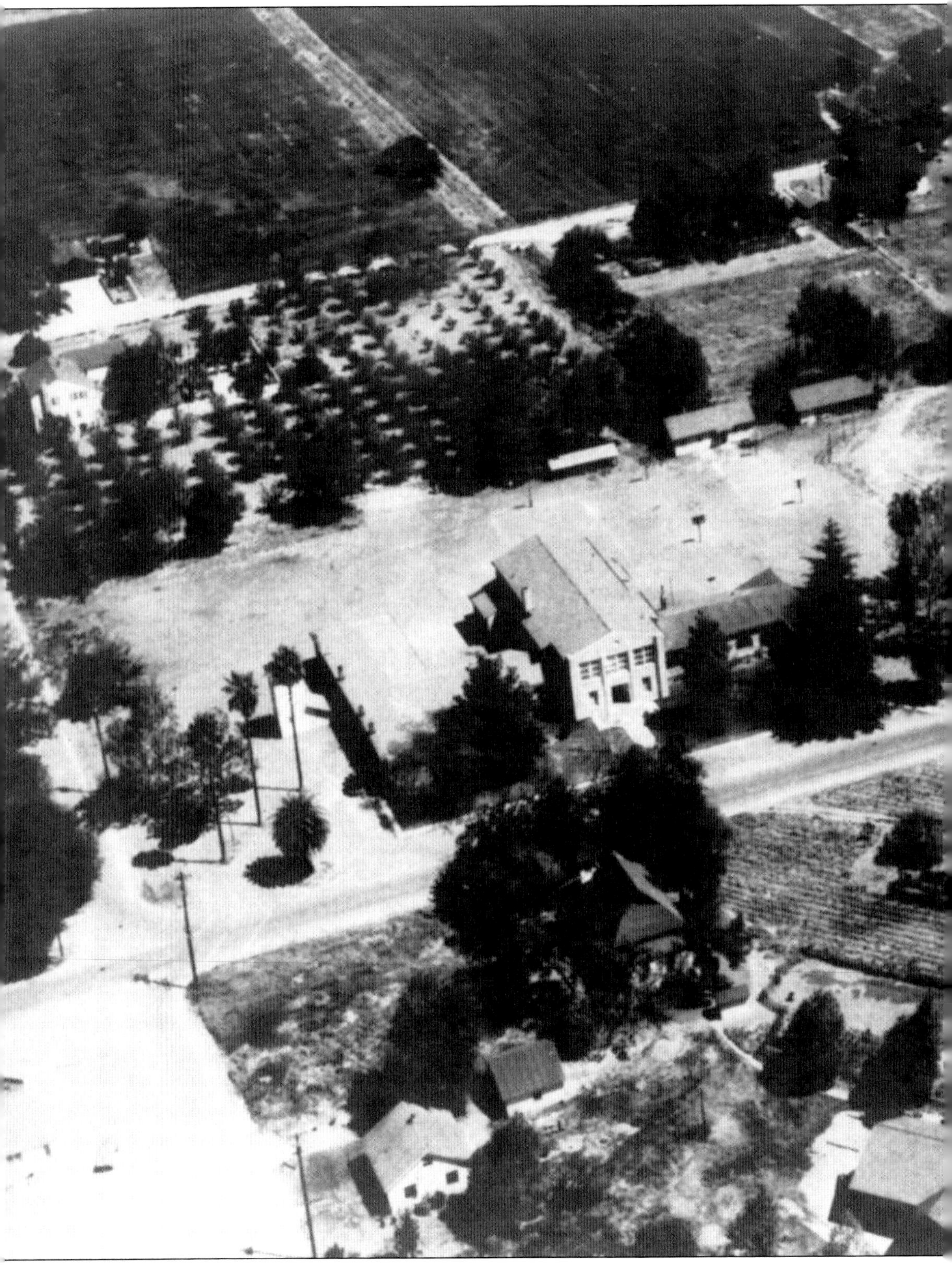

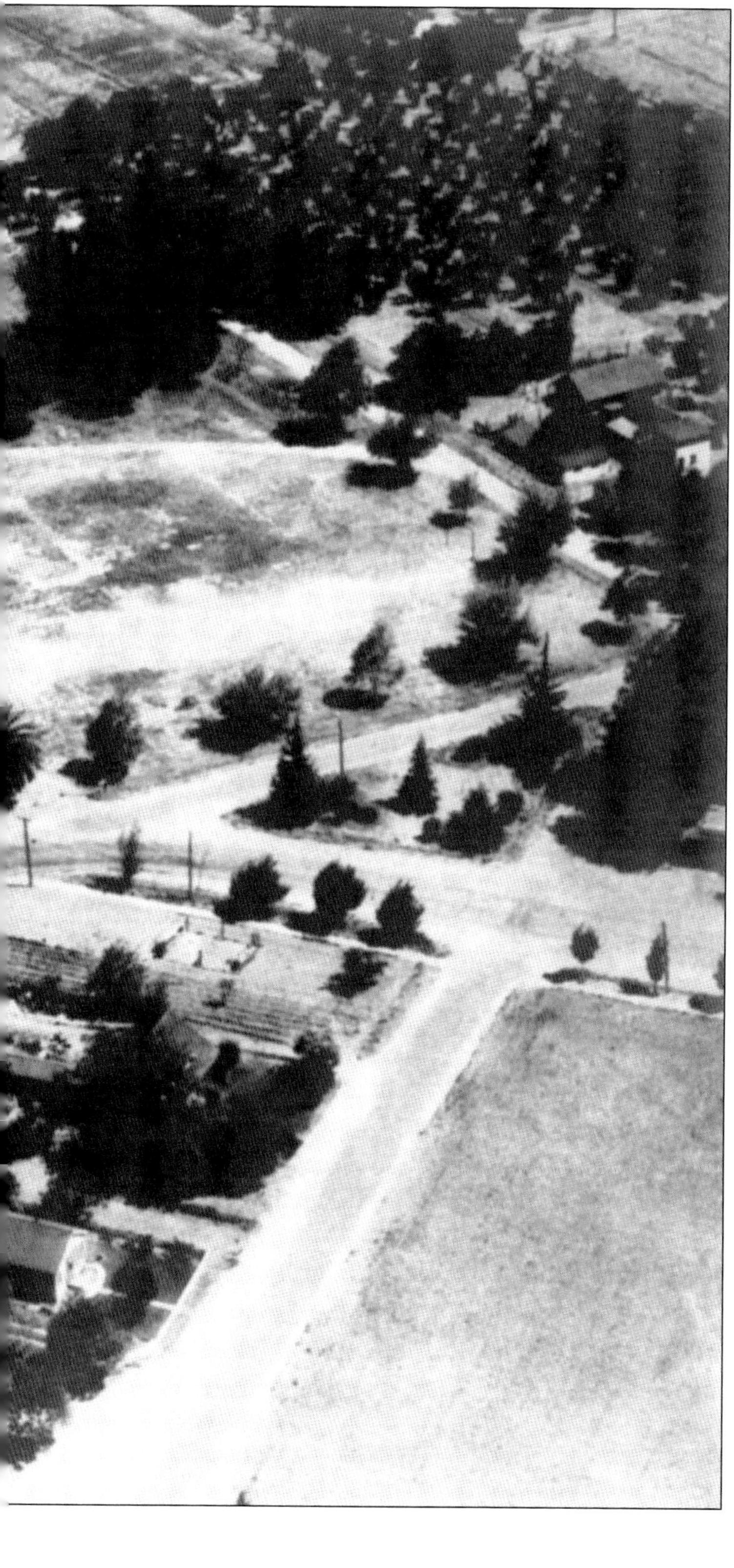

The Denair Grammar School site on Gratton Road quickly became too small for the growing population. A new elementary school was proposed across the railroad tracks at Hawthorne Street and Madera Avenue. After completion of the new elementary school, the classroom wings of the grammar school were removed, leaving just the auditorium, which became known as the Golden Gas Light Theater. Today, the Denair Community Service Center occupies the land to the south of the old grammar school, with the Denair Fire Department located to the north. (Courtesy of Denair Unified School District.)

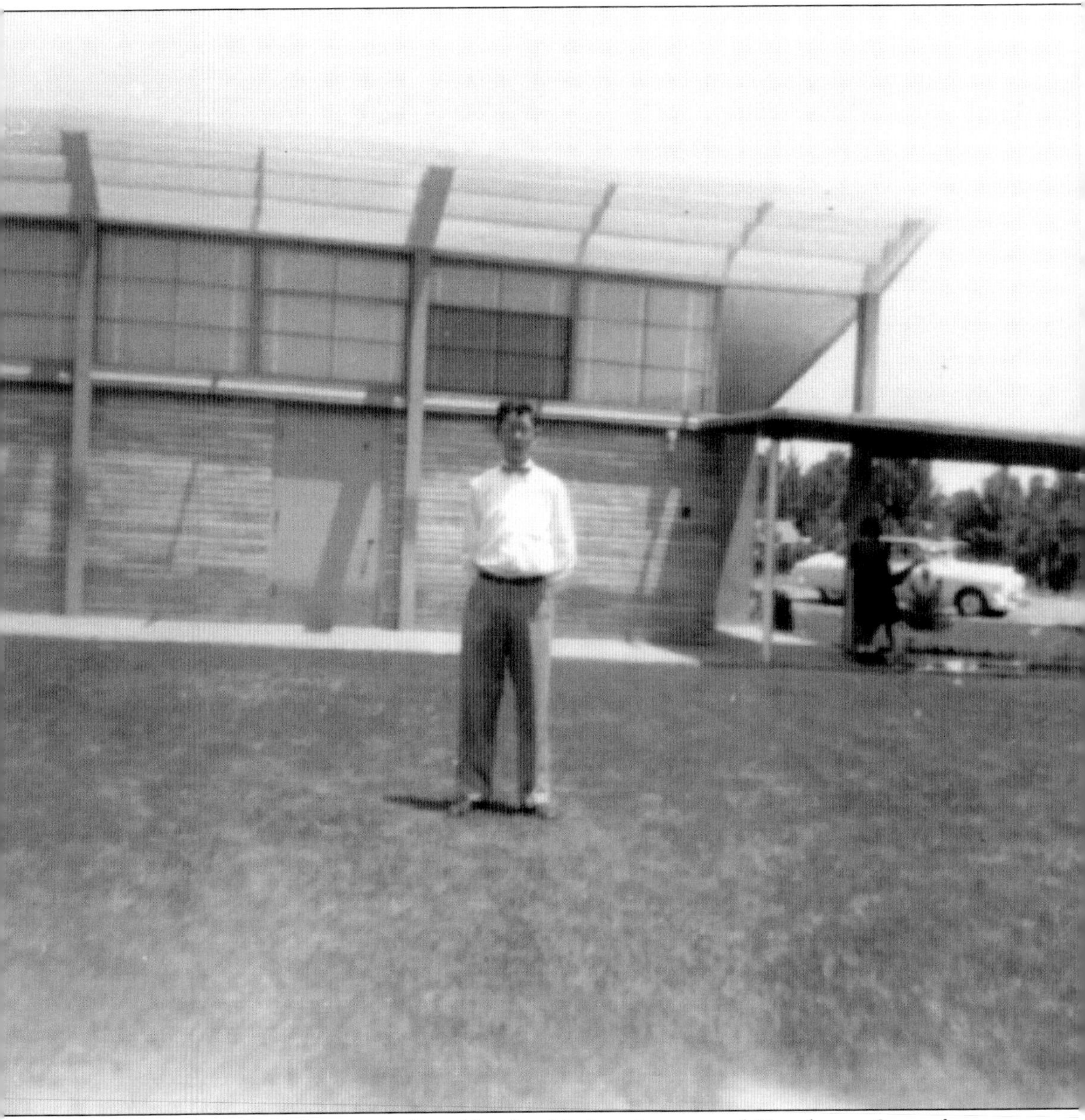

In 1947, the school district purchased land at Madera Avenue and Hawthorne Street for a new elementary school site. The first four classrooms, one wing, were completed in 1949, and the building featured a butterfly roof. In this photograph, Gilbert Ratcliff stands outside the first classroom wing. (Courtesy of Cheryl Cline.)

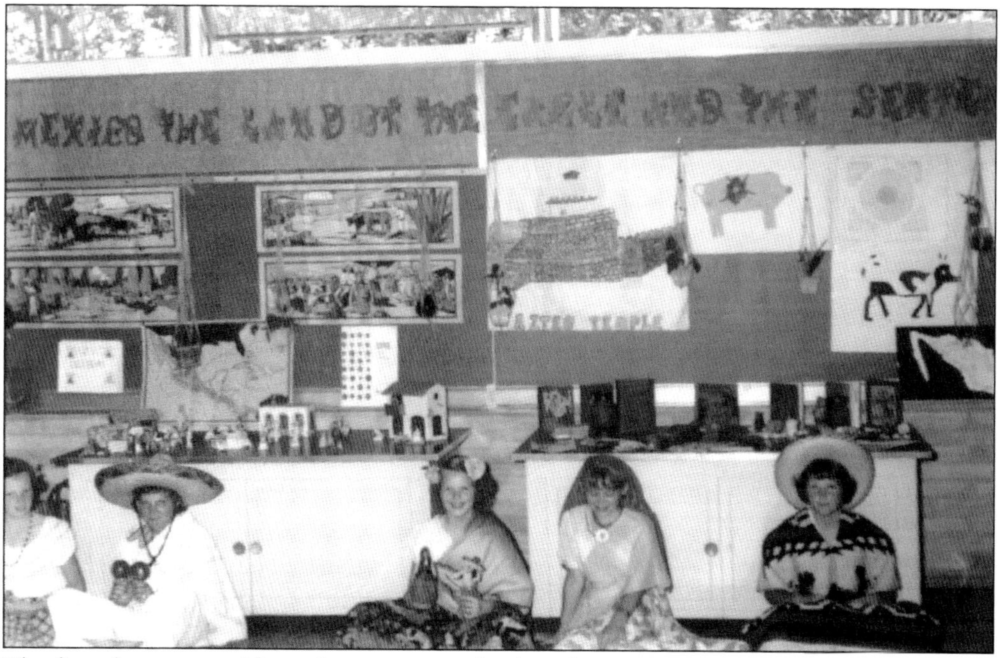

The first classes moved from the grammar school to the new site in 1950. Here is Doris Herr's sixth-grade class around 1951. Pictured are, from left to right, Mary Ann Agee, Ramona Steeley, unidentified, Loretta Burman, and Cheryl Montgomery. (Courtesy of Cheryl Cline.)

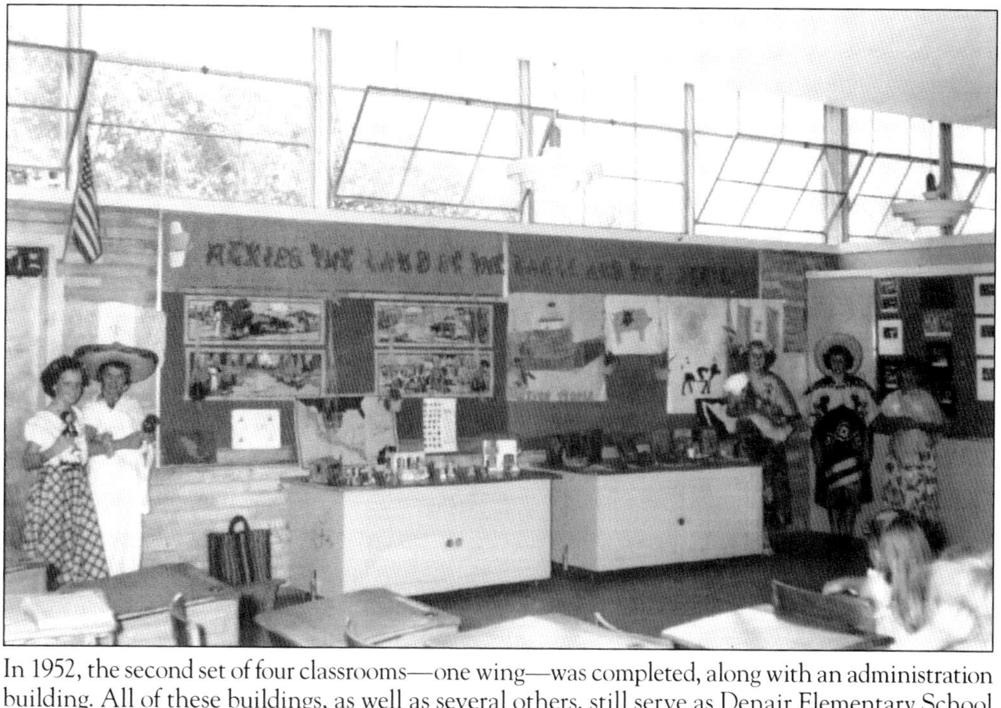

In 1952, the second set of four classrooms—one wing—was completed, along with an administration building. All of these buildings, as well as several others, still serve as Denair Elementary School today. (Courtesy of Cheryl Cline.)

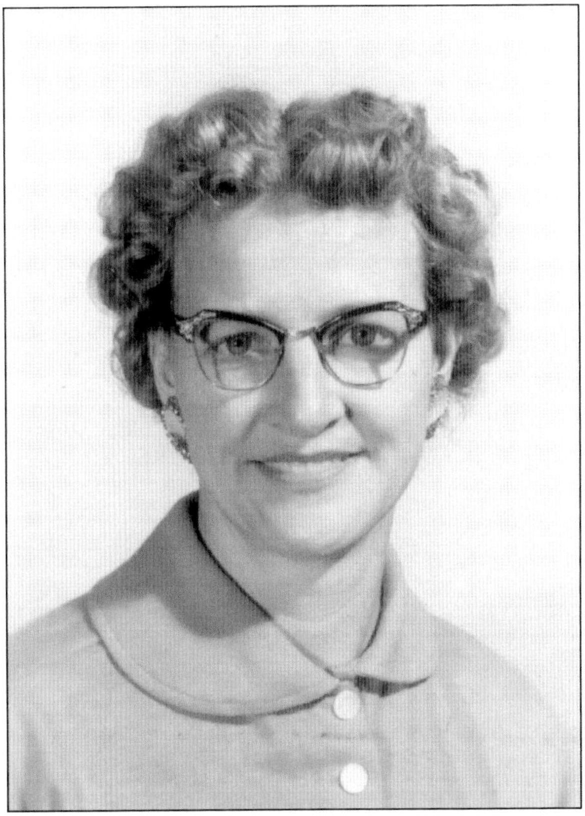

Hazel Wade began teaching from a one-room schoolhouse in Missouri in 1939 at the age of 17. In 1953, along with her husband and children, she moved to California. After teaching at several area schools, she was hired at Denair Elementary School in 1958. For 25 years, Hazel taught many of Denair's kindergartners before retiring. Every year, Hazel would prepare the children for the annual Easter parade. Some were happier to participate than others. (Both, courtesy of Hazel Wade Gomes.)

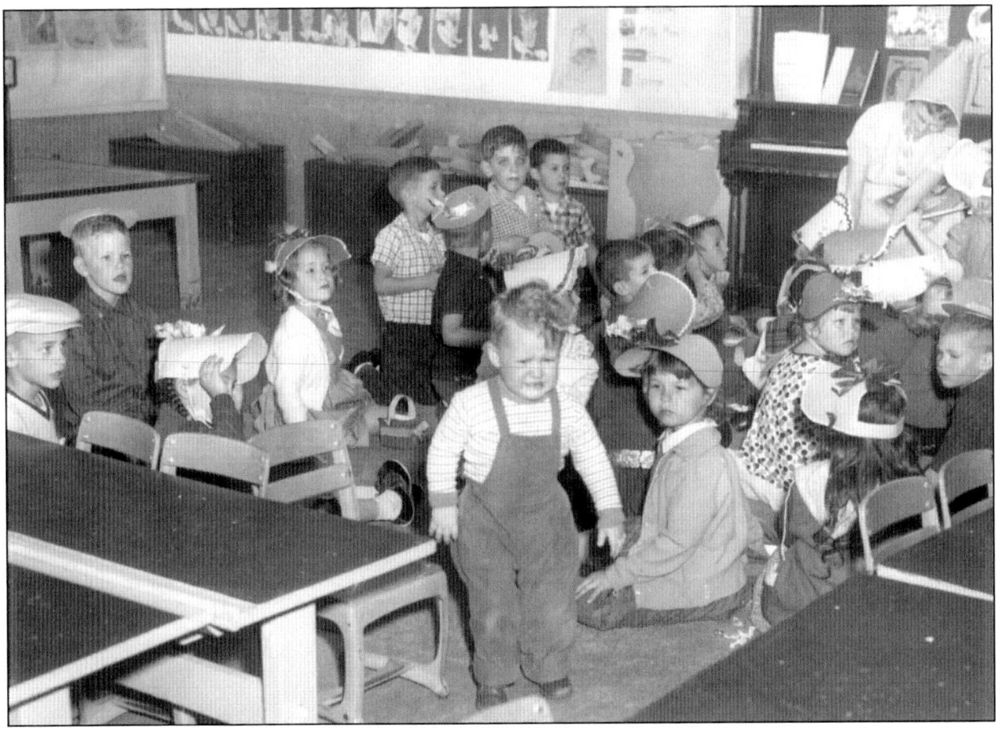

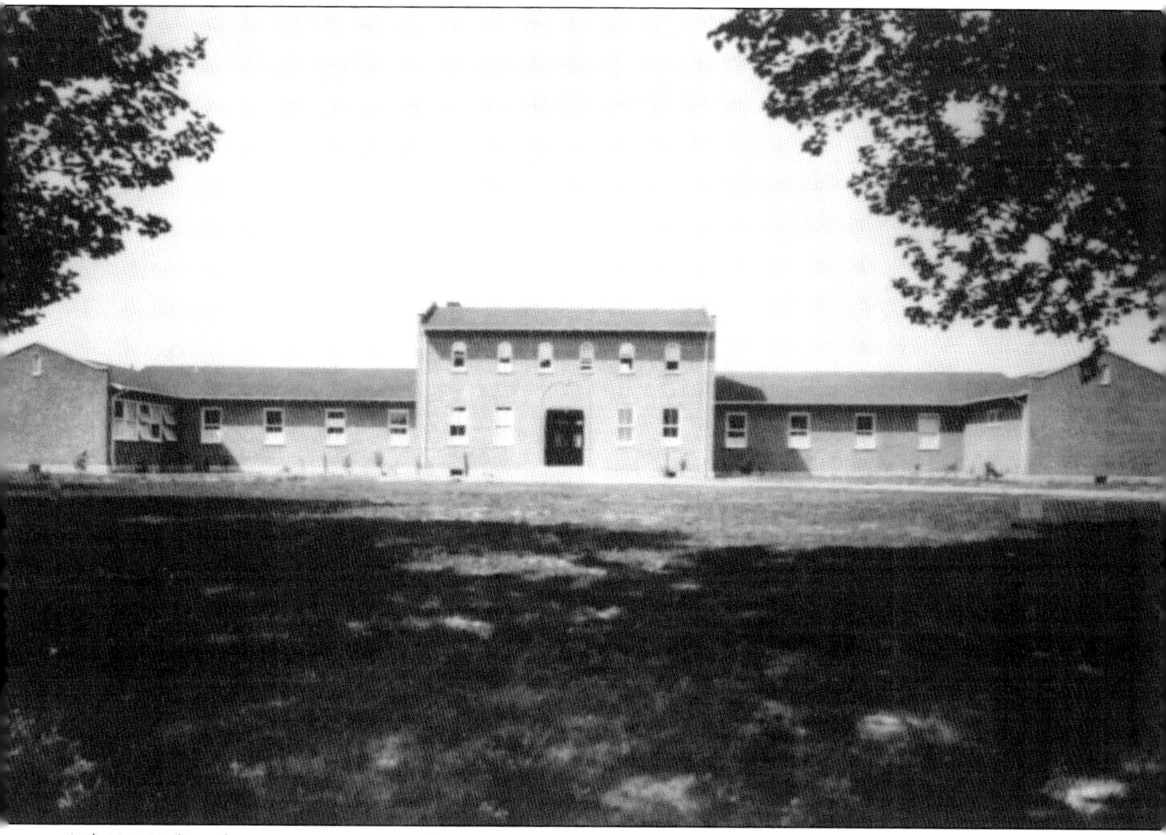

A $40,000 bond measure was passed in 1920 to support the cost of building a new high school. In 1921, a new brick high school was constructed on land purchased by the trustees in 1911 at the corner of Hawthorne and Fresno Streets. The school consisted of three classrooms, a typing room, shorthand room, laboratory, bathrooms, a small assembly hall (which doubled as a classroom), offices, a library, and other assorted rooms. (Courtesy of the Turlock Historical Society.)

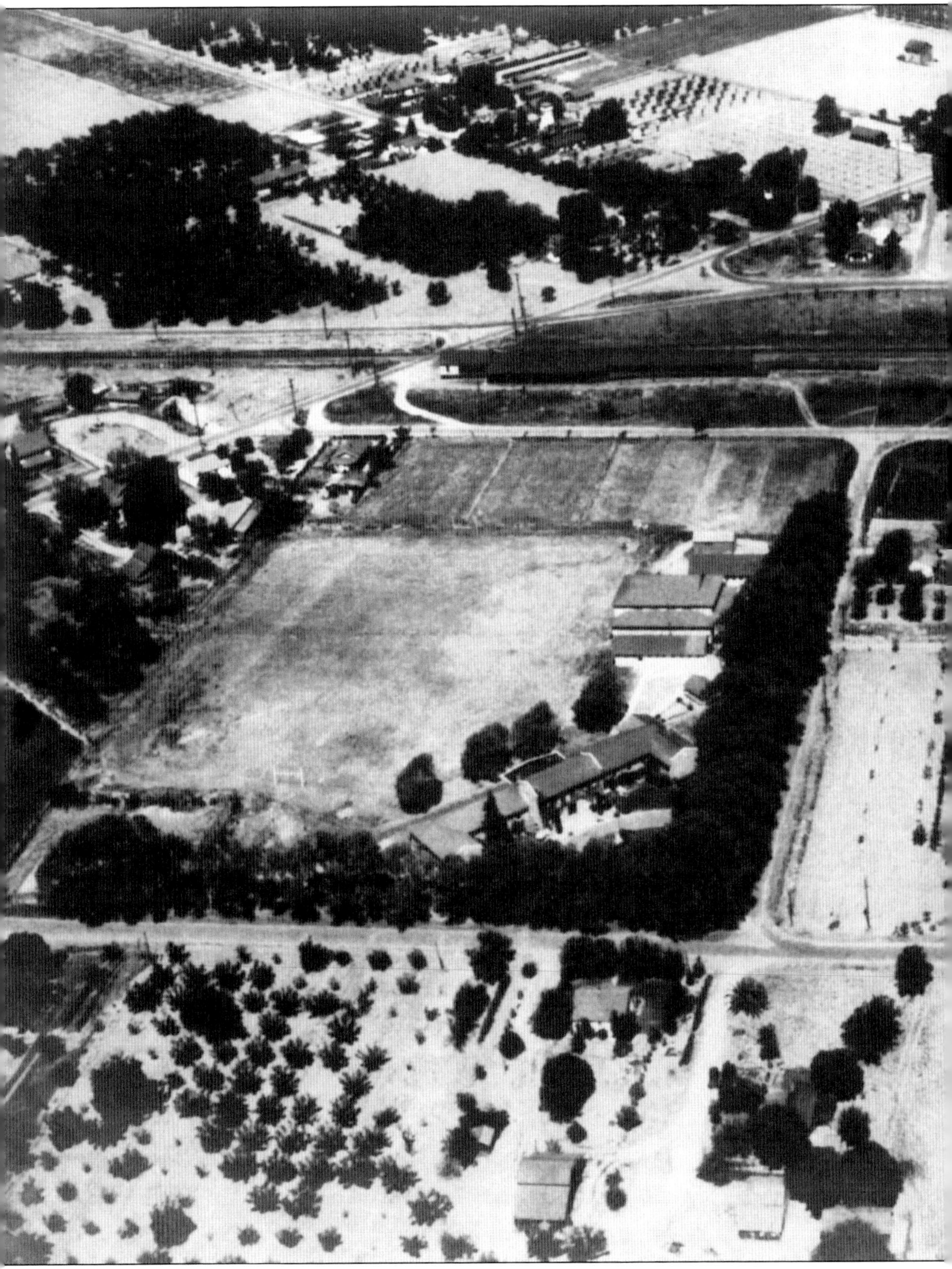

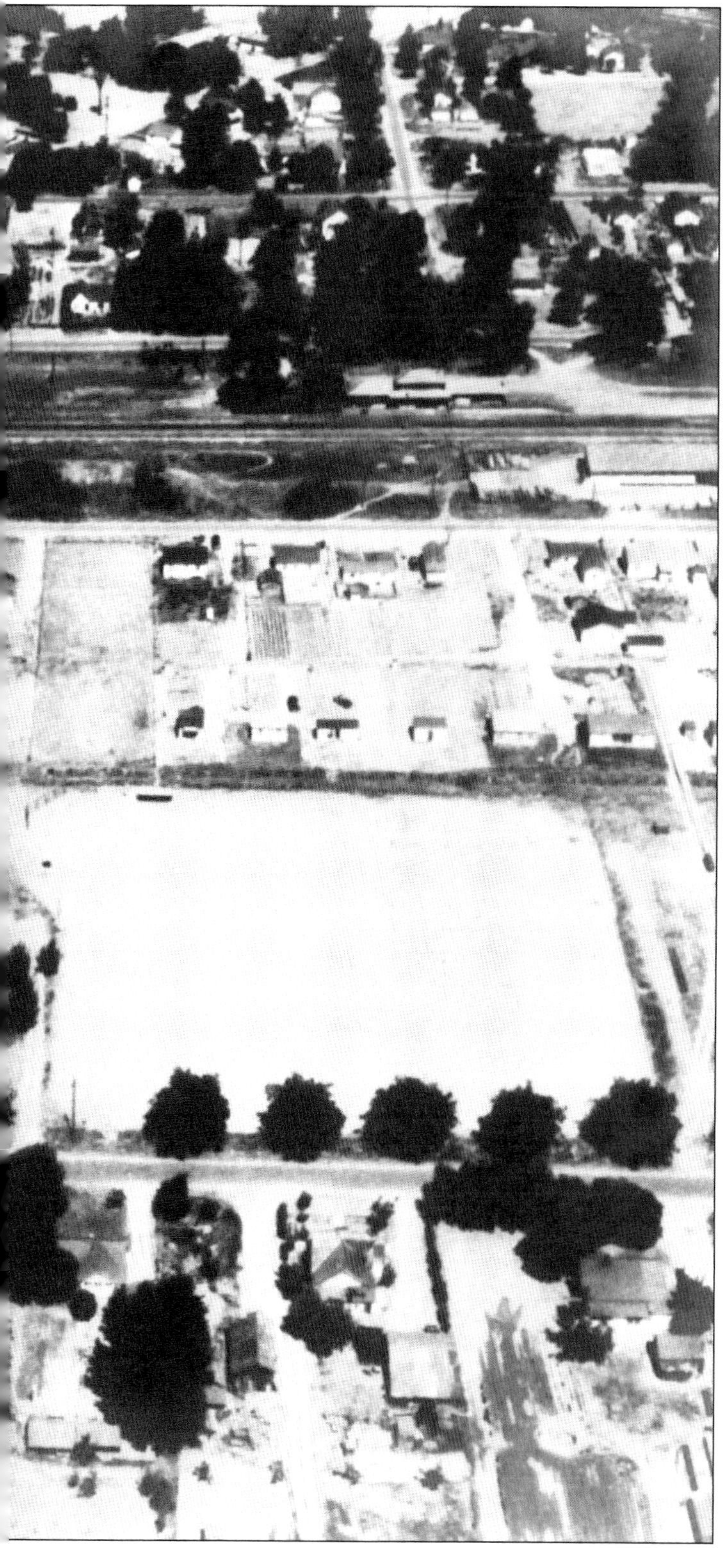

The Denair Union High School, located at Hawthorne and Fresno Streets, can been seen in the aerial photograph from 1946. Much of the land to the south (the right side of the photograph) and west (the bottom of the photograph) are now Denair Unified School District property, with the elementary school and other assorted facilities. (Courtesy of Denair Unified School District.)

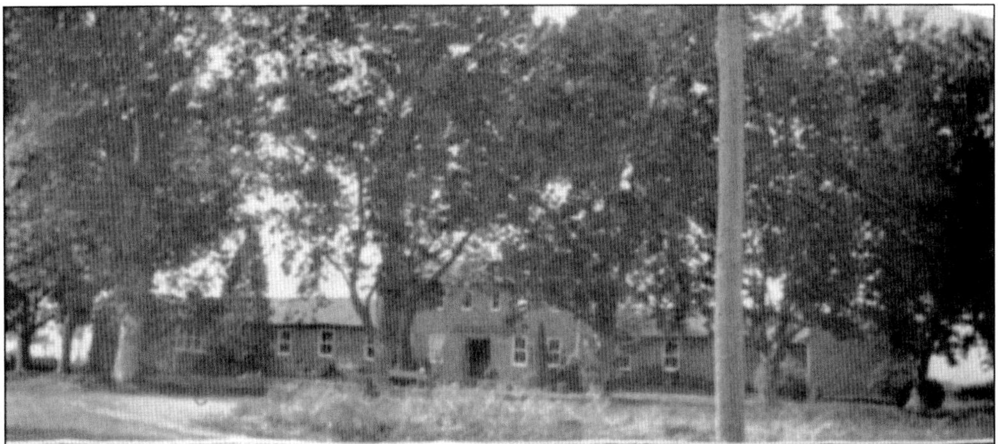

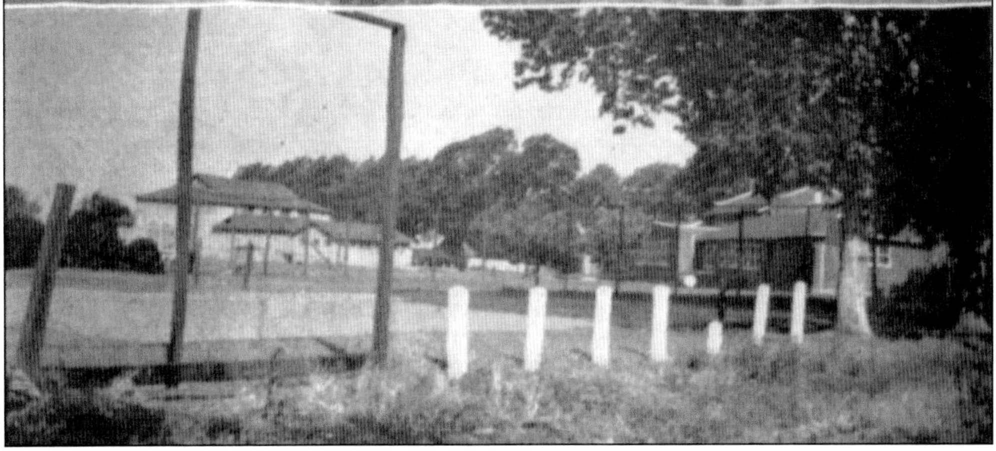

Denair Union High School had facilities for all types of sports. Seen here are some of the practice fields. To the left in this photograph, the "Barn," the school gymnasium, can be seen. It was nicknamed as such due to its resemblance to a large hay barn. It was built in 1927 for a cost of $4,000. (Courtesy of Denair Unified School District)

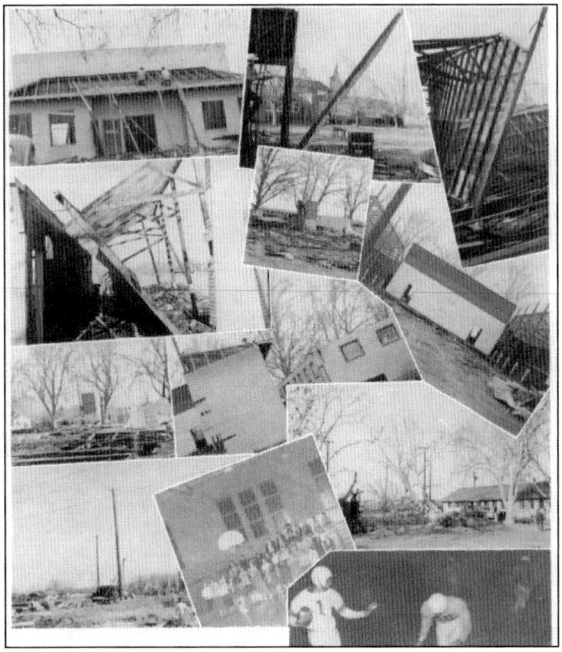

The Barn, as the gymnasium was known, was torn down in 1954. The boys' shop building, situated east of the gym, was moved to Lester road and currently serves as the bus shed. Here is a set of images from the 1954 *El Coyote* yearbook showing the demolition. (Courtesy of Joyce Morrissey.)

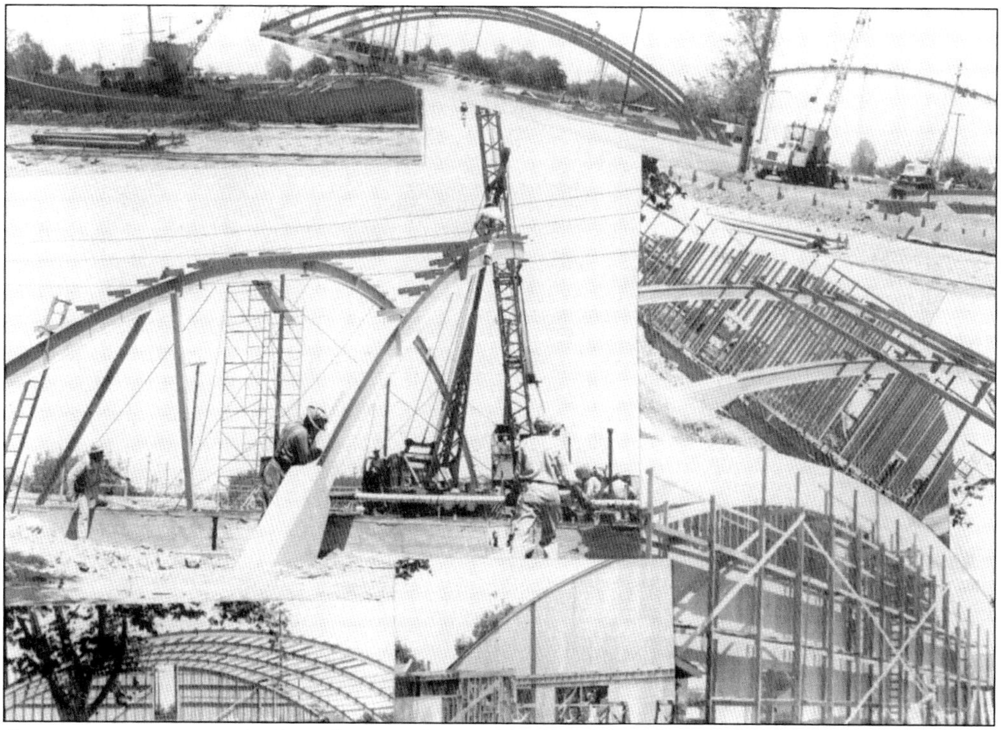

A new gymnasium was built in the same location as the old one. Construction was complete and the building was put to use in 1955. Here are a few photographs from 1955 *El Coyote* yearbook showing the construction of the new gym. (Courtesy of Joyce Morrissey.)

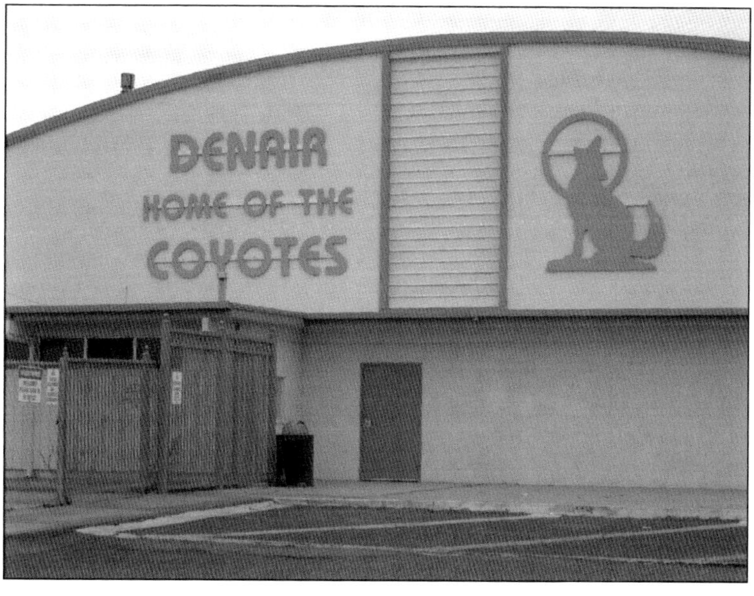

The east side of the new gym was used as a cafeteria until the new cafeteria, Larson Hall, was built in 1956. This gym is still used today by the elementary school. (Courtesy of Stephen Browning.)

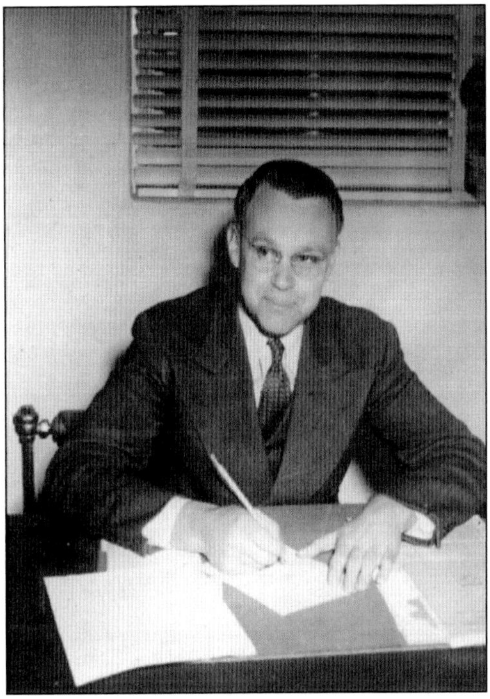

Thomas E. Simms began teaching at Denair High School in 1937. He served as a math and science teacher, basketball coach, bus driver, and, eventually, high school principal. When Denair Grammar School, Denair Union High School, and Montpellier Union School all unified in 1942, Simms was hired as the first superintendent of the new Denair Unified School District. He served in this position until his retirement in 1966. (Courtesy of Denair Unified School District.)

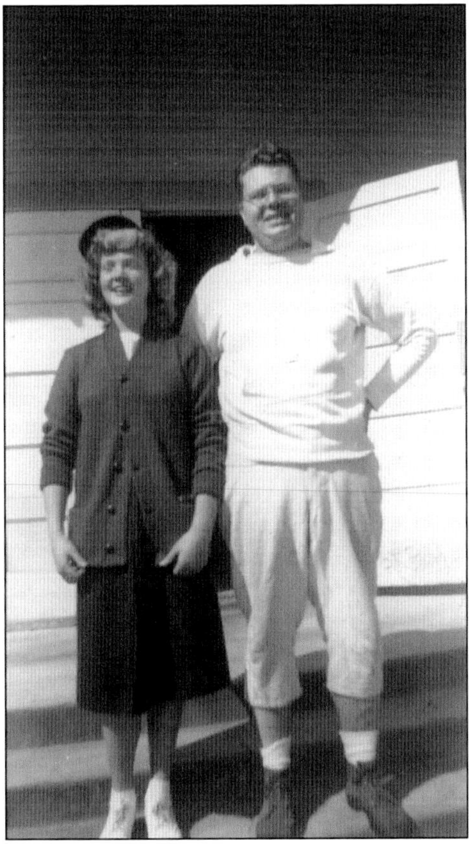

Jack W. Lytton was hired in 1947 as a teacher and coach for Denair High School. His tenure at the high school included 27 years: 6 years as a teacher, 6 years as a counselor, and 15 years as principal. He retired in 1974. In 1976, upon the completion of a new football field and stadium, the building committee and school district named it in honor of Lytton. Here, Coach Lytton poses with student Gail Russel. (Courtesy of Alma Jean Mills Coleman.)

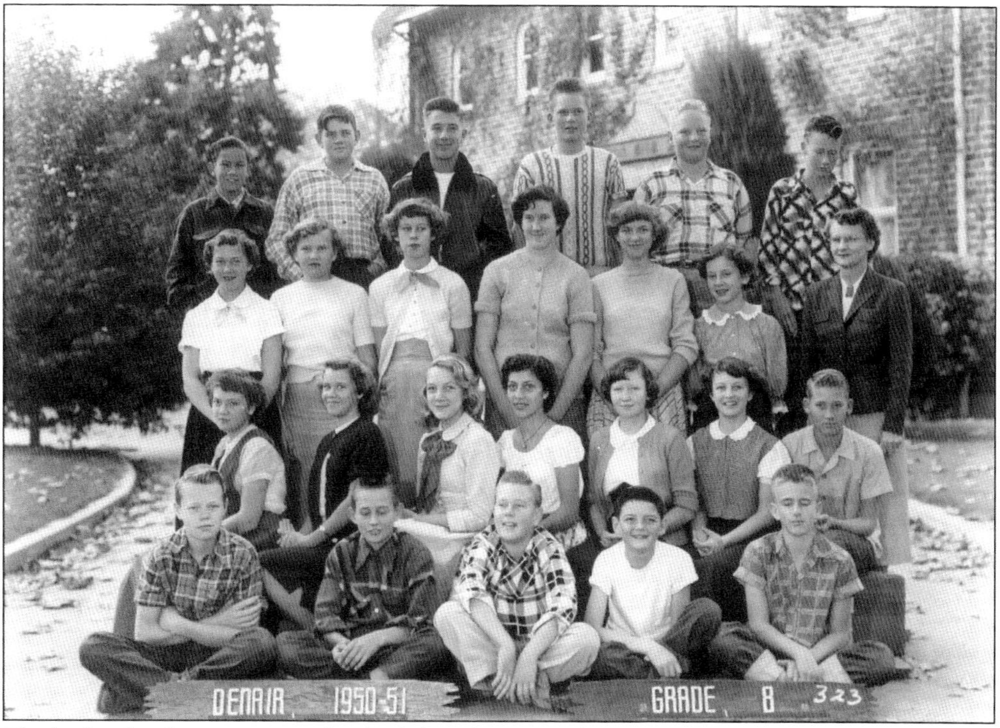

The high school campus served as backdrop for many photographs over the years. Not only was it used for high school photographs, but elementary school photographs were also often taken in front of the beautiful brick building. Seen here is the 1950–1951 eighth-grade class. (Courtesy of Joyce Morrissey.)

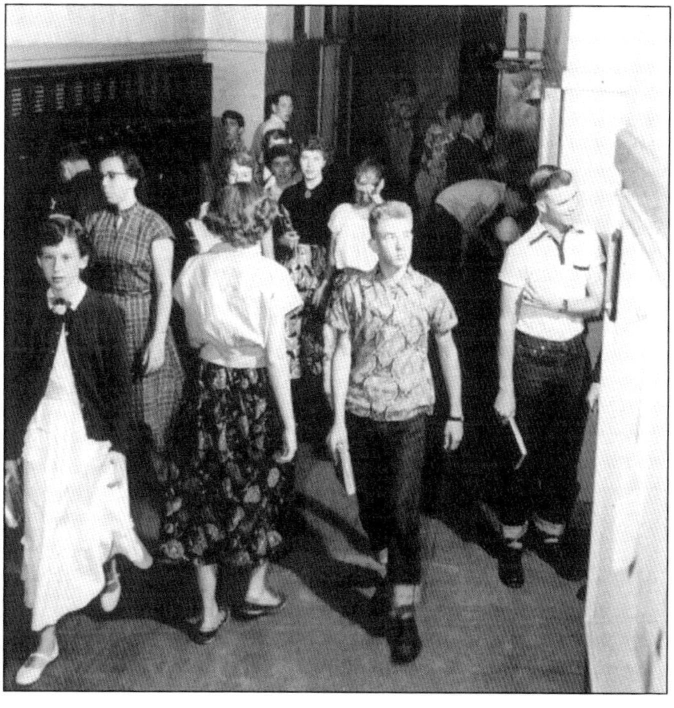

The halls of the high school could often be seen with students and faculty hurrying between classes, as seen in this image from the 1955 *El Coyote* yearbook. (Courtesy of Joyce Morrissey.)

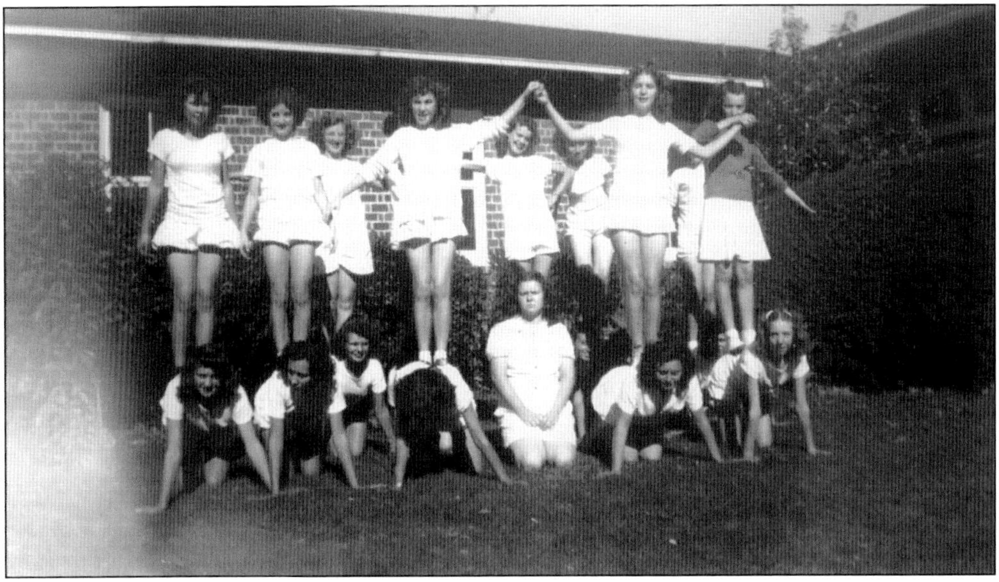

Physical education class has been an important part of the Denair High School education from the beginning. Here, girls practice stunts during a late-1940s physical education class. (Courtesy of Alma Jean Mills Coleman.)

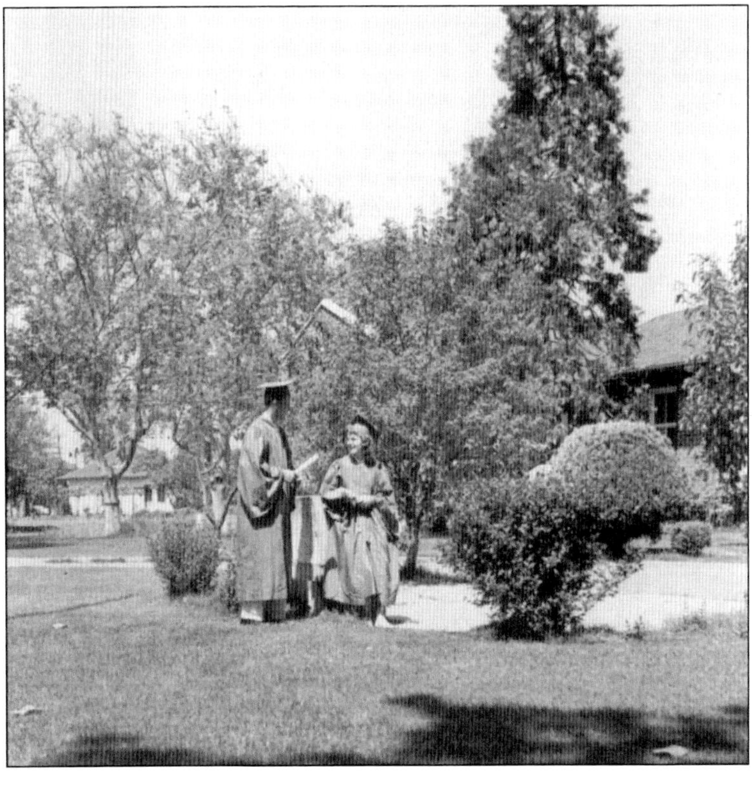

Denair Schools have strived to educate and build the leaders of tomorrow. This has been the foundation of the school from the start. This photograph is included in the 1955 *El Coyote* yearbook. (Courtesy of Joyce Morrissey.)

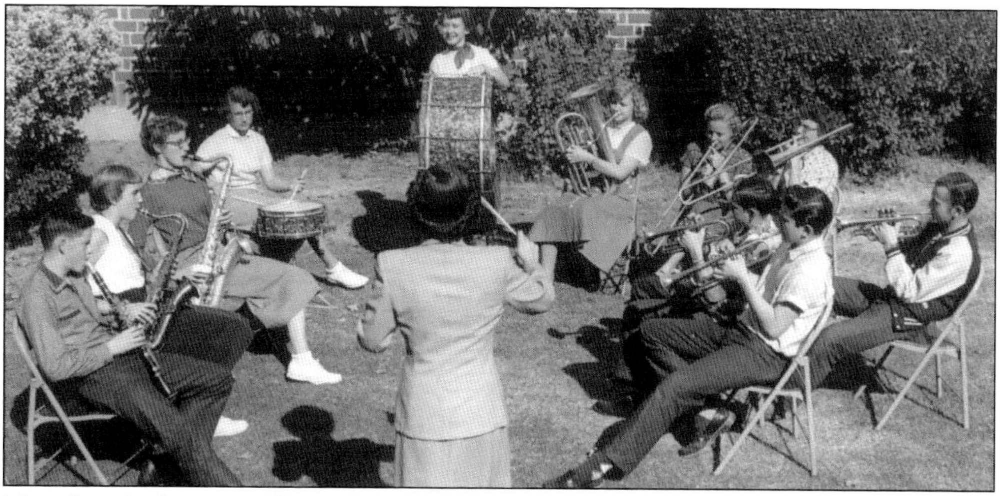

Music has also been a staple at Denair High School from the beginning. In this photograph taken from the 1955 *El Coyote* yearbook, a band made up of students practices. (Courtesy of Joyce Morrissey.)

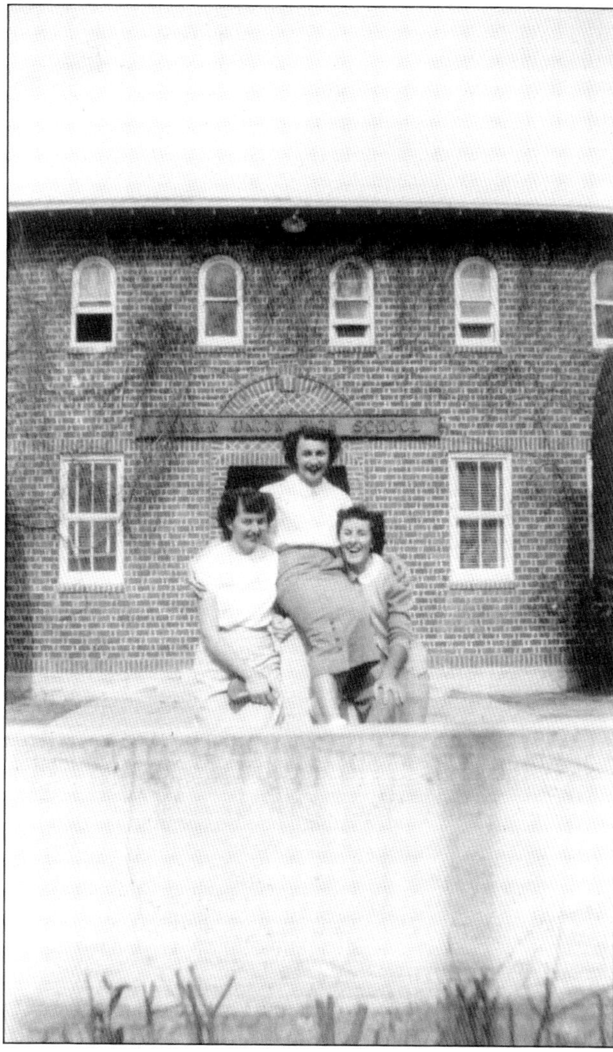

Gloria Murry (left), Virginia Brubaker (center), and Barbara Mills enjoy a warm day in front of the high school building in 1948. (Courtesy of Alma Jean Mills Coleman.)

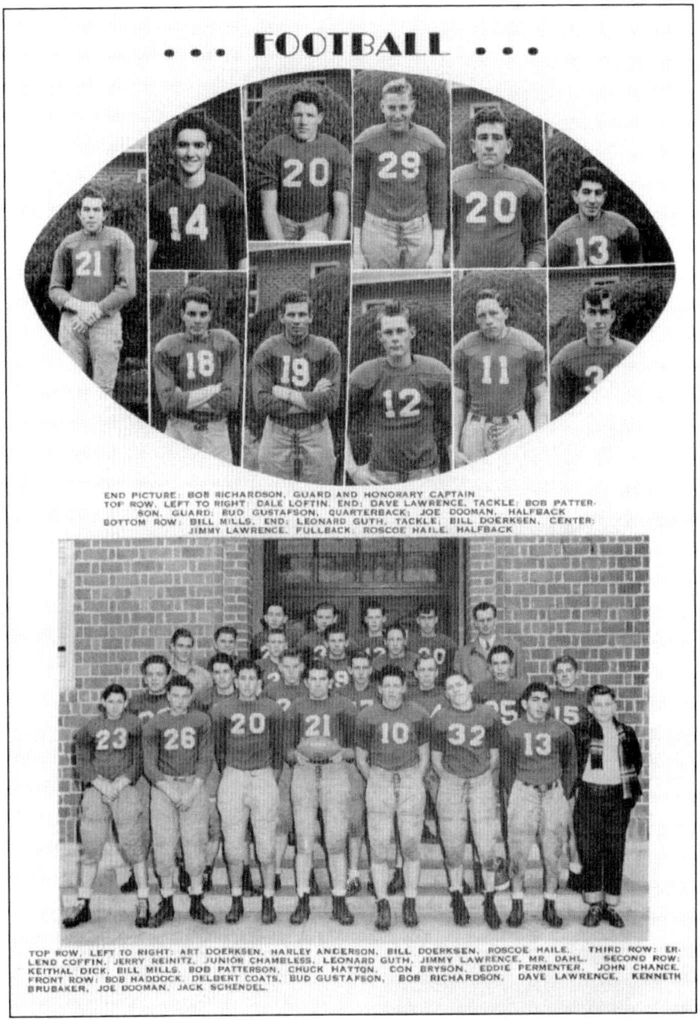

... FOOTBALL ...

END PICTURE: BOB RICHARDSON, GUARD AND HONORARY CAPTAIN
TOP ROW, LEFT TO RIGHT: DALE LOFTIN, END; DAVE LAWRENCE, TACKLE; BOB PATTERSON, GUARD; BUD GUSTAFSON, QUARTERBACK; JOE DOOMAN, HALFBACK
BOTTOM ROW: BILL MILLS, END; LEONARD GUTH, TACKLE; BILL DOERKSEN, CENTER; JIMMY LAWRENCE, FULLBACK; ROSCOE HAILE, HALFBACK

TOP ROW, LEFT TO RIGHT: ART DOERKSEN, HARLEY ANDERSON, BILL DOERKSEN, ROSCOE HAILE. THIRD ROW: ERLEND COFFIN, JERRY REINITZ, JUNIOR CHAMBLESS, LEONARD GUTH, JIMMY LAWRENCE, MR. DAHL. SECOND ROW: KEITHAL DICK, BILL MILLS, BOB PATTERSON, CHUCK HATTON, CON BRYSON, EDDIE PERMENTER, JOHN CHANCE. FRONT ROW: BOB HADDOCK, DELBERT COATS, BUD GUSTAFSON, BOB RICHARDSON, DAVE LAWRENCE, KENNETH BRUBAKER, JOE DOOMAN, JACK SCHENDEL.

Denair High School formed its first football team and played its first season in 1946. (Courtesy of Denair Unified School District.)

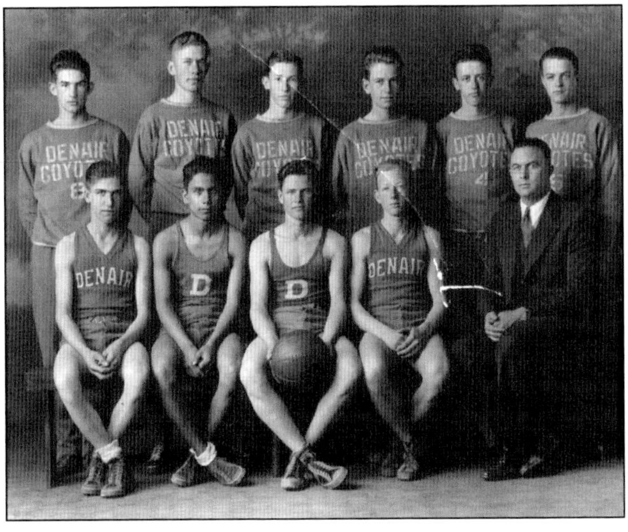

Athletics have long been a popular activity at Denair schools. Basketball, football, baseball, and track have long been enjoyed in Denair. (Courtesy of Denair Unified School District.)

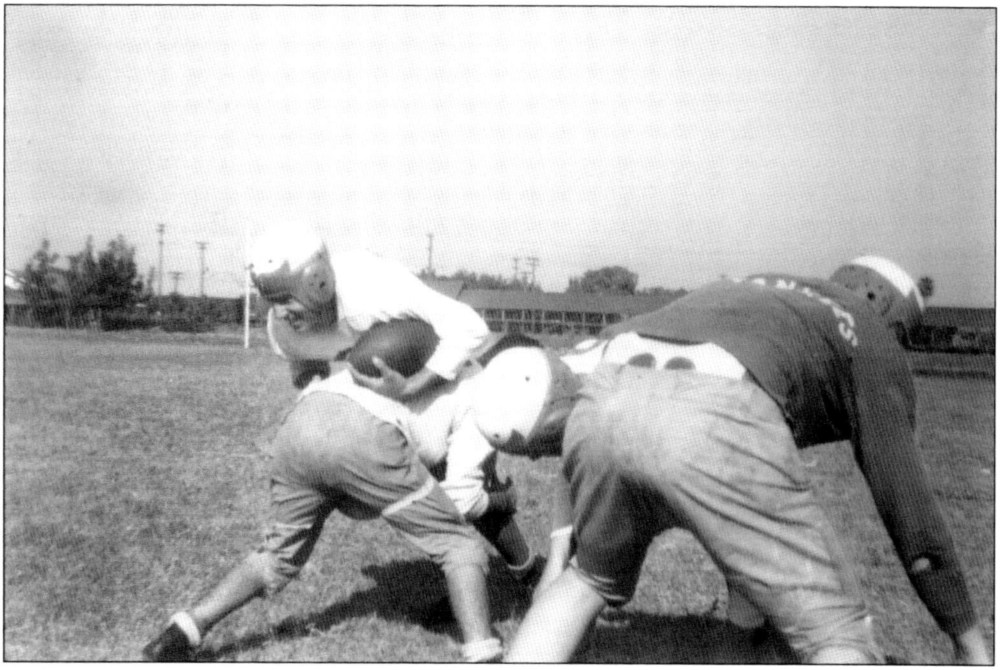

As anyone knows, a winning team needs to practice. Here, Bud Gustafson carries the ball while being tackled by other players. Off in the distance, behind the boys, the fruit packing sheds sit along the railroad tracks. (Courtesy of Alma Jean Mills Coleman.)

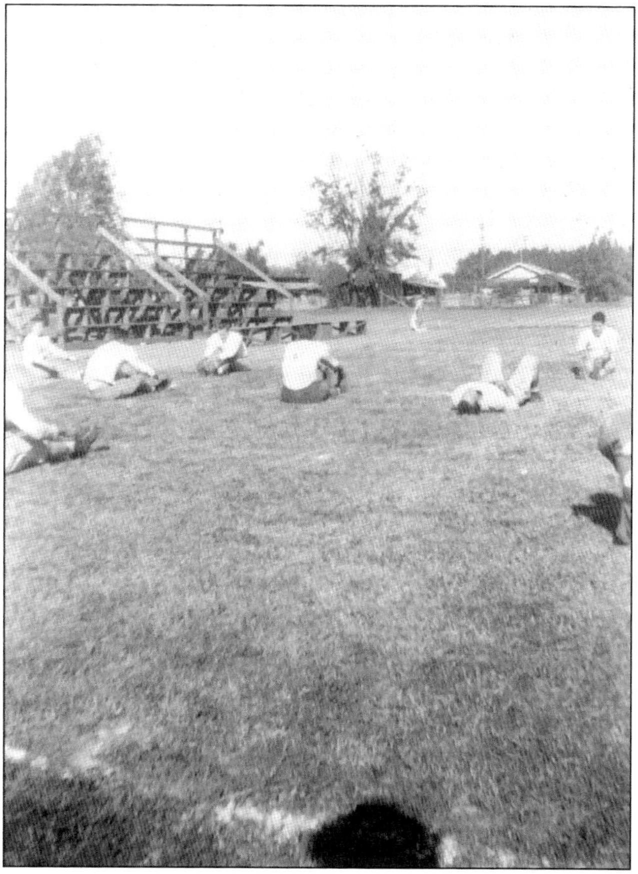

This photograph from around 1946–1947 shows players stretching before football practice to help prevent injury. (Courtesy of Alma Jean Mills Coleman.)

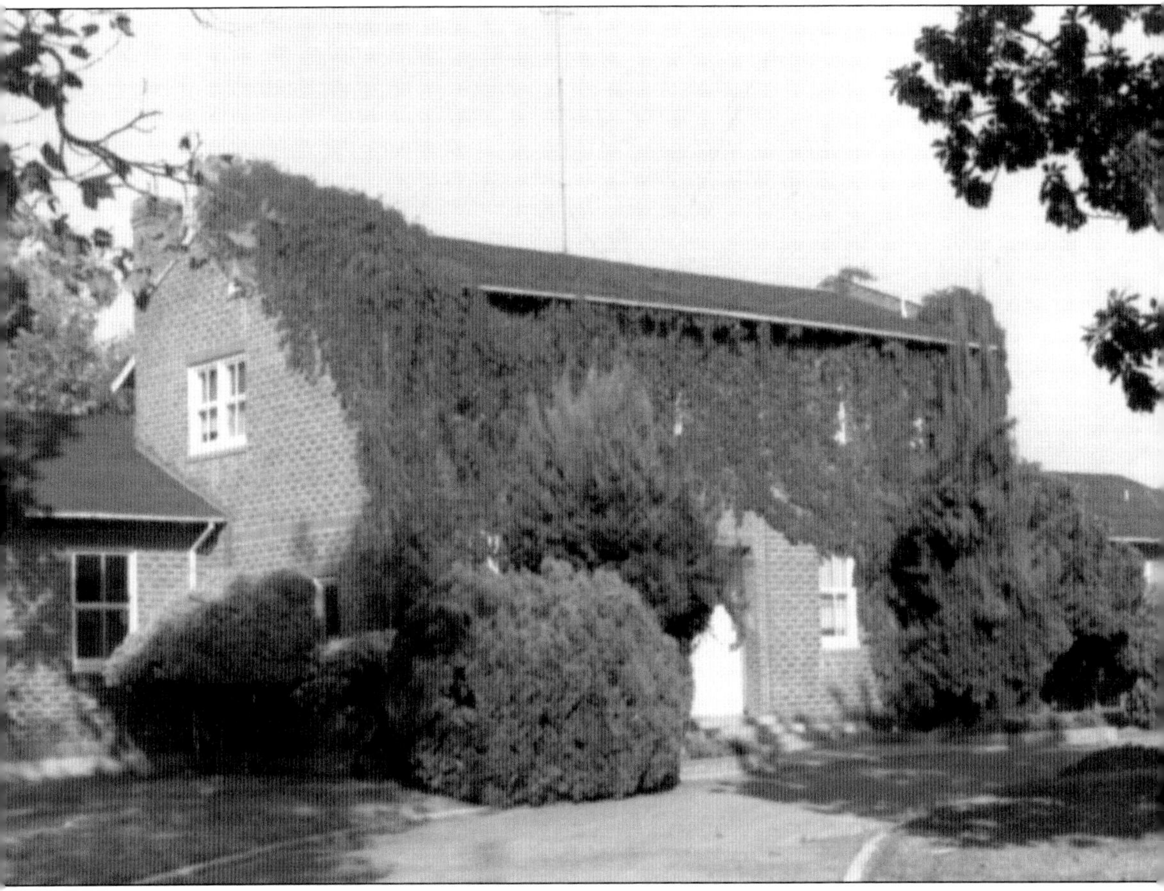

The school district purchased 40 acres from the descendants of John N. Lester on the west side of Lester Road in 1959, to be used for a new high school site. The new Denair High School on Lester Road opened in 1969 and students moved to the new facility, leaving the old brick building behind. (Courtesy of Denair Unified School District.)

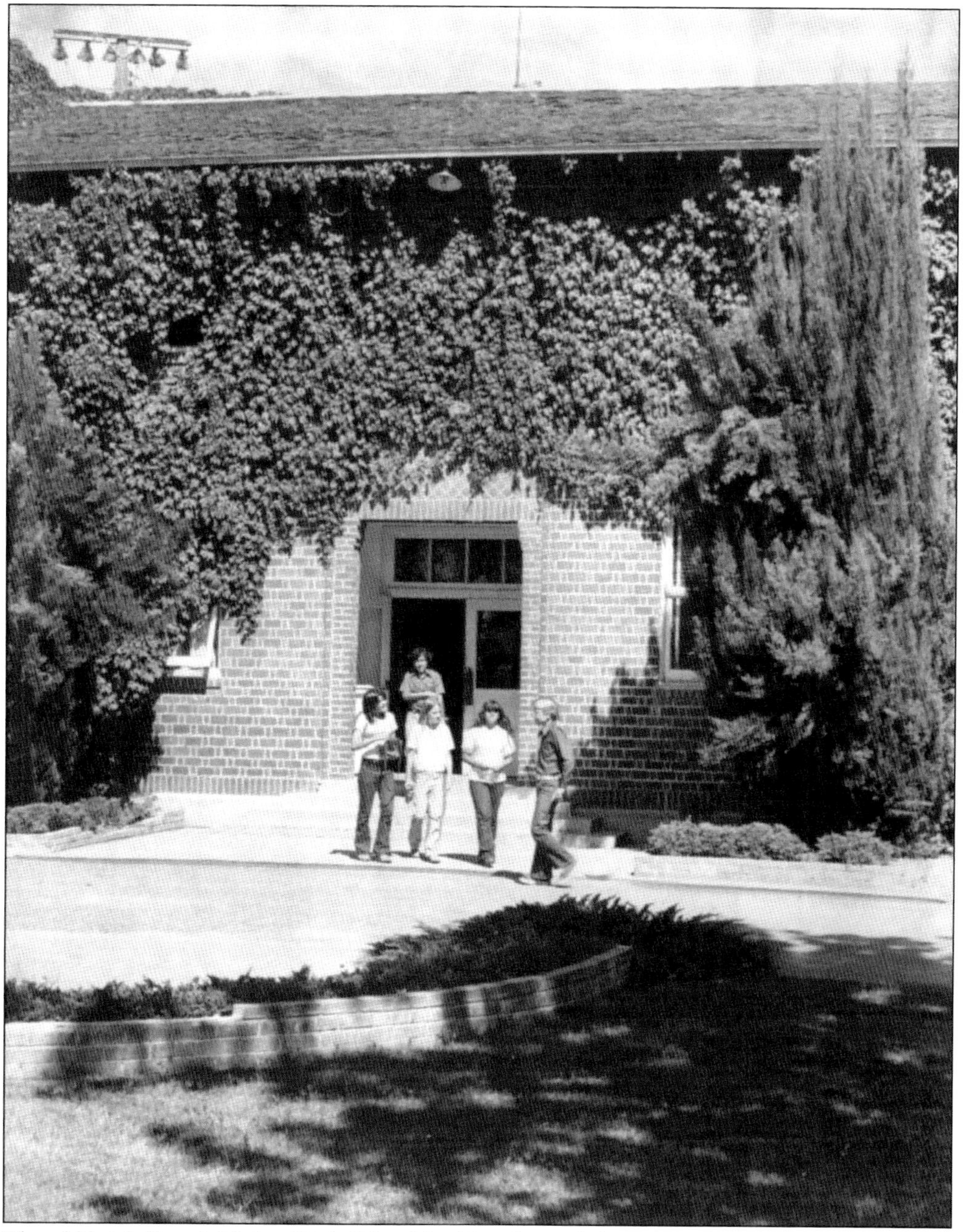

The old brick Denair Union High School building housed the Denair Junior High School from 1969 until 1974, when a new, more modern structure was erected just behind the brick building. (Courtesy of Denair Unified School District.)

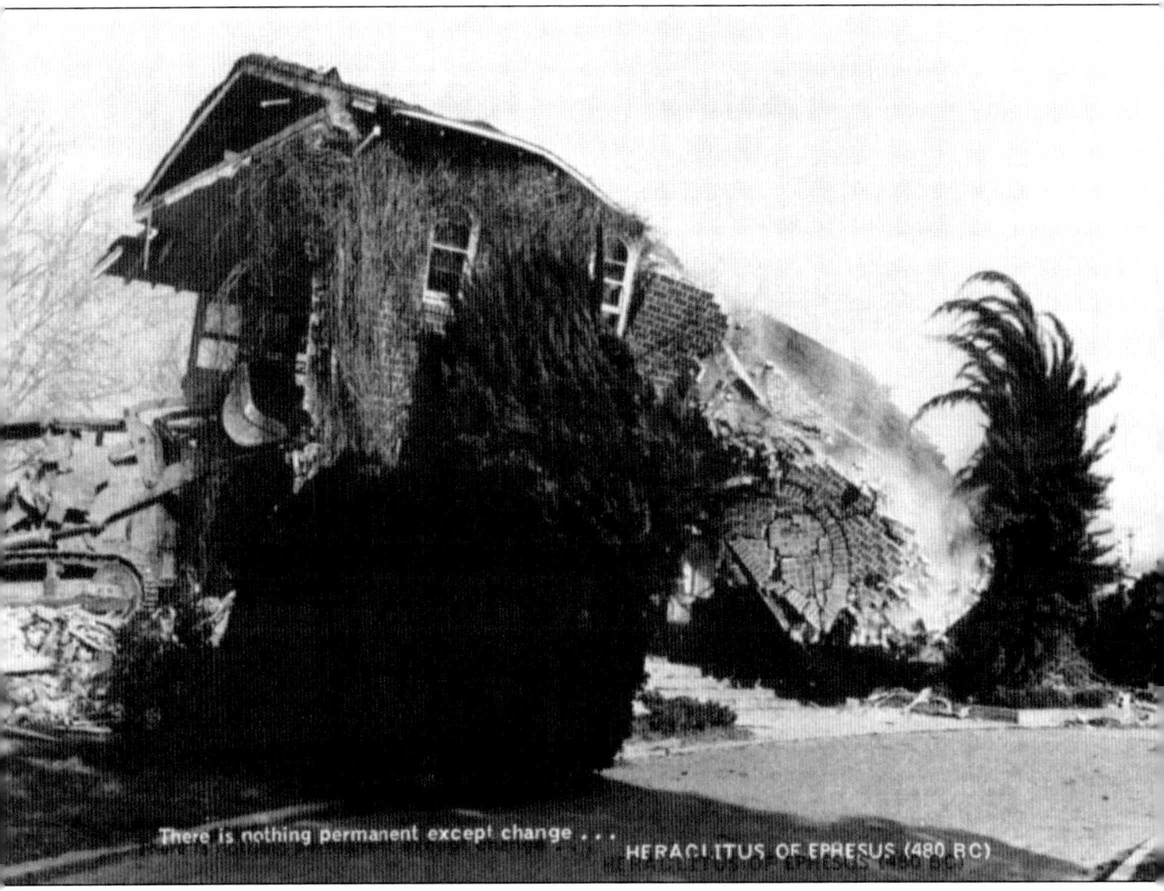

In 1975, because of more stringent California earthquake laws for schools, the old Denair Union High School building was demolished. (Courtesy of Denair Unified School District.)

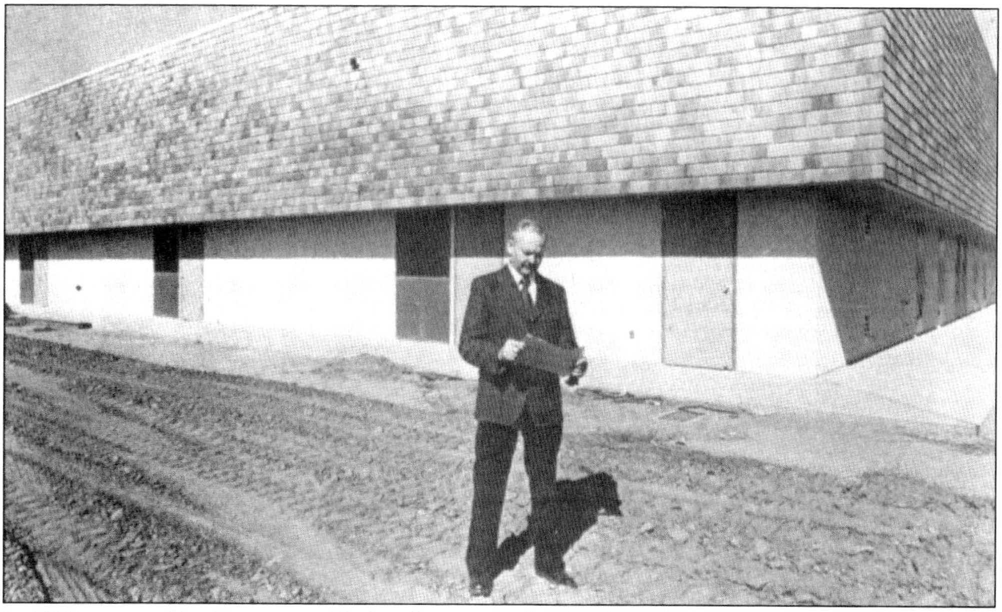

In 1974, a second building was added to the new high school. In this 1974 photograph, high school principal Daniel DuFrane checks landscaping plans designed to complete the campus. (Courtesy of the *Turlock Daily Journal.*)

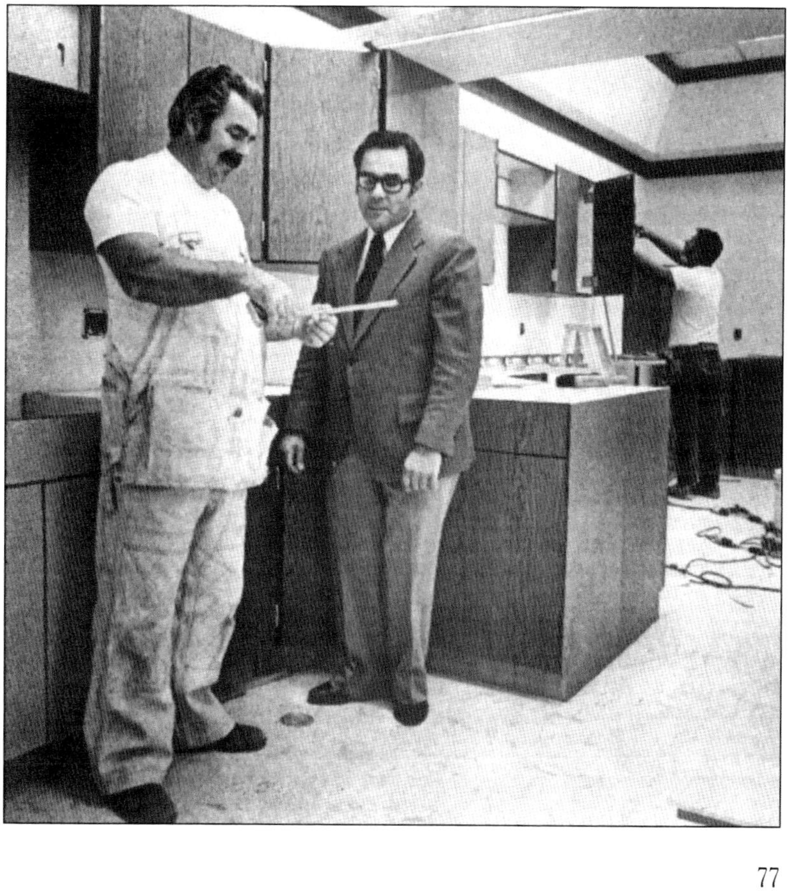

The new middle school building was also constructed in 1974. Here, middle school principal Lee Fernandes (right) checks with carpenter Dave Kidwell on the progress of the home economics classroom at the new middle school. (Courtesy of the *Turlock Daily Journal.*)

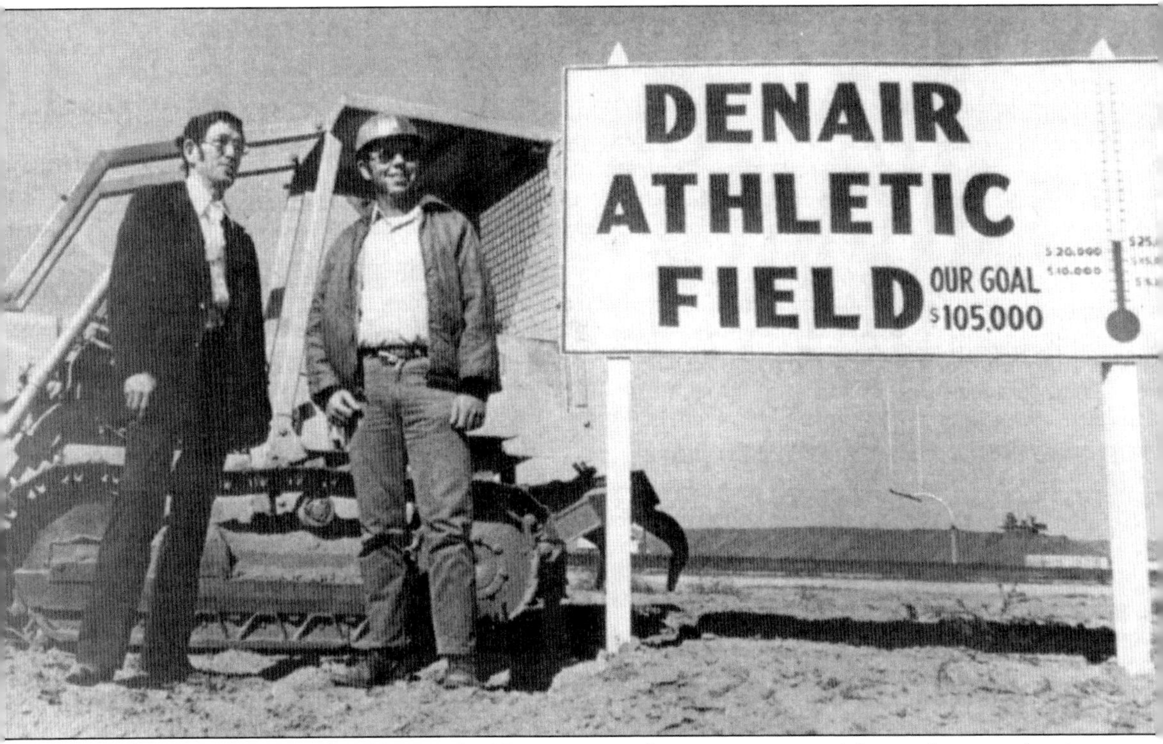

A $650,000 Denair School District building program that same year taxed district finances, leaving no room in the budget for a football stadium. Denair citizens started an athletic field fund to raise the money to build the stadium. Casey Construction provided labor at no charge—such as Bub Sanders (right), who helped construct portions of the stadium and drive donated equipment. The completed stadium was named in honor of former teacher, coach, and principal Jack Lytton. This image appears in the October 30, 1974, issue of the *Turlock Daily Journal.* (Courtesy of the *Turlock Daily Journal.*)

Four

CHURCHES

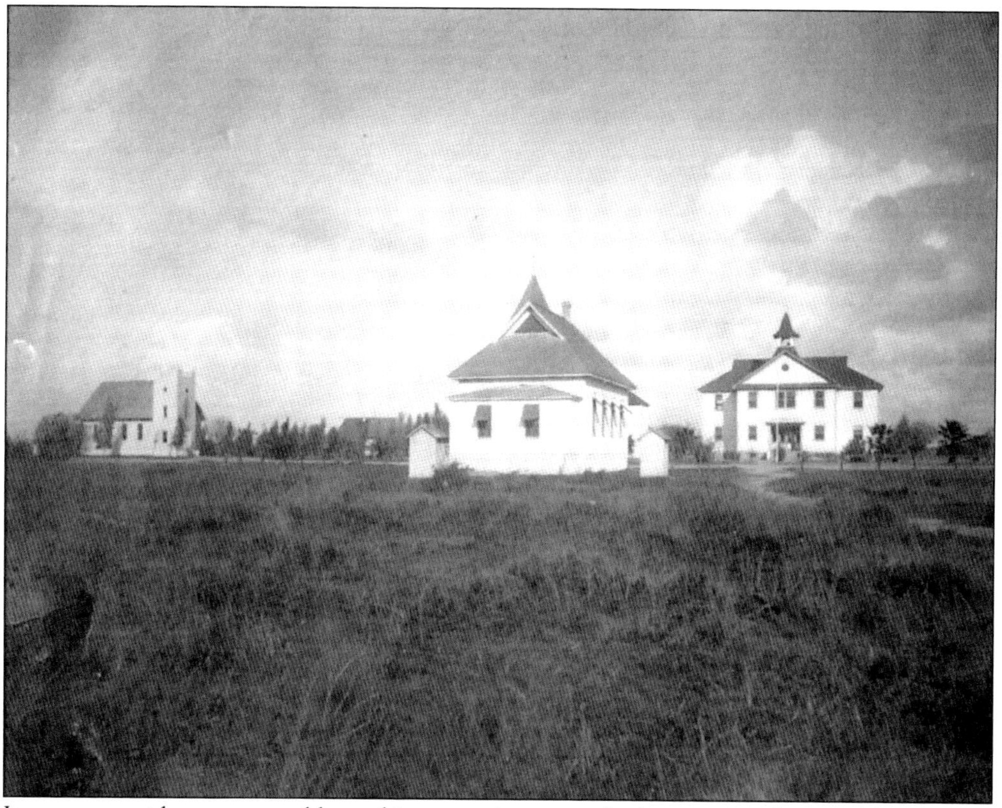

It was once said a person could stand in a certain area and take a picture that would include all three buildings in town, as proven in this photograph of the Denair Friends Church on the left, Christian Church (original schoolhouse) in the middle, and the two-story schoolhouse on right. (Courtesy of John Chance.)

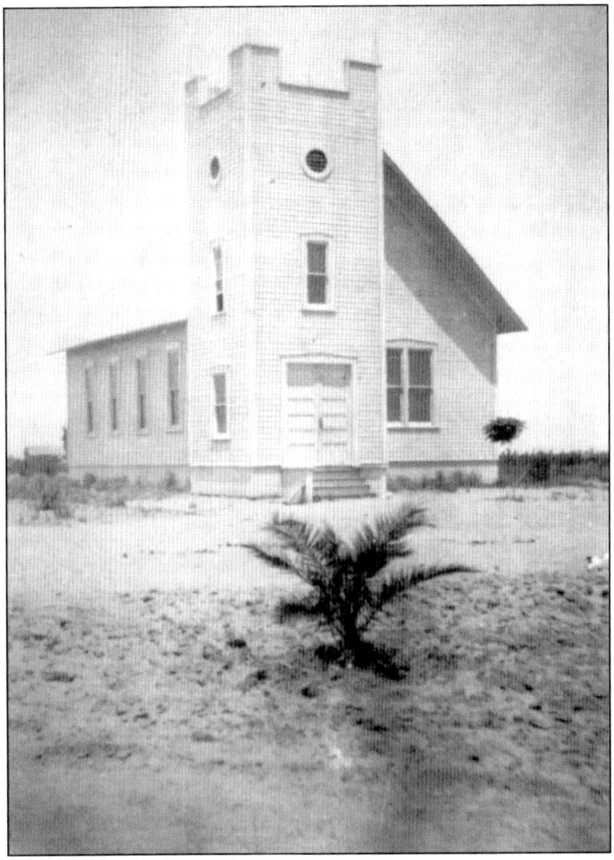

In 1907, a small group of Quakers moved into the area, with the promise of fertile land and a place to start a Quaker colony. The Denair Friends Church was built a year later at the corner of Gratton Road and Zeering Road. (Courtesy of John Chance.)

Elwood Mills, an ordained minister, answered the call to become the first minister of the Denair Friends Church. (Courtesy of John Chance.)

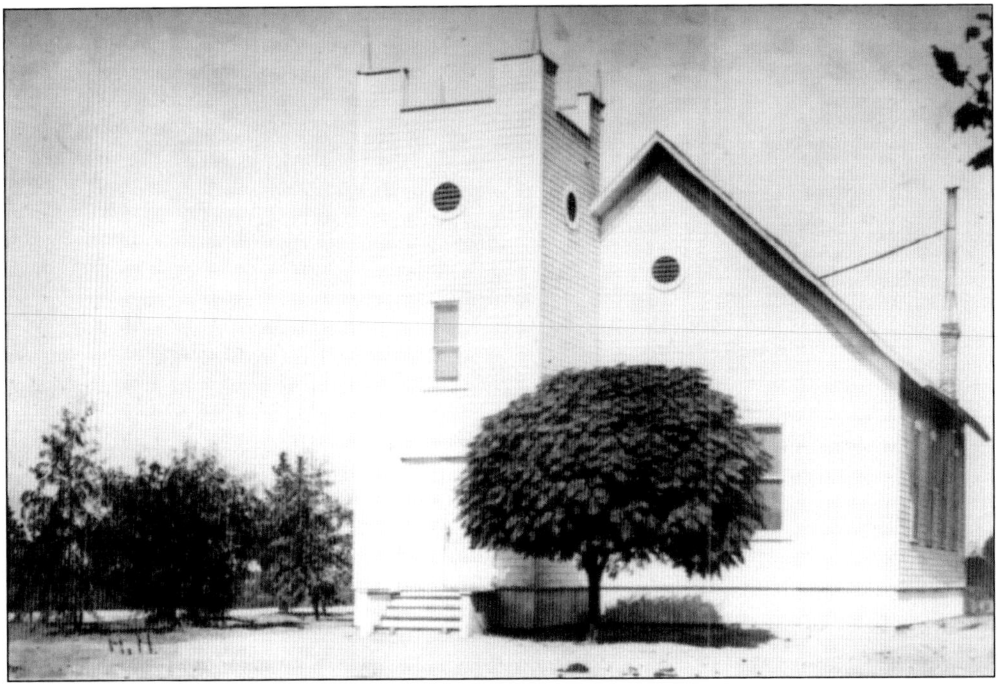

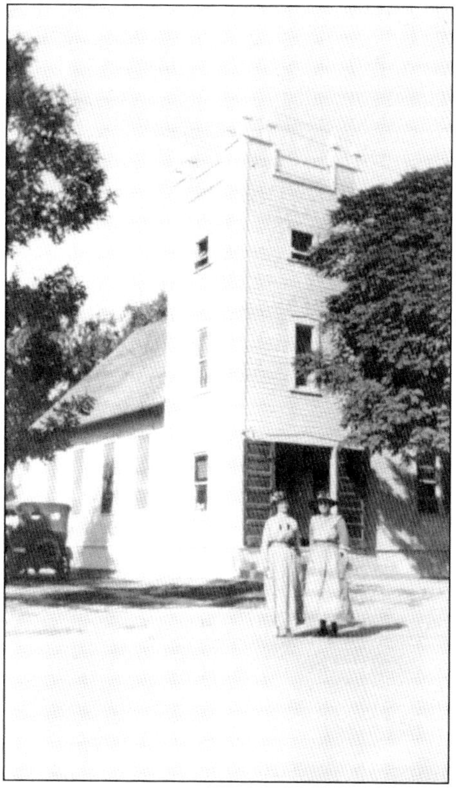

Although a Quaker colony never developed, the little Friends Church thrived with members from the area and held Sunday services under kerosene lamps with organ music playing. (Both, courtesy of John Chance.)

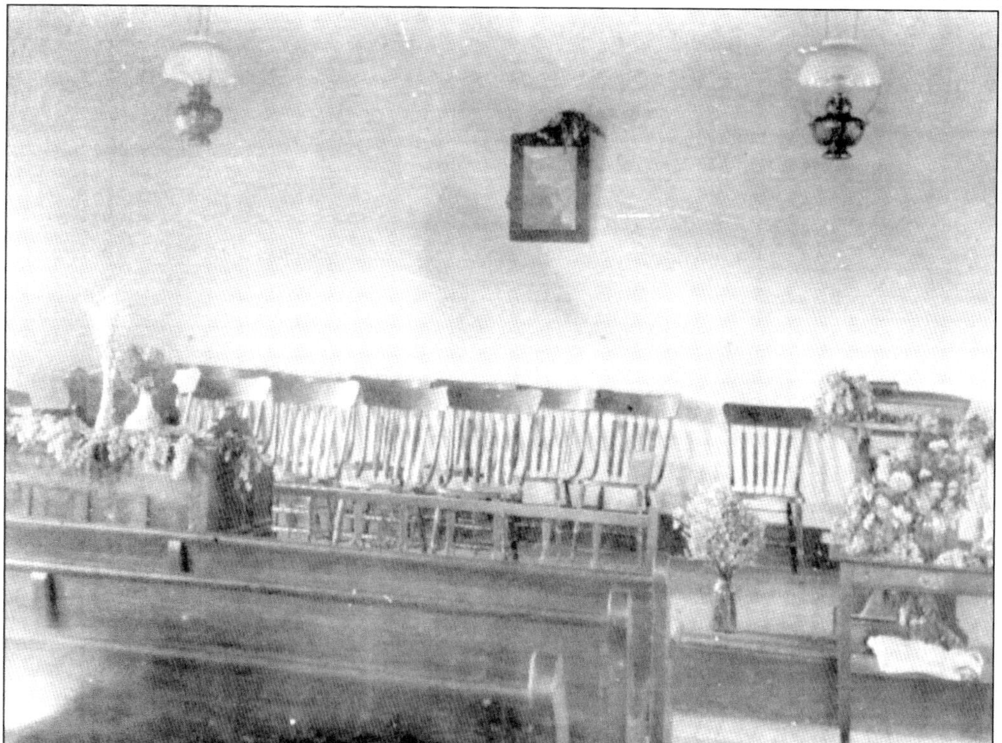

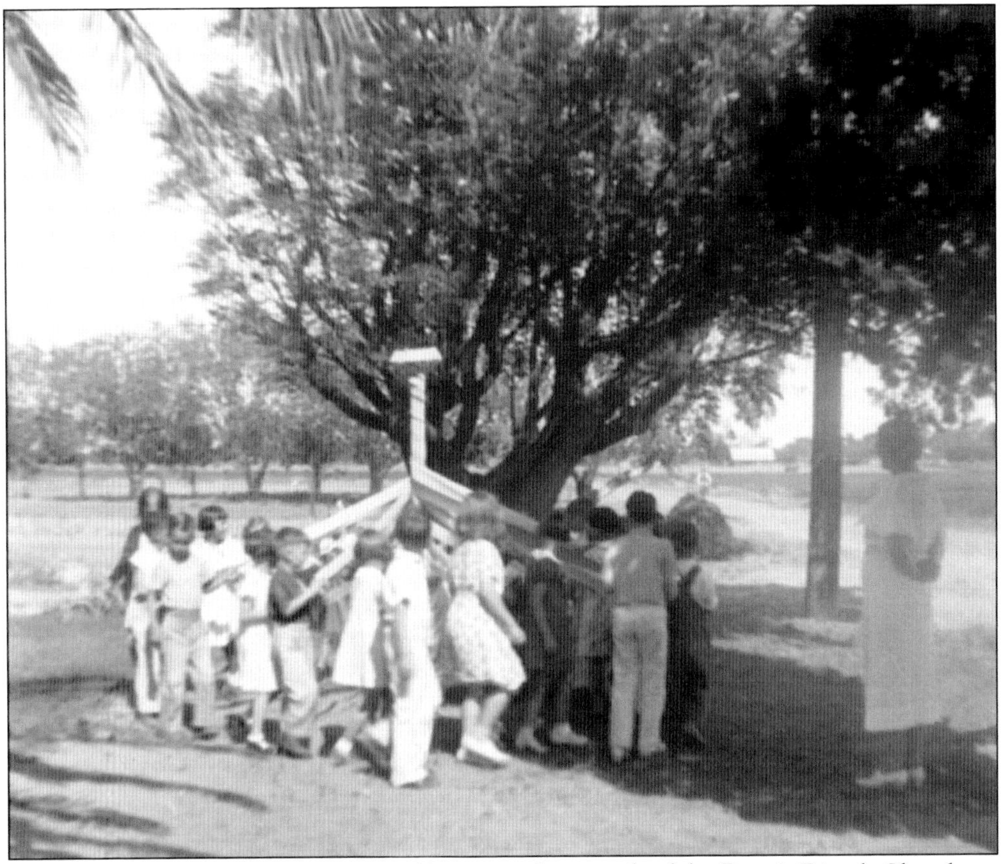

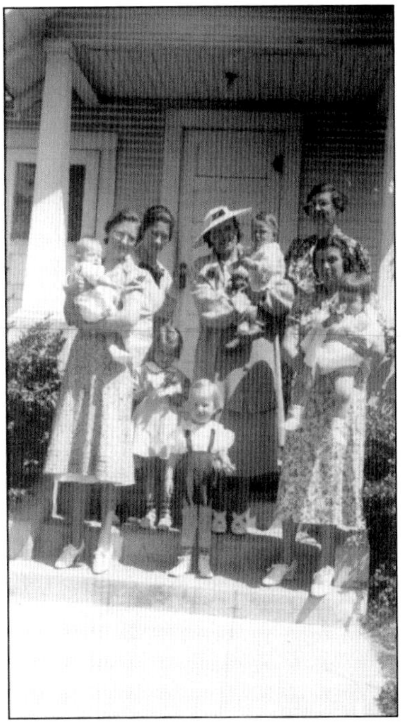

Above is a photograph of the Denair Friends Church Sunday schoolchildren celebrating May Day with a maypole dance in the early 1930s. Many families have worshiped every Sunday at the little Denair Friends Church, including the Chances, Domecqs, Bonners, and Terrels. (Both, courtesy of John Chance.)

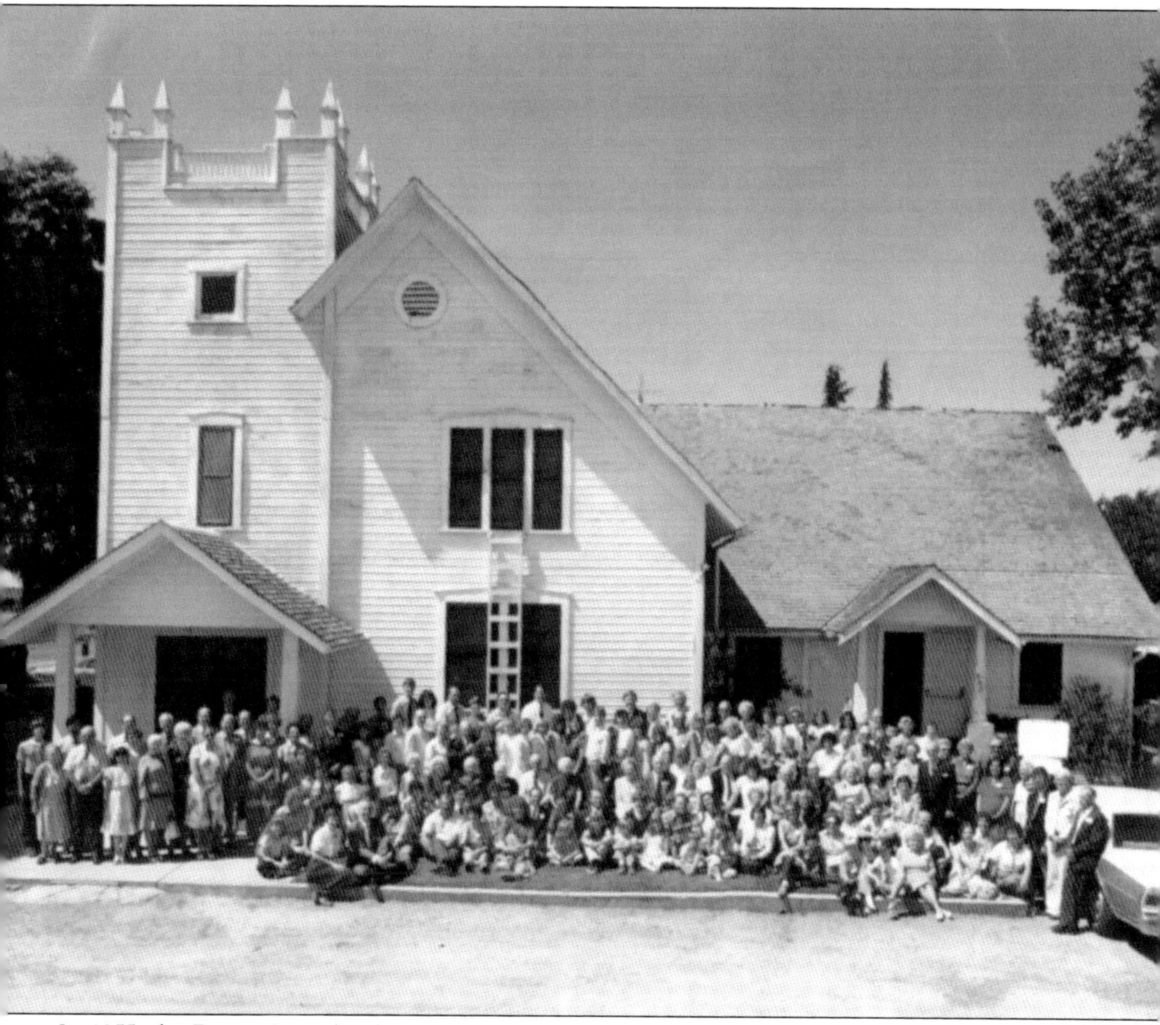

In 1955, the Denair Friends Church, having outgrown their small community church, saw the need for a larger facility. A more modern structure was built just a block north of the old church on Zeering Road. Here, church members celebrate the church's 50th anniversary around 1957. (Courtesy of John Chance.)

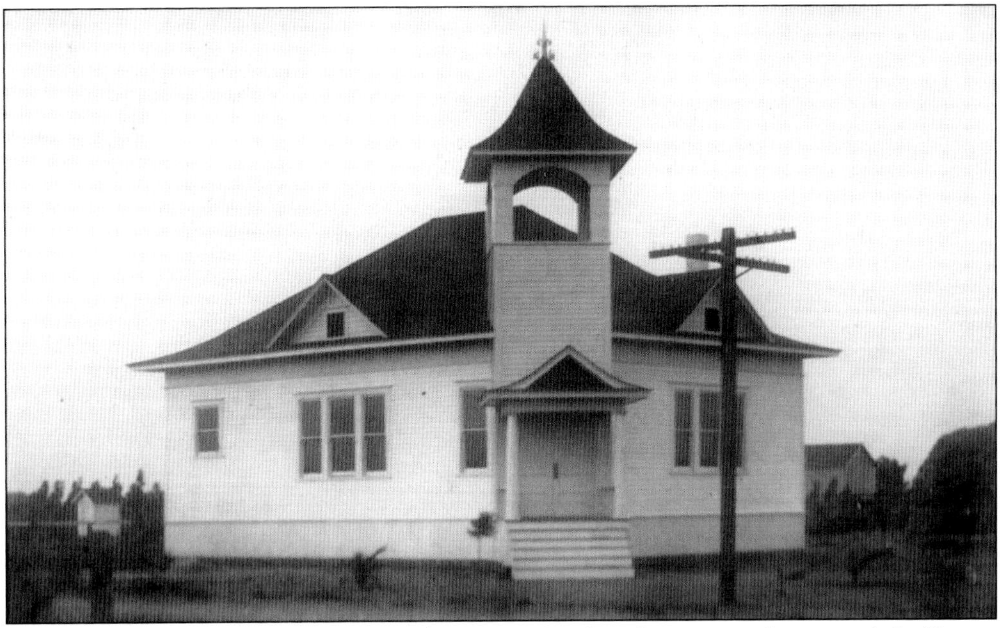

In March 1906, a group of about 20 people met one Sunday afternoon and organized the Denair Missionary Baptist Church. The church building was constructed four years later in 1910, with Rev. N.J. Witmer as pastor. (Courtesy of the Witmer family.)

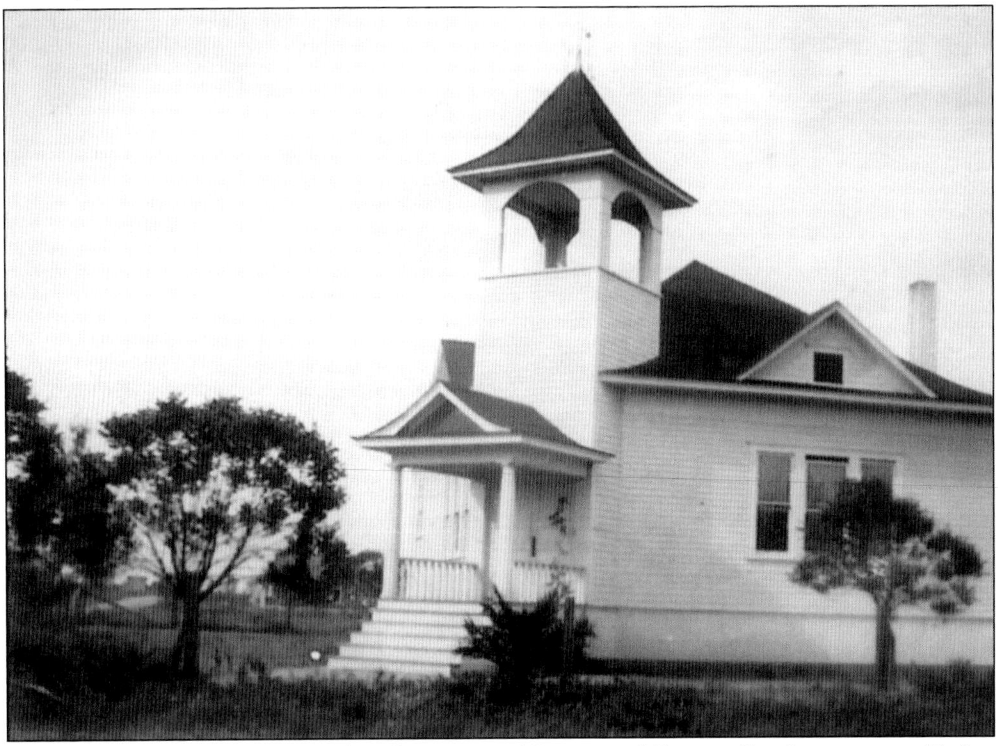

The missionary church has stood at the corner of Sperry and Zeering Roads ever since. Today, the building is used by the Denair Bilingual Seventh-day Adventist Church, but the structure remains the same. (Courtesy of Denair Community Service District.)

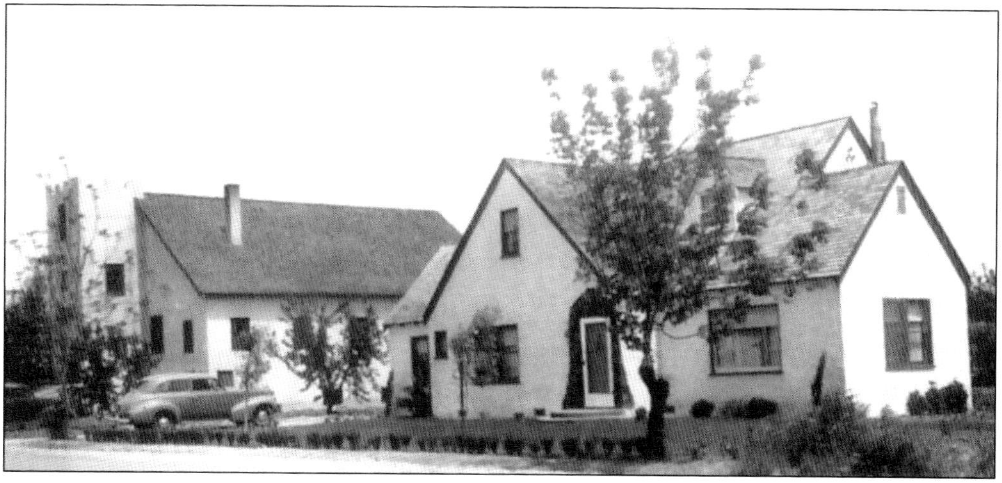

The Denair Church of the Nazarene was organized in June 1933. Mr. and Mrs. Bob Story gave the church one acre of land at the corner of Gratton and Walton Roads. Below is the Denair Church of the Nazarene congregation in 1944. (Above, courtesy of the Connecting Point Church of the Nazarene; below, courtesy of Alma Jean Mills Coleman.)

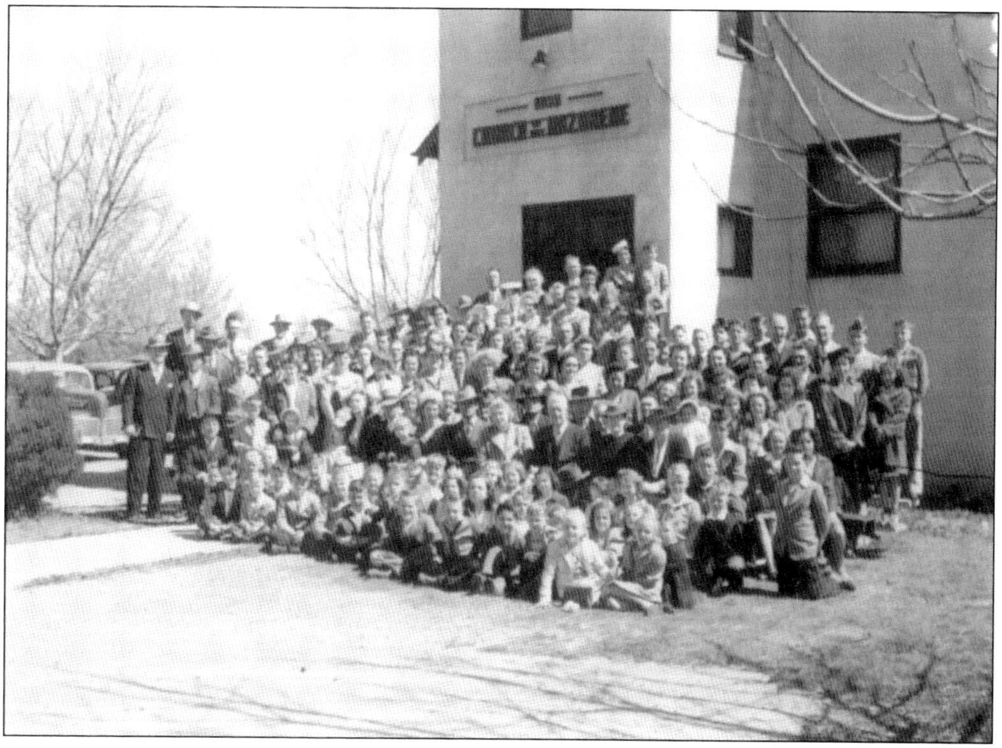

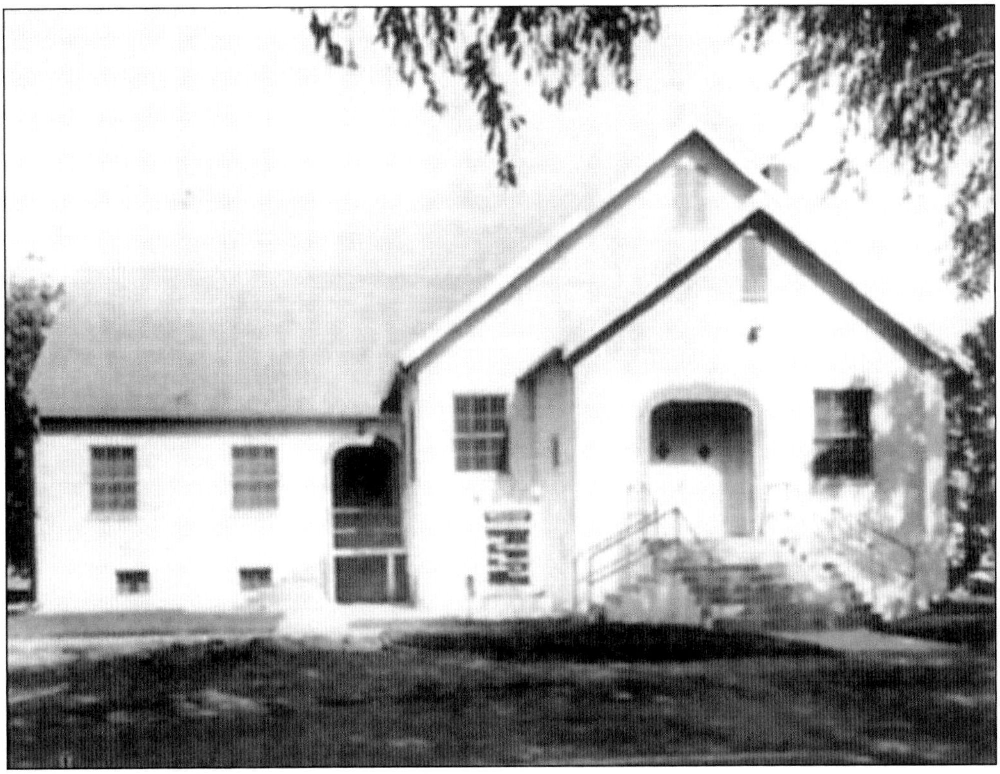

The Church of the Nazarene was expanded in the late 1940s and celebrated its 25th anniversary in 1958, as seen in this photograph. In 1982, the church moved to a larger facility built at its current location on the corner of Monte Vista Avenue and Waring Road. (Both, courtesy of the Connecting Point Church of the Nazarene.)

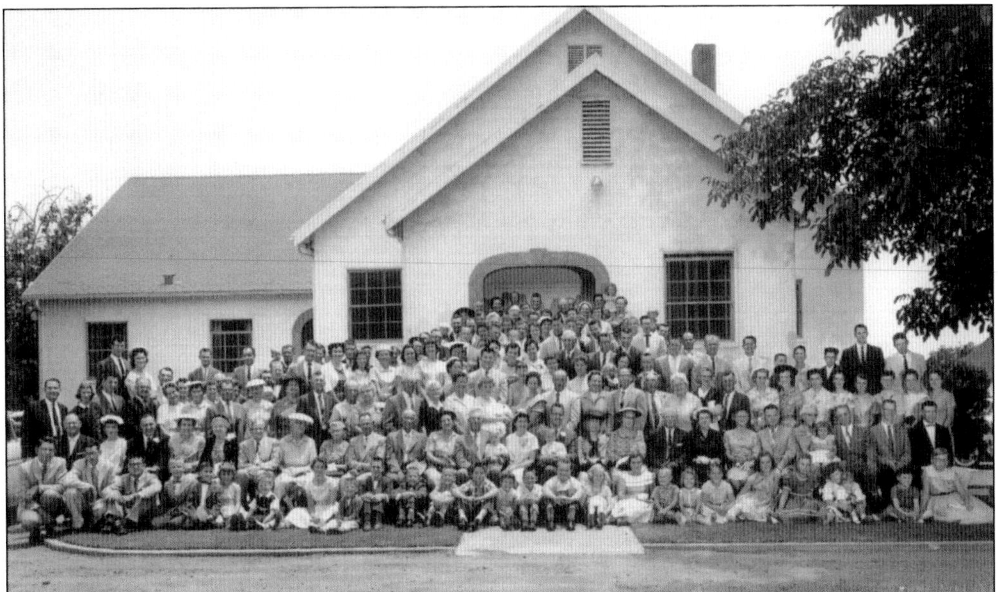

Five

Around Town

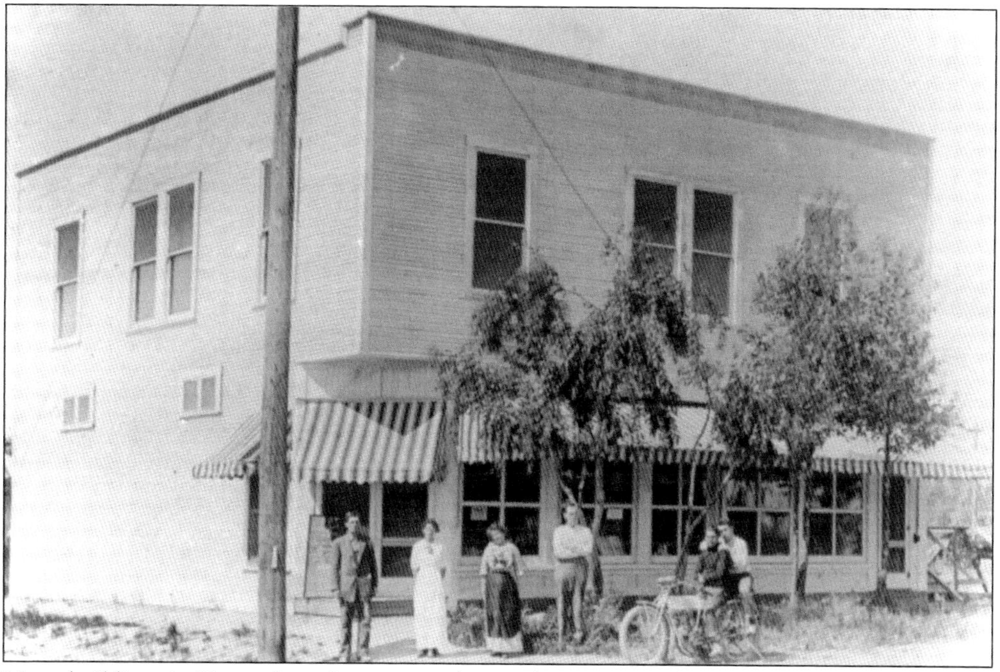

Many buildings in Denair have been erected, torn down, or even burned down and then rebuilt. The face of Main Street and the surrounding area has changed a lot over the years. This building sits at the corner of Main Street and Santa Fe Avenue; however, it looks much different today. Since being built in 1914, it has housed many businesses throughout years. Most people today know it as a single-story building that was once home to a garage and gas station. The gentlemen on the motorcycle are known to be Walt and Tom Harmon, and one of the ladies pictured is named Grace. (Courtesy of Denair Community Service District.)

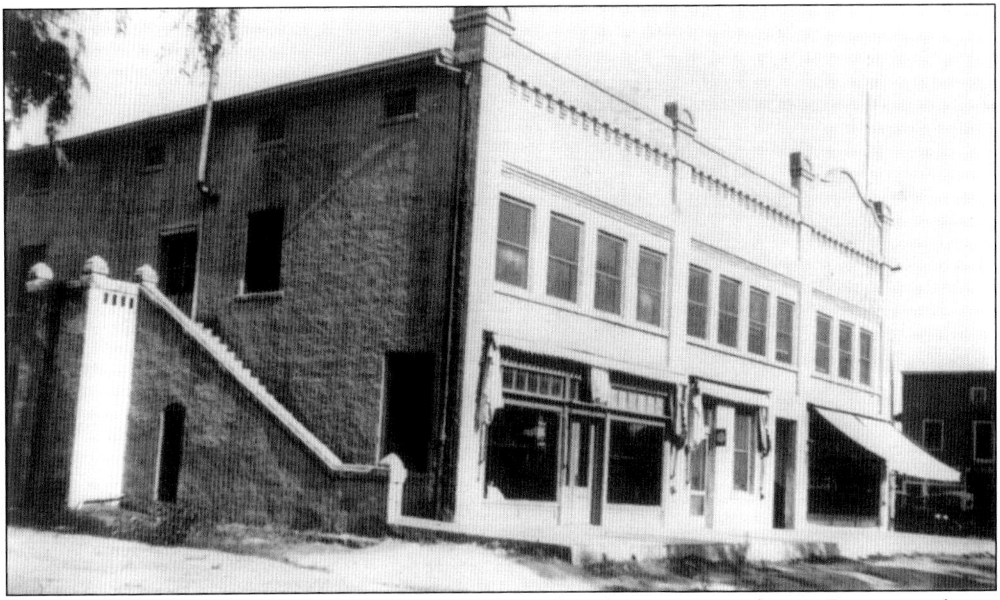

The old Bank Building, while no longer standing, is still in the memories of many Denair residents. When the building was demolished in 1981, many of the bricks were used in construction of the new Bank Building, which stands today in its place. (Courtesy of Denair Unified School District.)

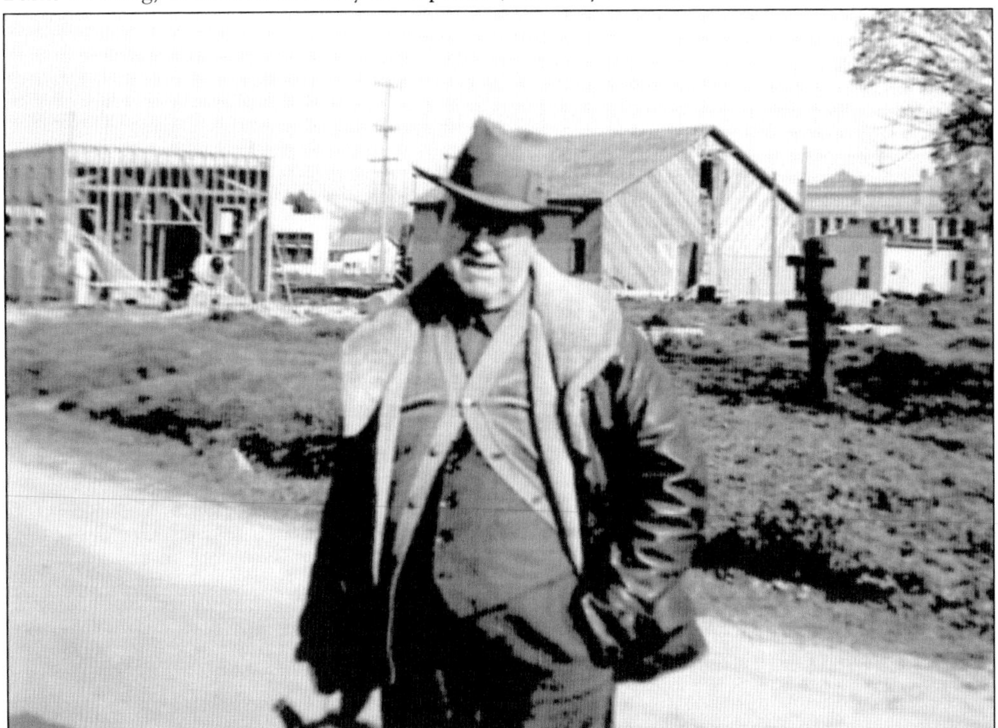

Tim Foley, section boss for the Santa Fe Railway, stands on Santa Fe Avenue. Construction of buildings along Main Street can be seeing in the background. In this 1934 picture, one can see the old Bank Building at far right, with the corner of the original post office and library just left of Foley. (Courtesy of John Chance.)

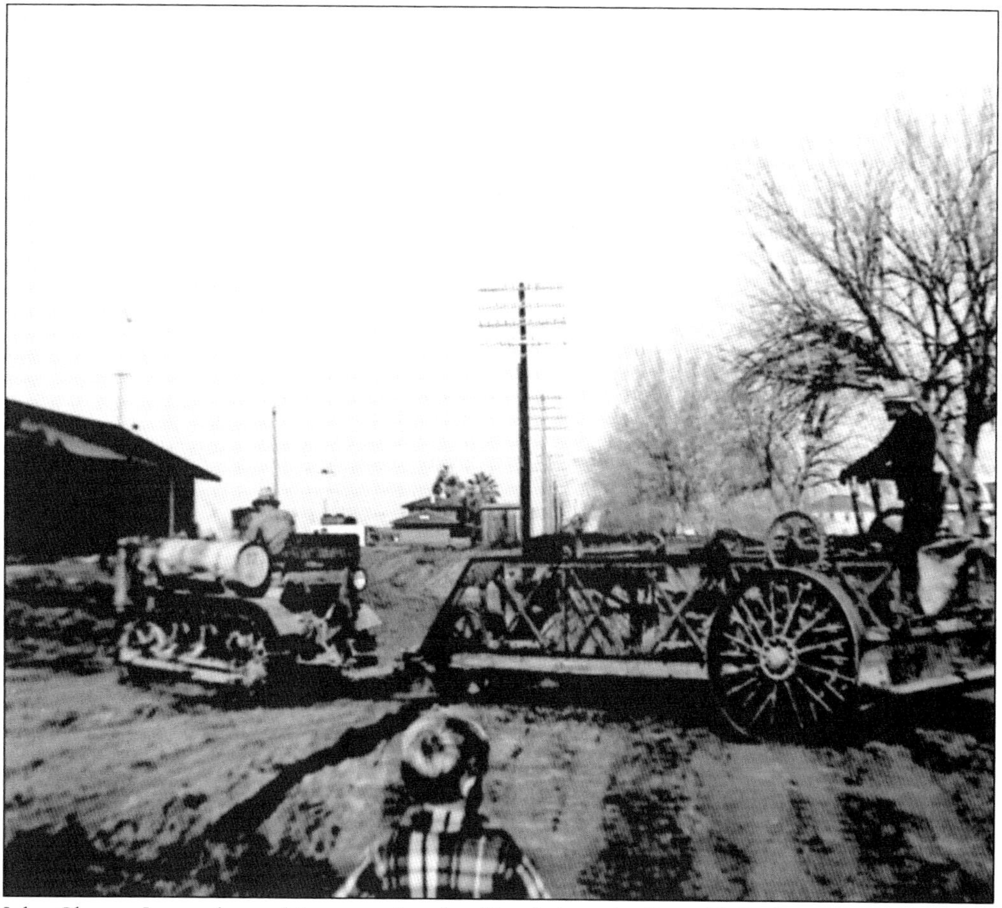

John Chance Jr. stands watching as workers level land along the Santa Fe Railway to make way for a new shipping warehouse. This photograph was taken around 1934. (Courtesy of John Chance.)

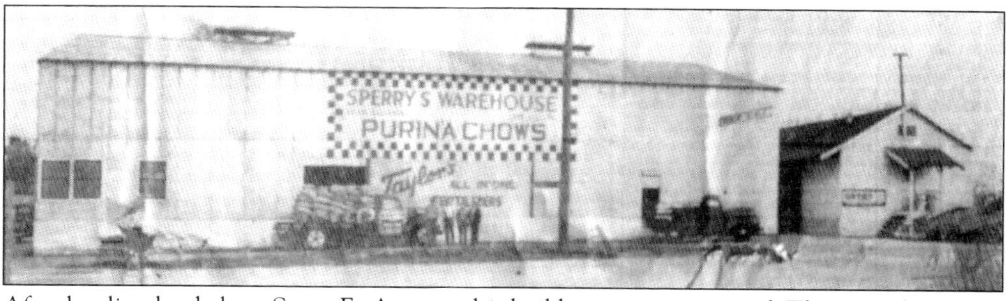

After leveling land along Santa Fe Avenue, this building was constructed. The "Warehouse," as it was known, served local farms needing to ship out their produce and crops for years until it burned down one foggy night. This image appears in the February 24, 1947, *Turlock Daily Journal.* (Courtesy of the *Turlock Daily Journal.*)

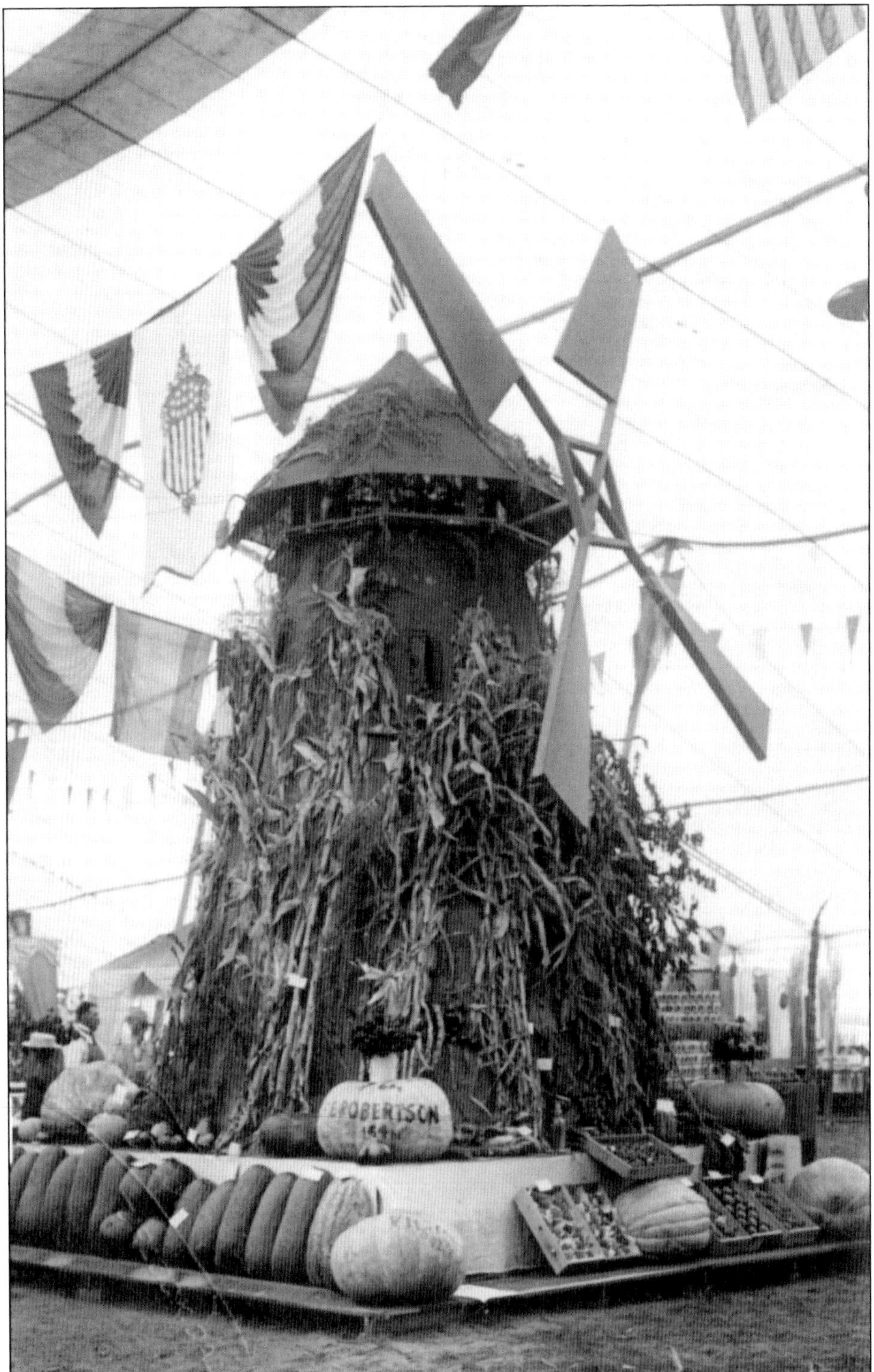

Denair's display at the Turlock Melon Carnival won first place in 1911. The carnival was the predecessor to the Stanislaus County Fair. (Courtesy of John Chance.)

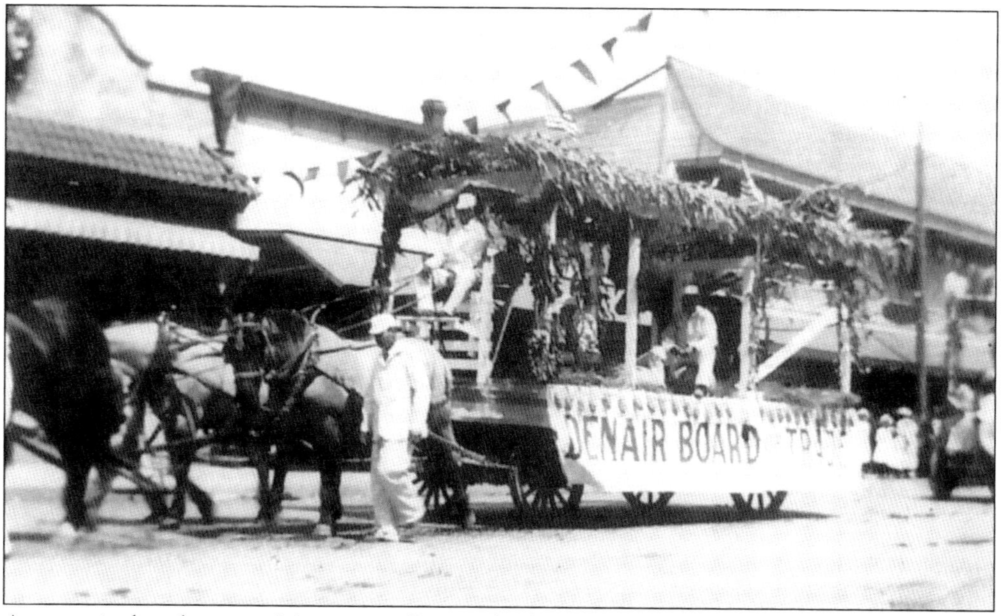

As an agricultural center of the county, Denair displayed its abundance of crops. This photograph is from the Turlock Melon Carnival and shows a float being pulled by horse. (Courtesy of the Witmer family.)

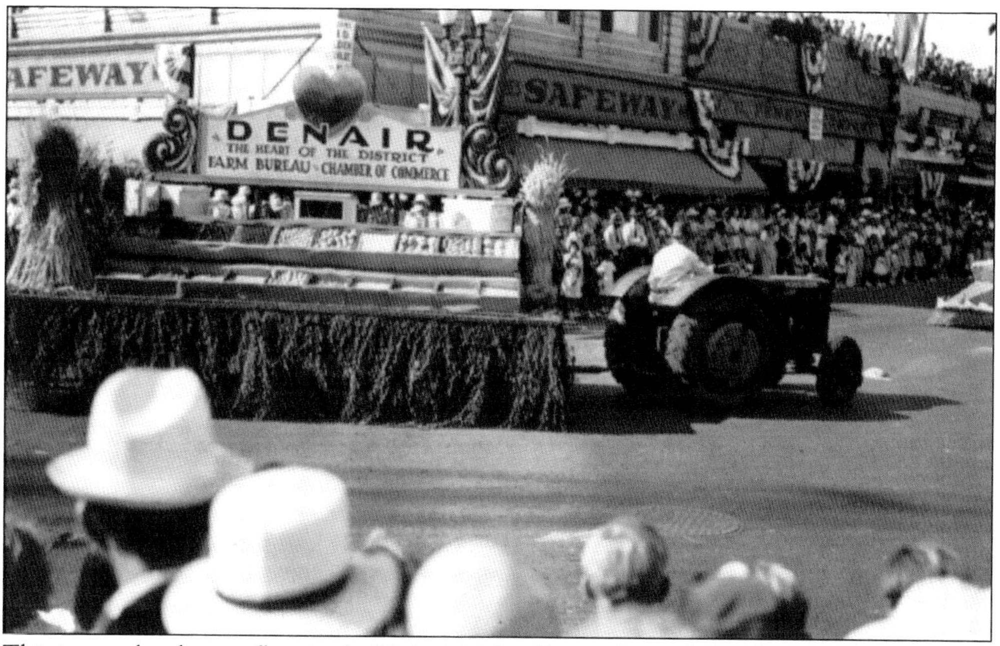

This image also shows a float in the Turlock Melon Carnival parade, but from several years later. Denair upgraded from horse-drawn to a tractor-pulled float. (Courtesy of Cheryl Cline.)

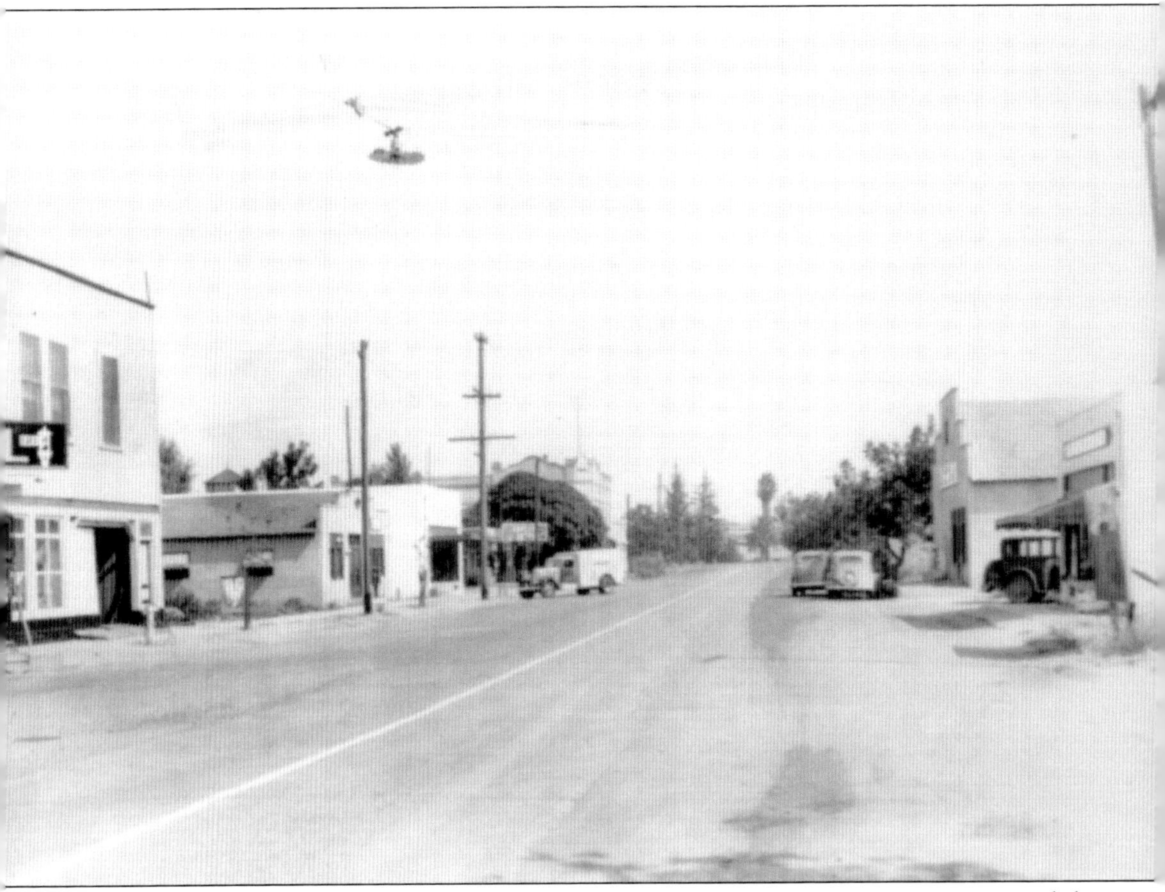

The view in this image of Main Street in Denair looks east from Santa Fe Avenue toward the grammar school, with palm trees in the distance. This photograph was taken in the 1930s. (Courtesy of the Turlock Historical Society.)

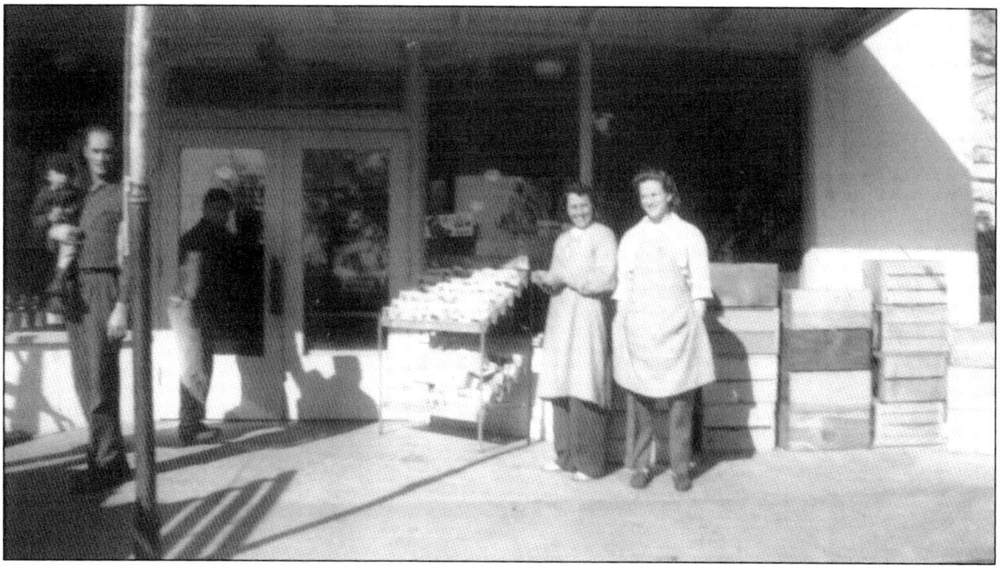

The Village Market has been a staple in Denair for many years, supplying residents with groceries, meats, fresh fruits and vegetables, and, of course, candy. This c. 1930s photograph shows Lorene Mills Haworth (second from right) and Grace Anderson (right). Many remember Anderson as a Denair High School teacher for many years. In the 1960s, Albert and Martha Kastner purchased Village Market. (Above, courtesy of Alma Jean Mills Coleman; below, courtesy of Martha Kastner.)

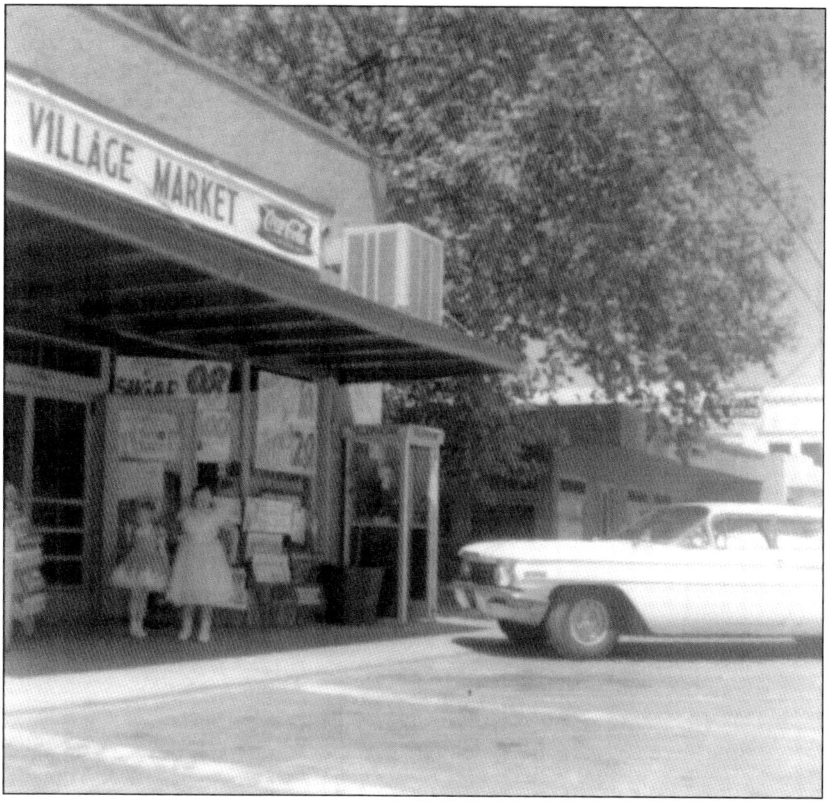

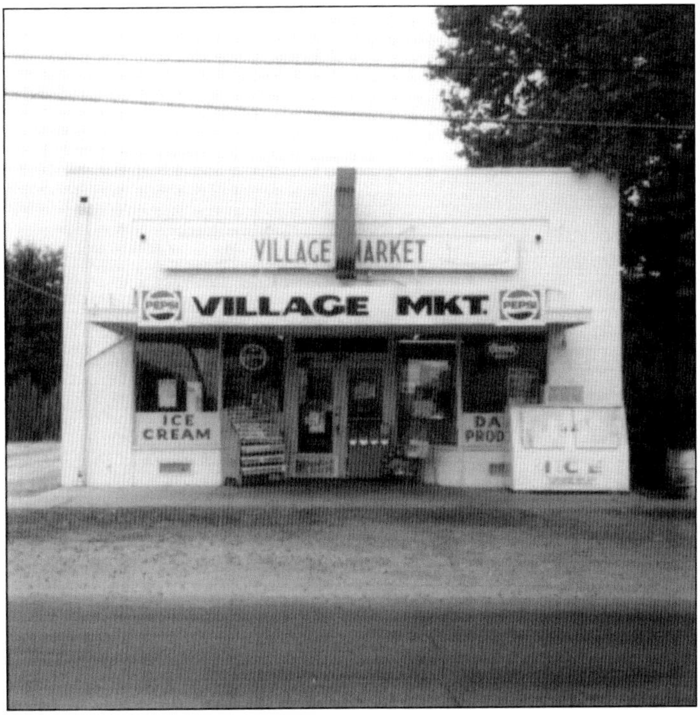

Albert and Martha Kastner ran Village Market until the early 1980s. The meat counter was always stocked with the freshest meat, poultry, and cheeses. (Both, courtesy of Martha Kastner.)

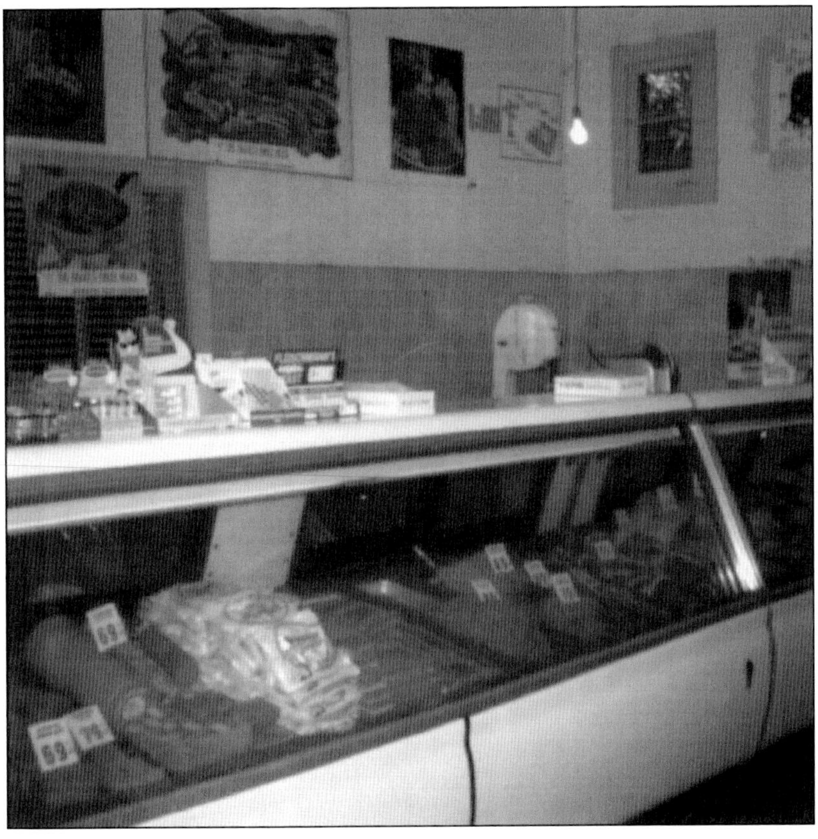

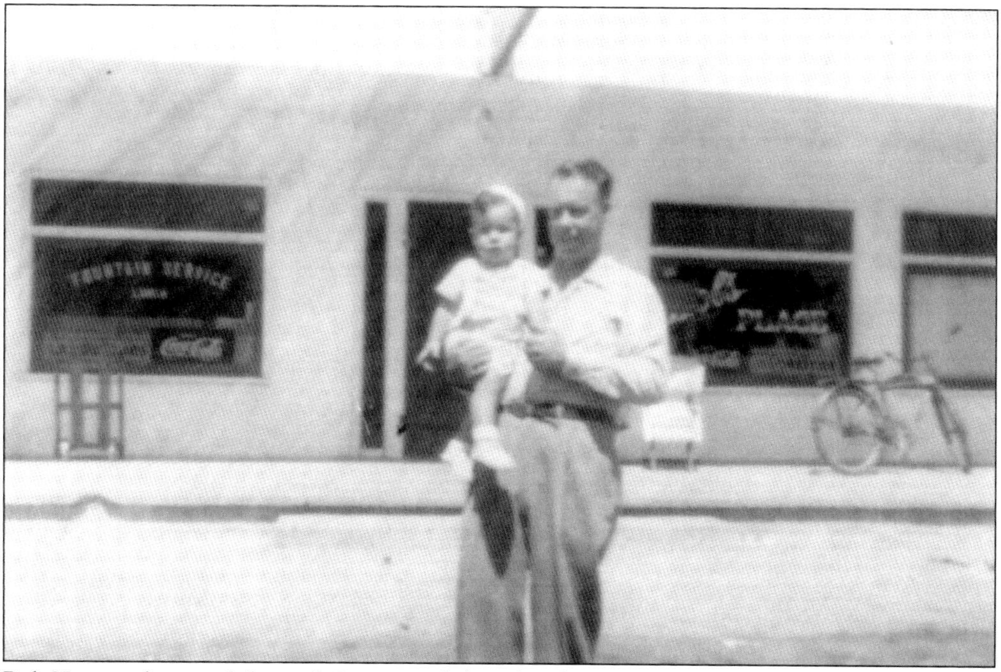

Bob Heans, along with his wife Leone and their family, moved to Denair in 1945. Bob tried his hand as a restaurateur, but he soon learned that the long days did not pay off. Bob's Place was only open about a year. (Courtesy of Carole Royster.)

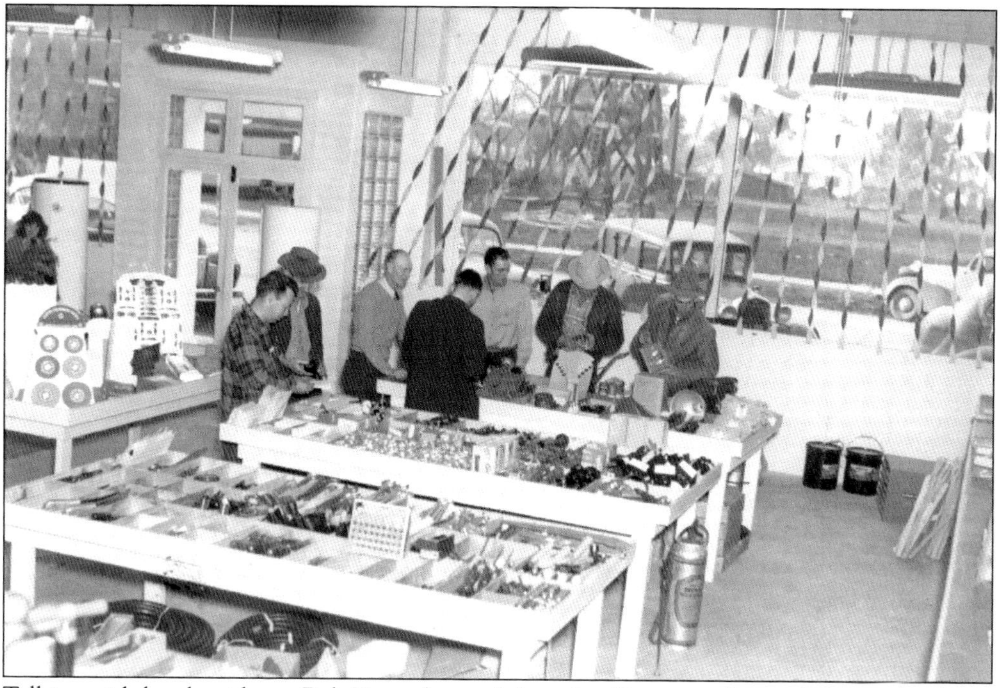

Talking with local residents, Bob Heans learned that what Denair really needed was a hardware store. So, with the help of partner Pete McCauley, he opened one. This photograph was taken on opening day in 1947. (Courtesy of Carole Royster.)

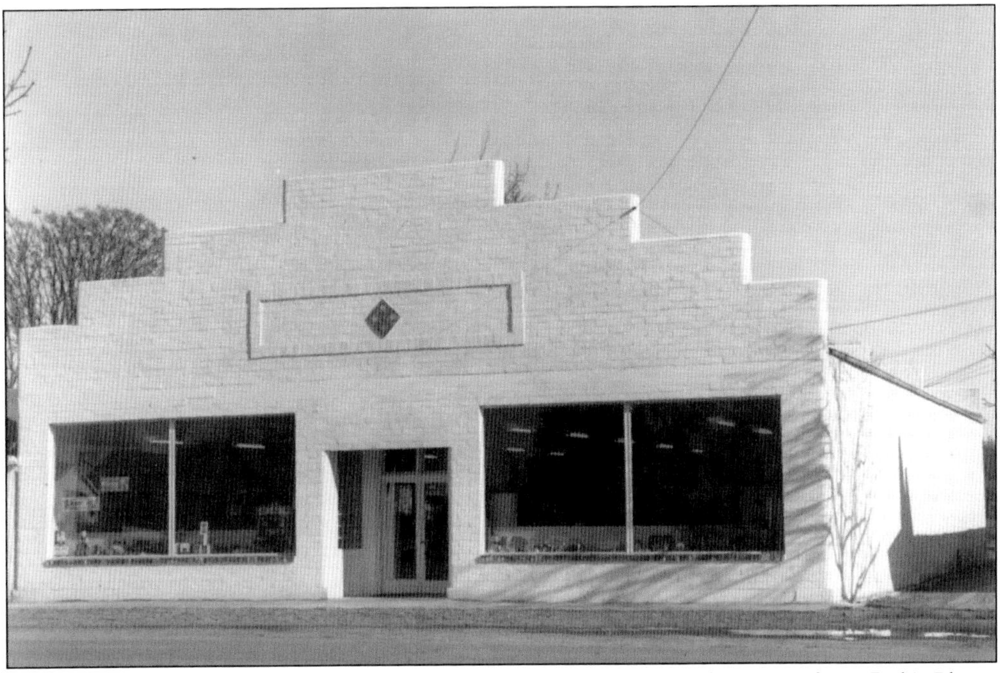

The hardware store opened in a brand-new building just down the street from Bob's Place. (Courtesy of Carole Royster.)

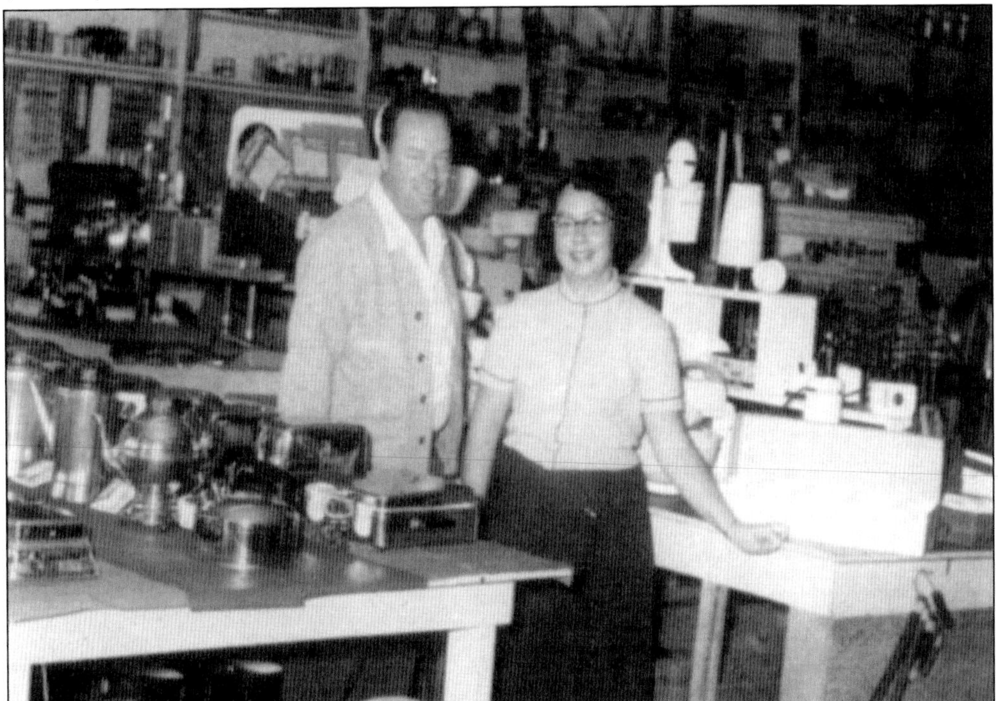

Pete McCauley soon decided that the hardware business was not for him. Bob Heans built a small apartment on the back of the hardware store, sold his home to buy out McCauley, and moved his family into the apartment. Here is Bob with his daughter Carole. (Courtesy of Carole Royster.)

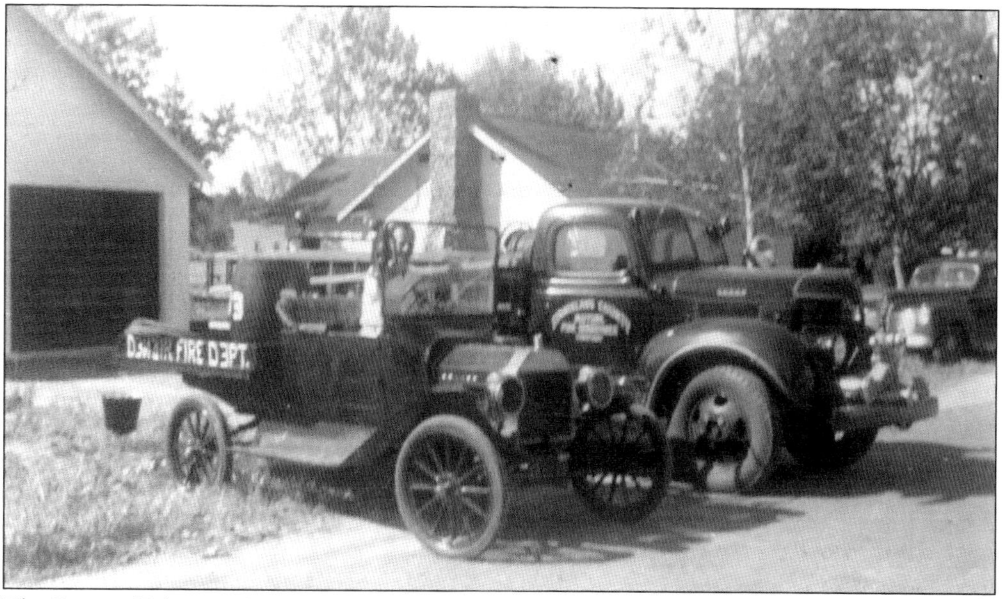

The Denair Volunteer Fire Department was established in 1942 with a 17-man volunteer crew, made up of 12 volunteer firemen and 5 commissioners. Shortly before the department received its first fire truck, the firehouse was constructed behind the community clubhouse at Alameda Avenue and Elm Street. (Courtesy of Denair Fire Department.)

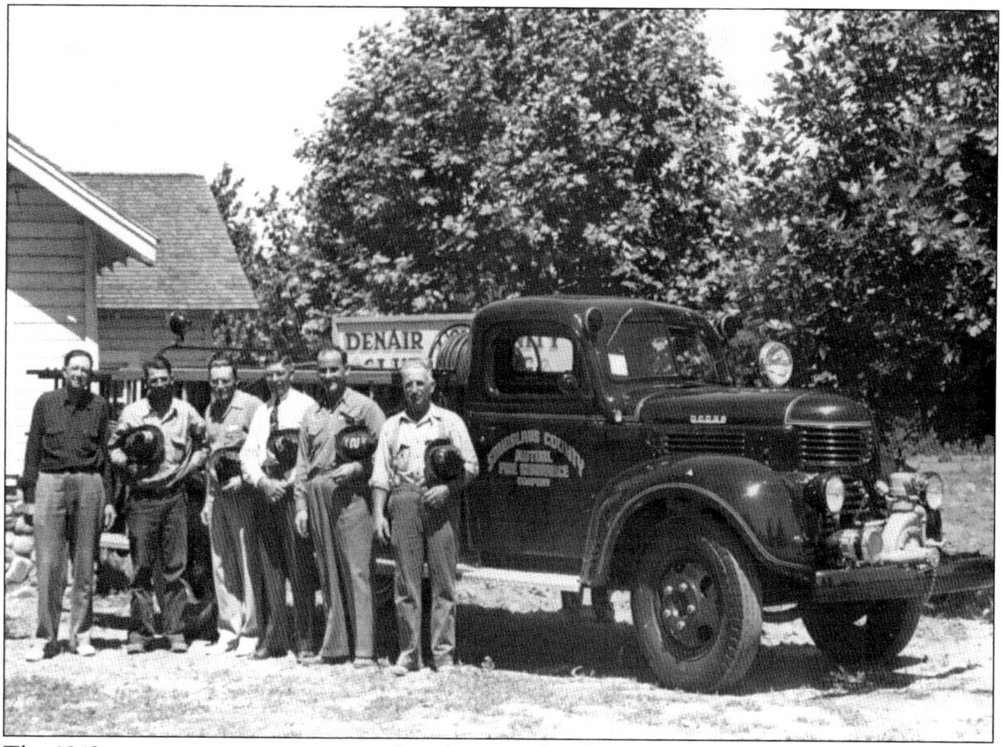

The 1942 commissioners are seen in this photograph, taken on June 2, 1942. Pictured are, from left to right, Lew Burwell, Joe Domecq, Chas Pratt, Guy Brown, Don Scott, and Dave Houeck. (Courtesy of Denair Fire Department.)

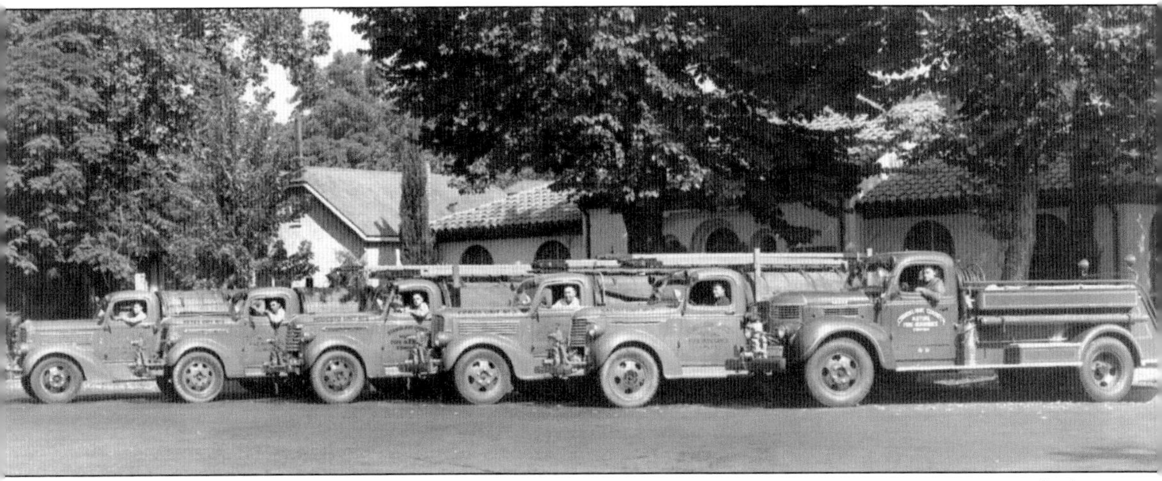

Denair was the first community to organize a volunteer fire department in conjunction with the Stanislaus County Mutual Fire Insurance Company. The insurance company paid for the initial cost of the fire truck. The department would fight all fires it was called to, but properties not insured by the company would be billed for the service of the truck and crew. Denair's truck is at the far right in this photograph. (Courtesy of Denair Fire Department.)

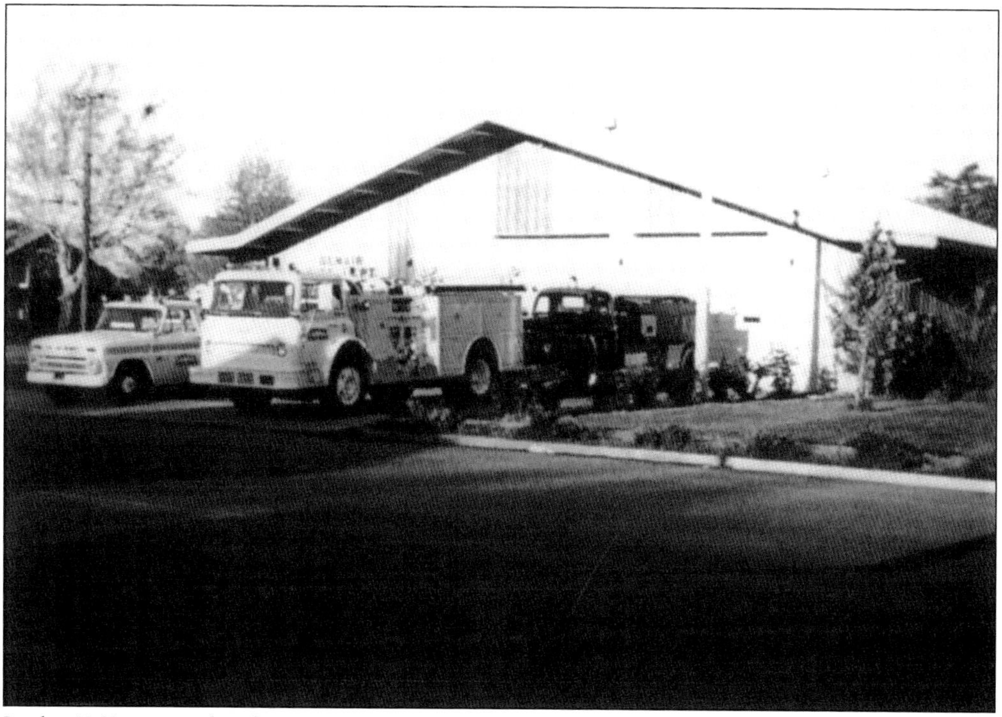

In the 1960s, a new fire department was built at the corner of Zeering and Gratton Roads on land previously occupied by the Denair Grammar School. (Courtesy of Denair Fire Department.)

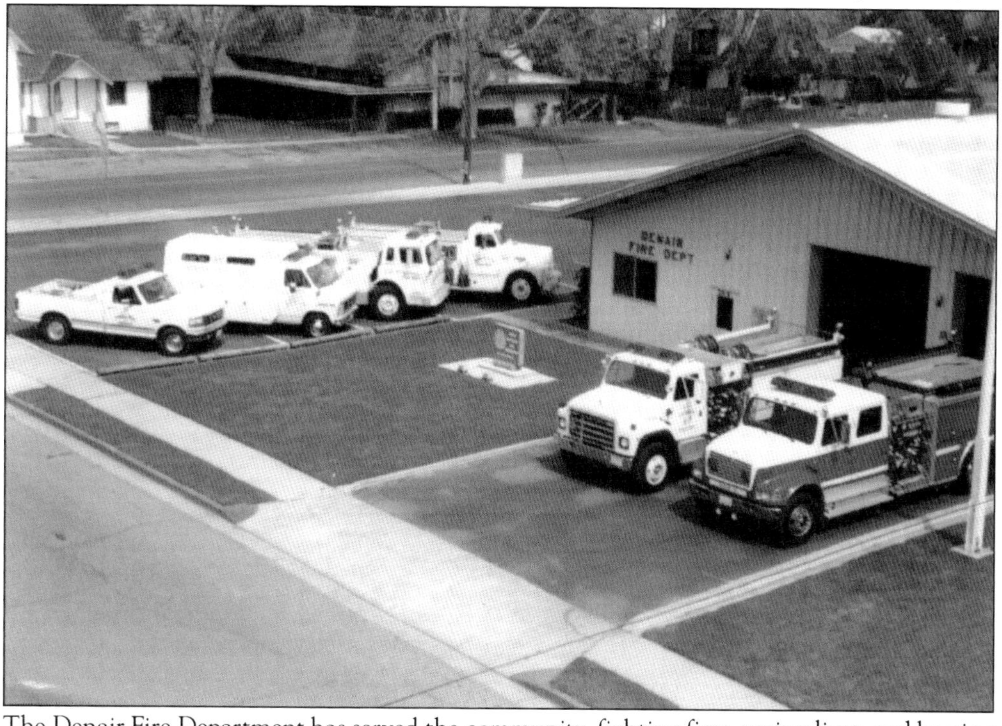

The Denair Fire Department has served the community, fighting fires, saving lives, and hosting an annual deep-pit barbecue at the new location. (Courtesy of Denair Fire Department.)

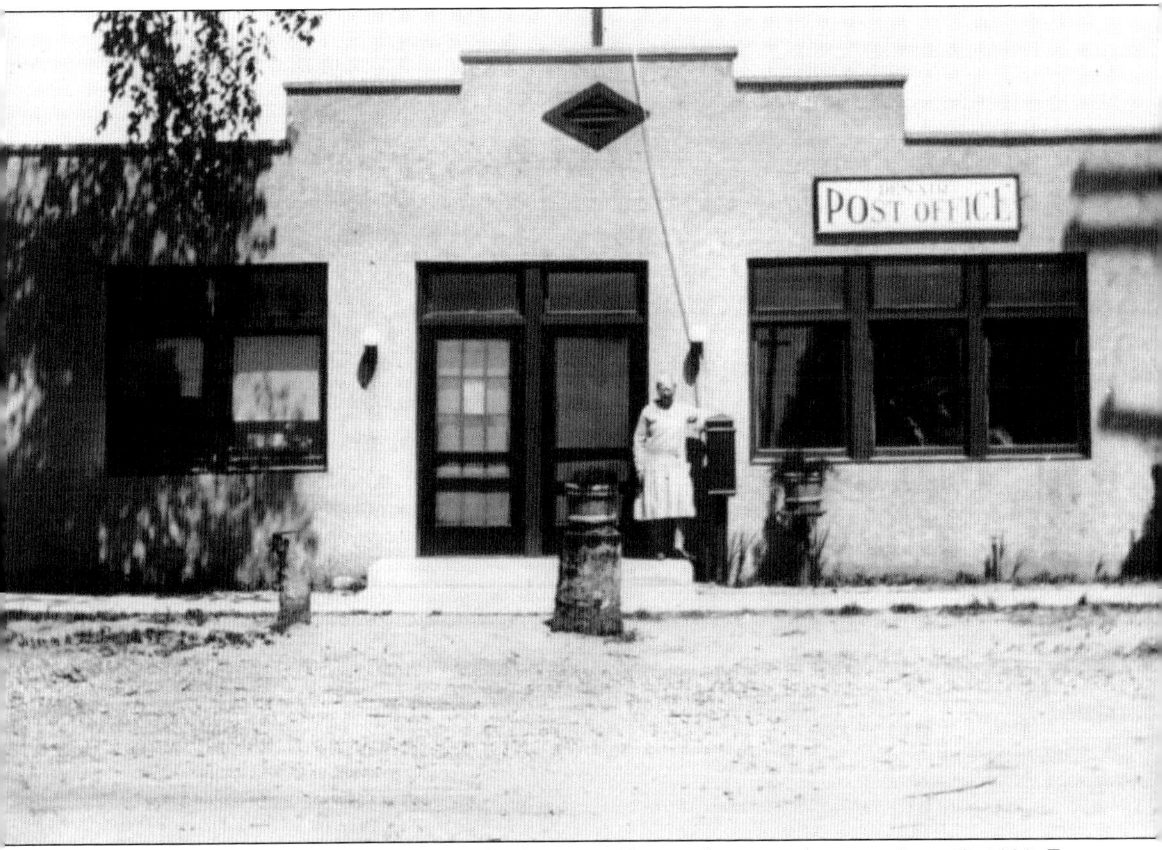

The Post Office Department established a post office in the train depot on June 17, 1898. Even though the area was known as Elmwood, the post office suggested the name Elmdale, as it already had an Elmwood elsewhere in California. Eventually, in 1904, the name was changed to Elmwood, and the post office moved into the Crouch-Warner General Store a year later. The name was changed again in 1907, to Denair. In 1915, the post office moved to the northeast corner of the Bank Building, and in 1929, moved yet again to the structure seen here. This building also housed the library. (Courtesy of Bill McClure.)

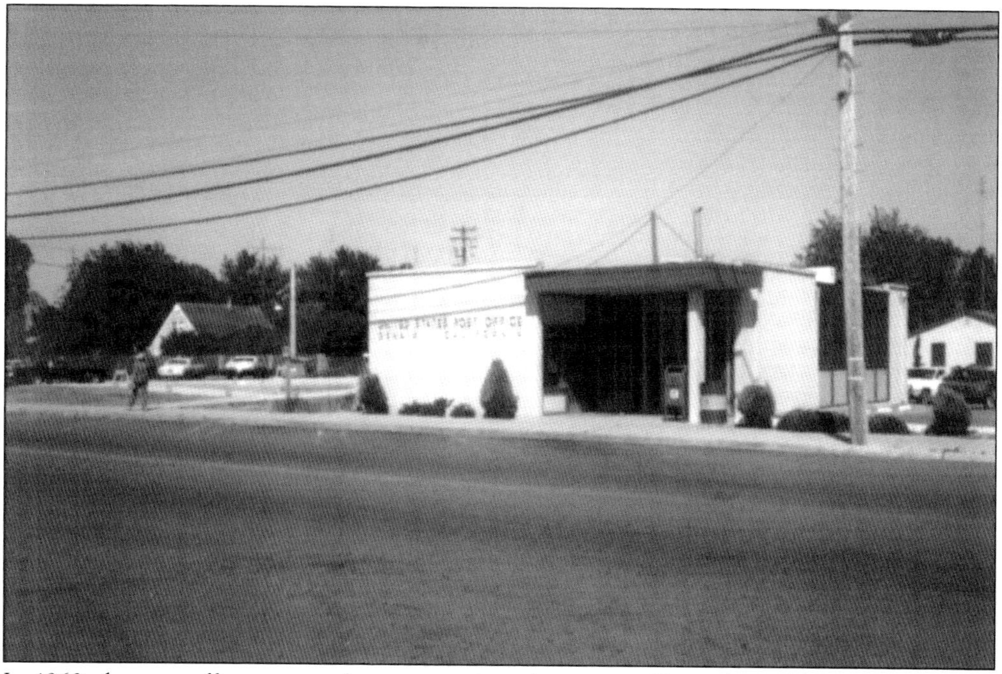

In 1960, the post office was on the move again, relocating in December of that year to a more modern facility on the corner of Alameda Avenue and Main Street. (Courtesy of the Denair Post Office.)

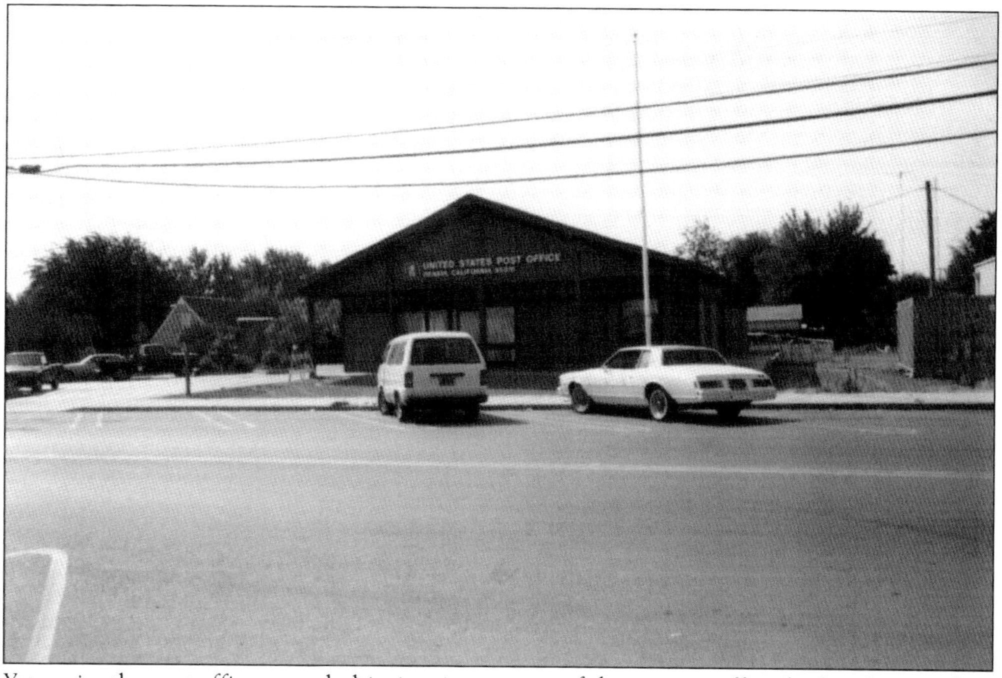

Yet again, the post office moved, this time into a state-of-the-art post office, built right next door to the 1960 building. The new building opened in August 1986. The old 1960s building was torn down, and the land became the parking lot for the existing post office. (Courtesy of the Denair Post Office.)

Sound Insurance

At a Saving in Cost

List Your Property With Us

Two Offices to Serve You

Denair Office	Turlock Office
Myrtle St.	239 W. Main

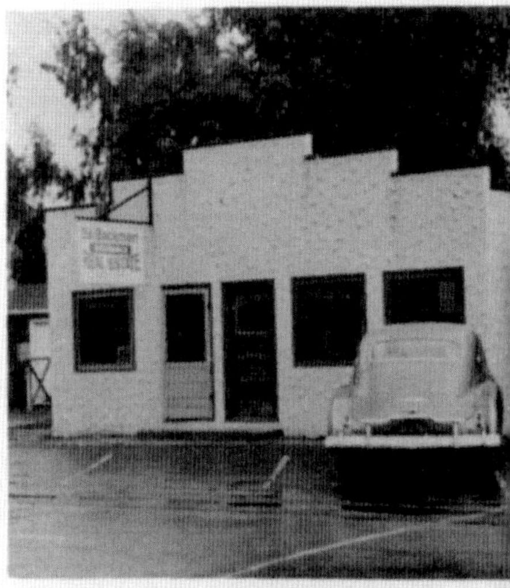

ED BACKMAN
INSURANCE AND REAL ESTAT

The town of Denair and its streets have had many name changes over the years. Elmwood, Elmdale, Elms, and Denair are just a few of the names of the town. Main Street has seen its share of name changes as well. Originally Alameda Avenue, it later became Myrtle Street and eventually Main Street, as it is known today. (The Alameda Avenue that exists today was named so after the original Alameda Avenue had become Myrtle Street.) This advertisement for Ed Backman Insurance and Real Estate lists its location as Myrtle Street. This building sits across from the existing post office, next to the old hardware store. (Courtesy of Denair Unified School District.)

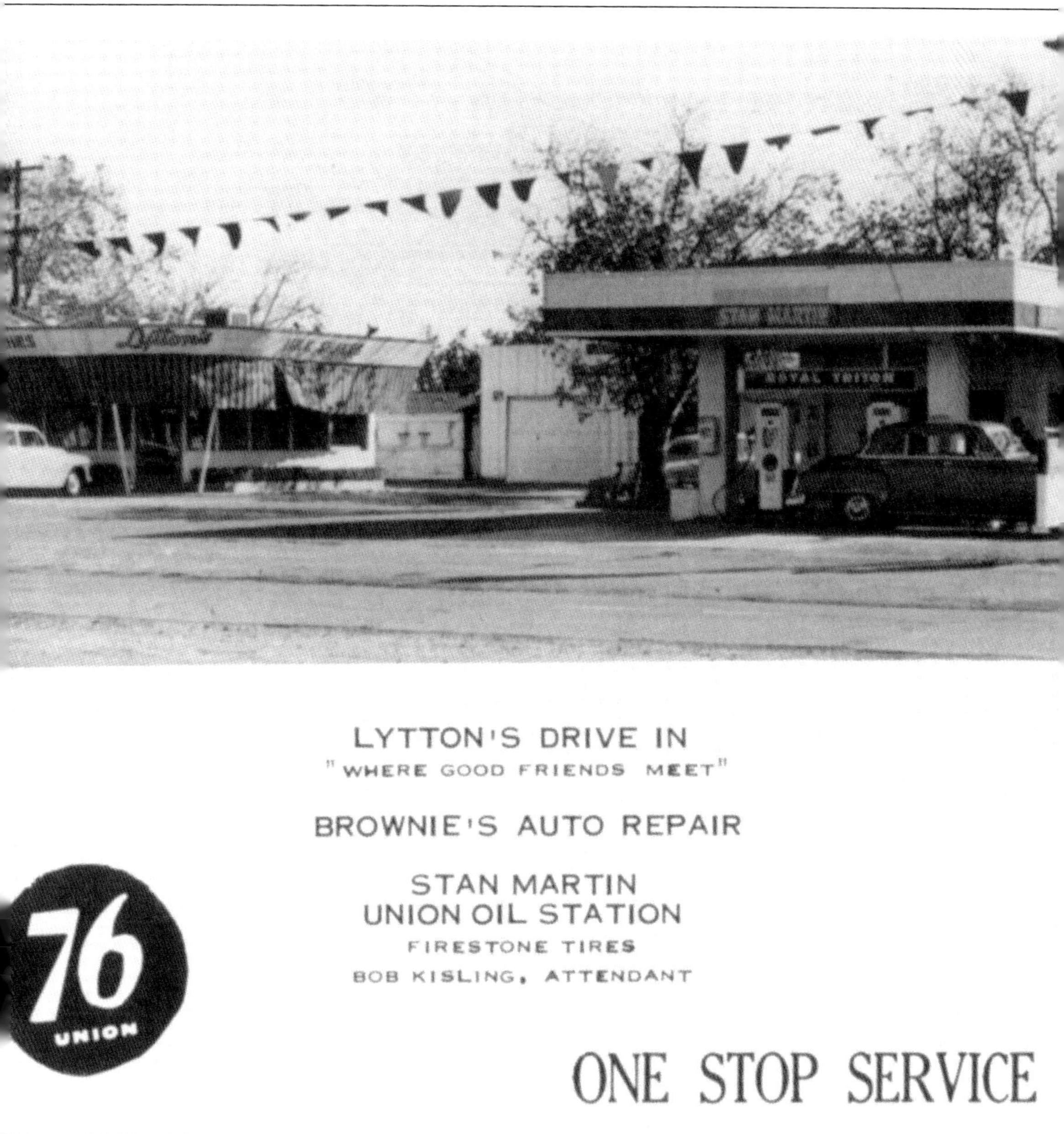

The land at the southeast corner of San Joaquin Avenue and Main Streets has had many businesses over the years. This advertisement from 1954 shows, from right to left, Stan Martin's Union Oil Station, Brownie's Auto Repair, and Lytton's Drive In. (Courtesy of Denair Unified School District.)

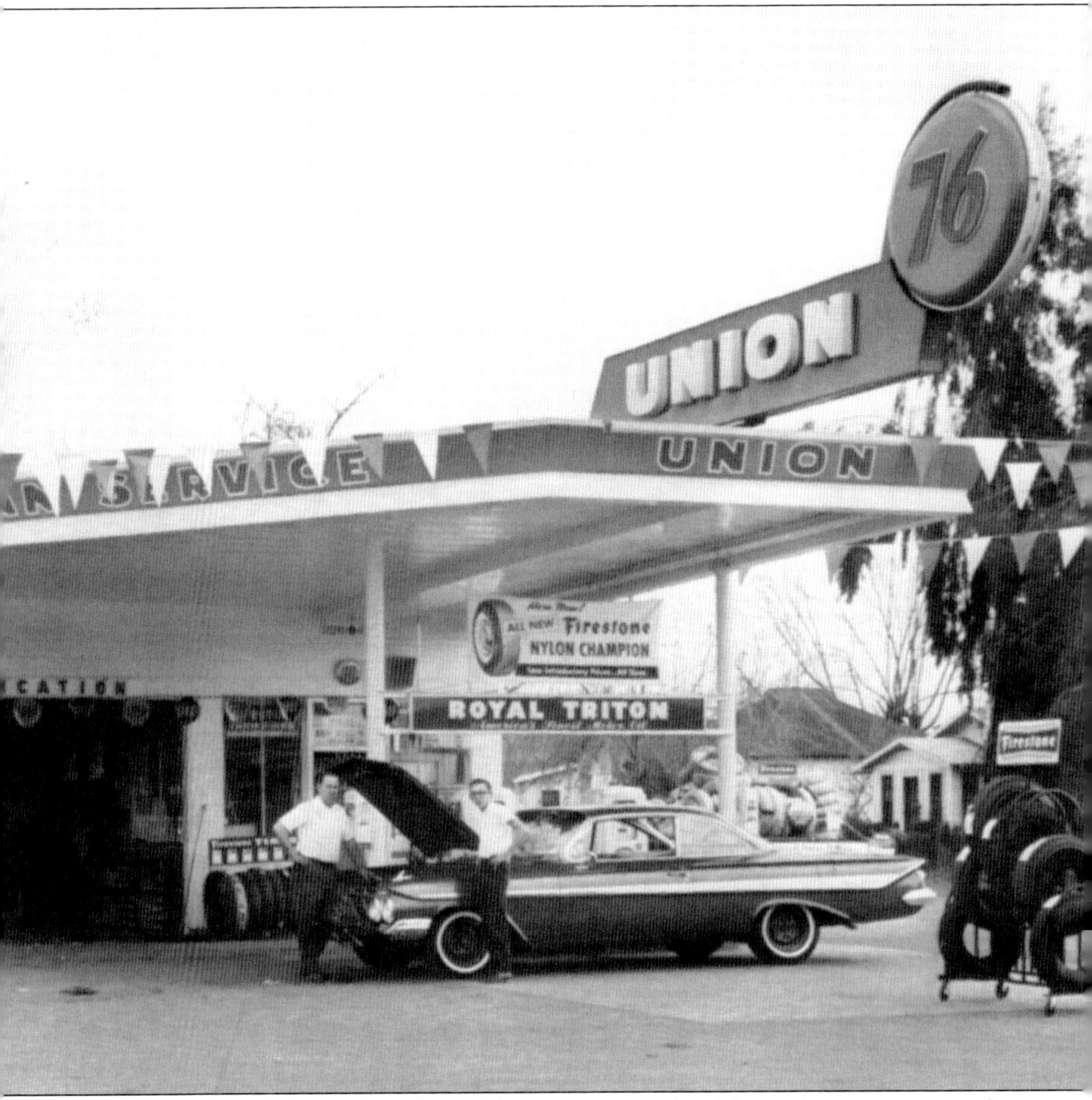

Several years later, Stan Martin's Service Station received a face-lift to make it look more modern. (Courtesy of Denair Unified School District.)

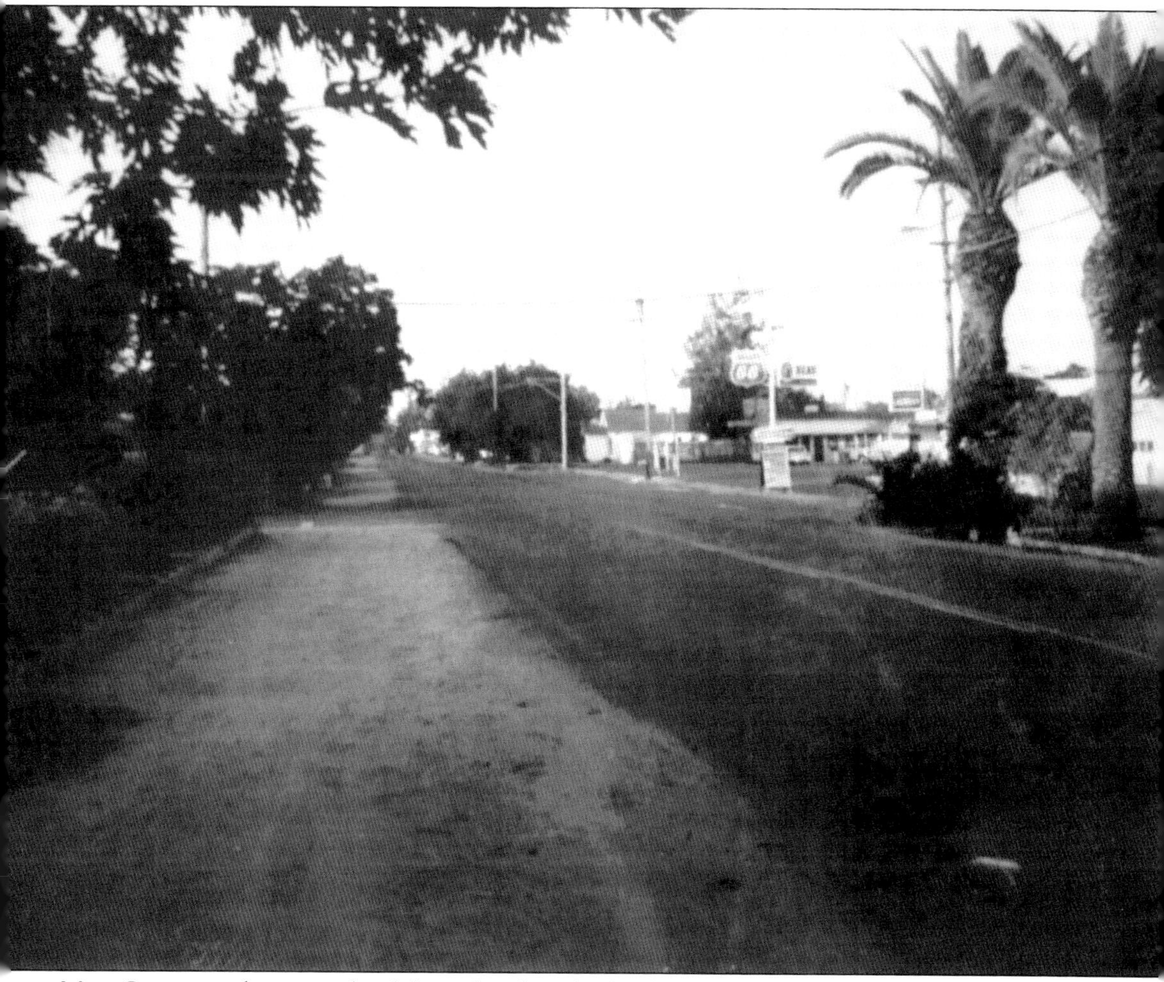

Main Street, on the west side of the railroad tracks, has had its share of changes over the years as well. This 1960s photograph shows the Denair Village shopping center on the right, with the 66 Station and sign in front. The palm trees at the right were later removed when Quick Stop was built in the 1980s. (Courtesy of the Oasis Grill and Deli.)

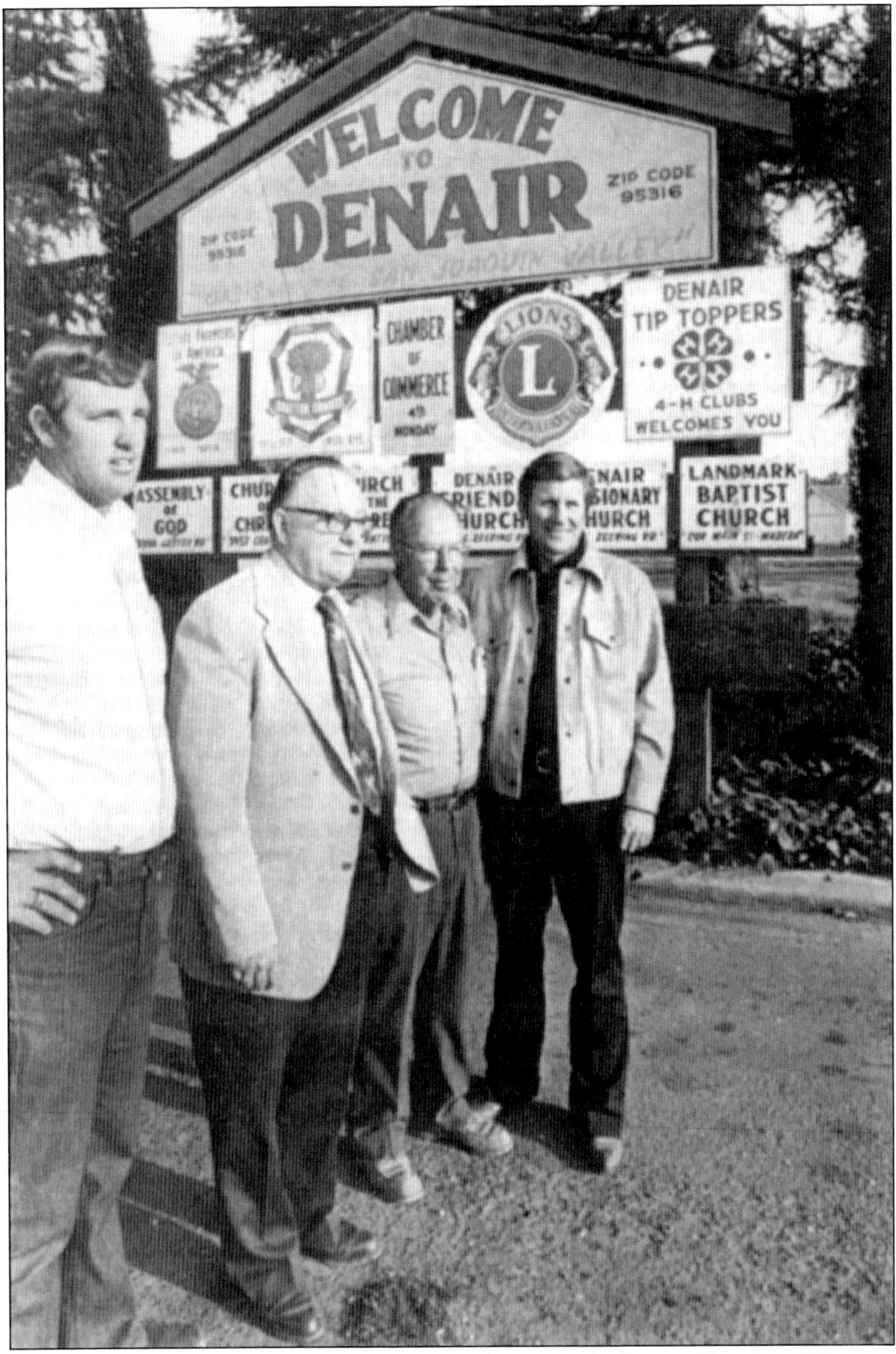

The Denair Board of Trade was formed in 1911, later becoming the Denair Chamber of Commerce in 1923, with 45 members. This 1974 photograph shows chamber members, from left to right, Bob Runyan, Ken Bratten, Bob Heans, and Jerry Schell. The Denair Chamber of Commerce is no longer operational. (Courtesy of the *Turlock Daily Journal*.)

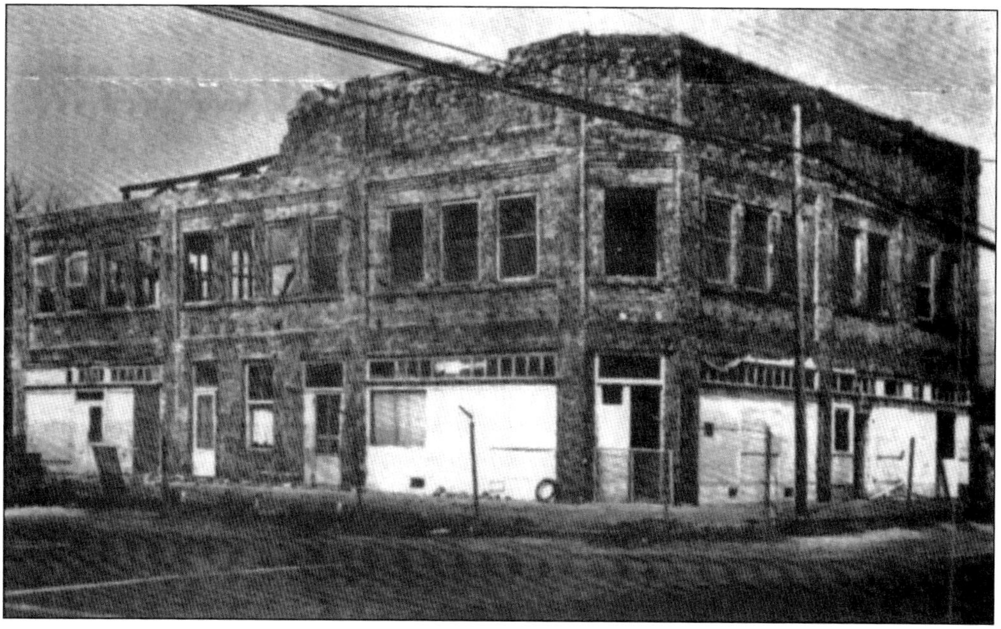

Following years of disrepair and neglect, the old Bank Building was torn down in 1981. Tractors were used to pull the heavy brick walls down. Leftover bricks were used to construct the new Bank Building that still stands today. (Both, courtesy of the *Turlock Daily Journal*.)

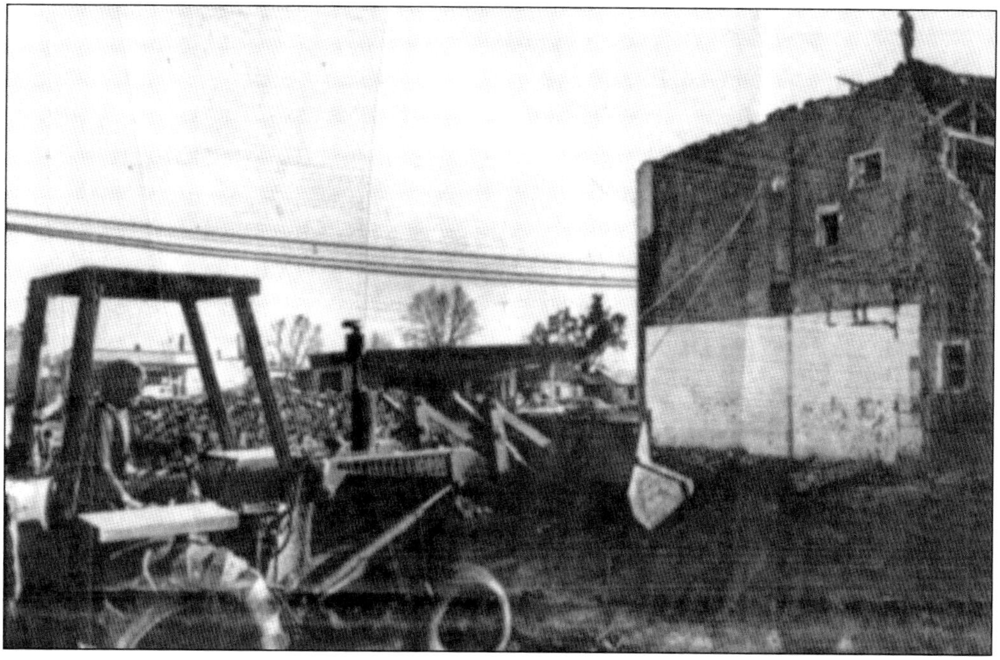

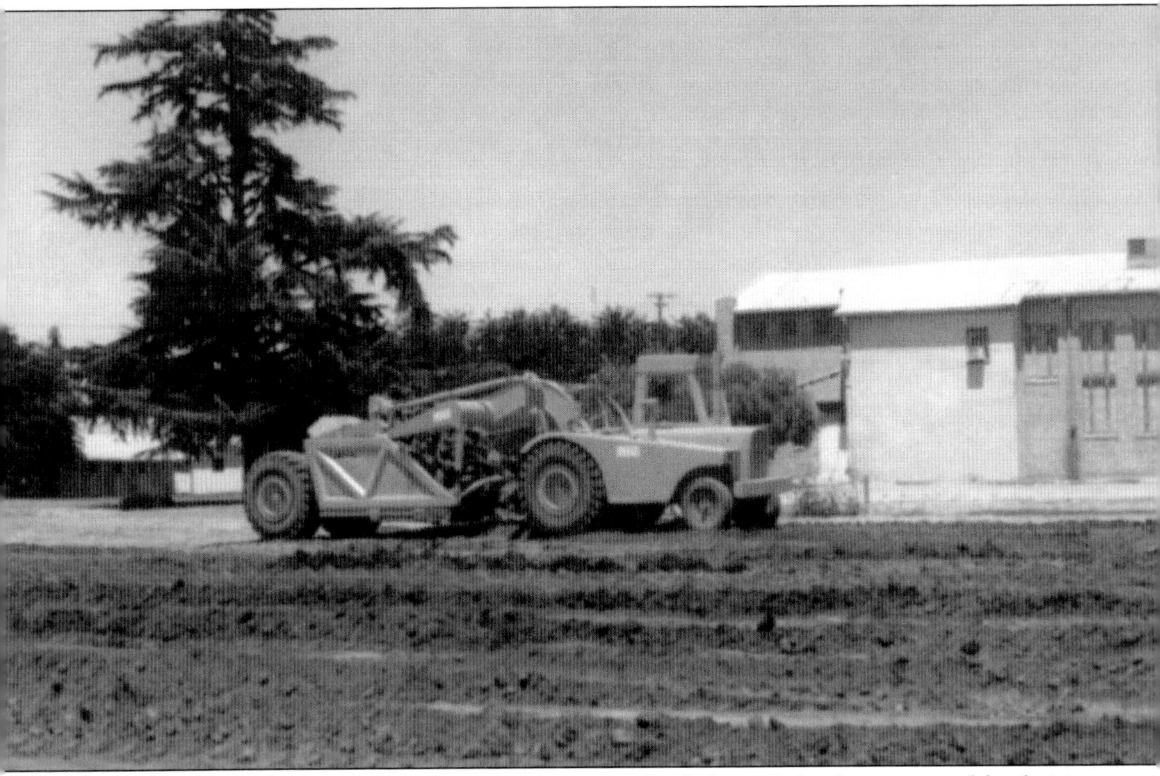

In 1983, the Denair Community Services Center was built through the donations and fundraising by the Denair Lions Club. The structure was erected with the help of volunteer labor and materials. (Both, courtesy of Denair Lions Club.)

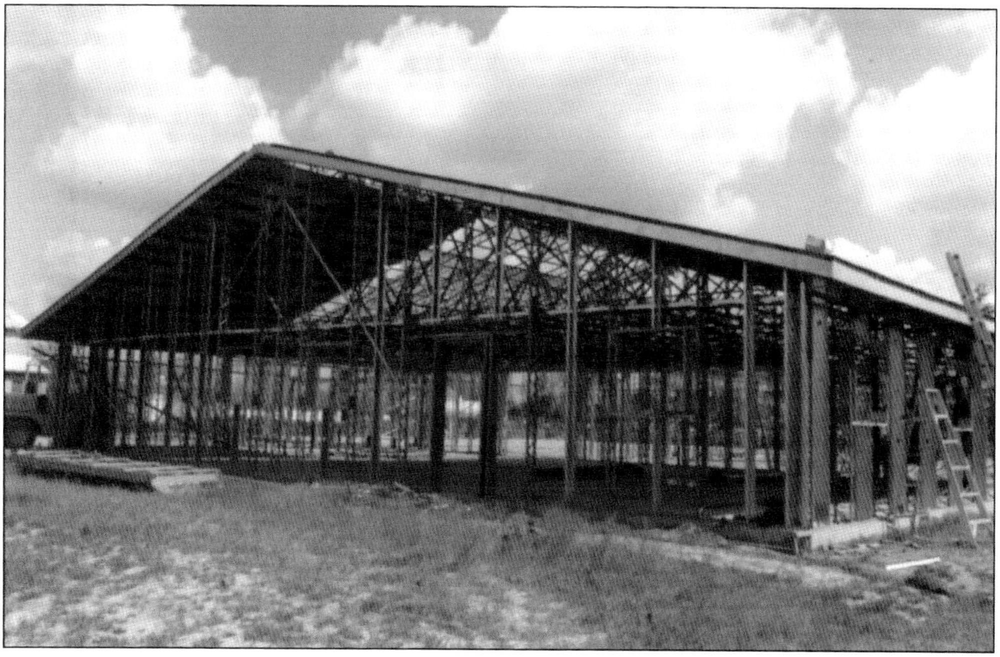

The building serves as home to the Denair Community Services District, the Denair Lions Club, and a community hall, which is available for parties and gatherings. (Above, courtesy of Denair Lions Club; below, courtesy of Stephen Browning.)

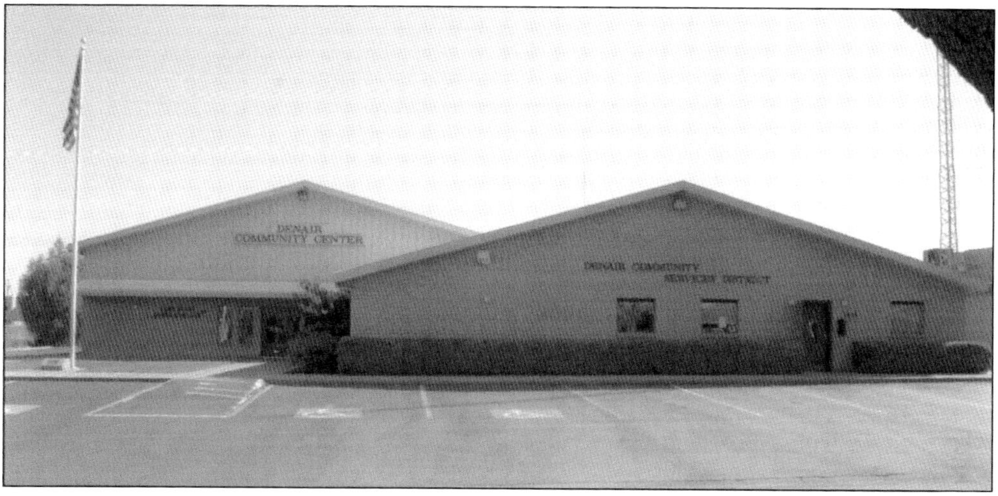

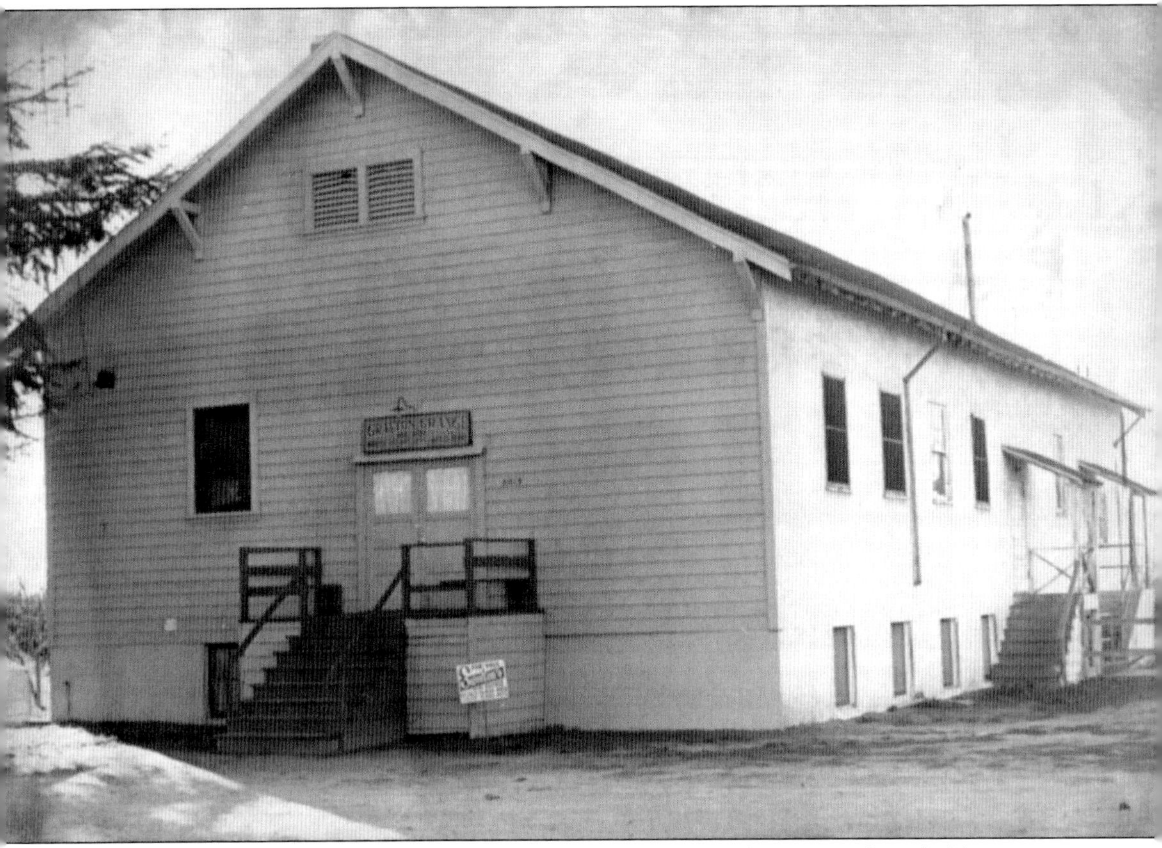

Gratton Grange No. 528, organized August 2, 1933, with 50 charter members, held its meetings and events in this building located a few miles north of Denair on Gratton Road. The Grange operated from this location until the mid-1970s, when the building was sold and converted into a private residence. (Courtesy of the Turlock Historical Society.)

Six

THE DENAIR COMMUNITY

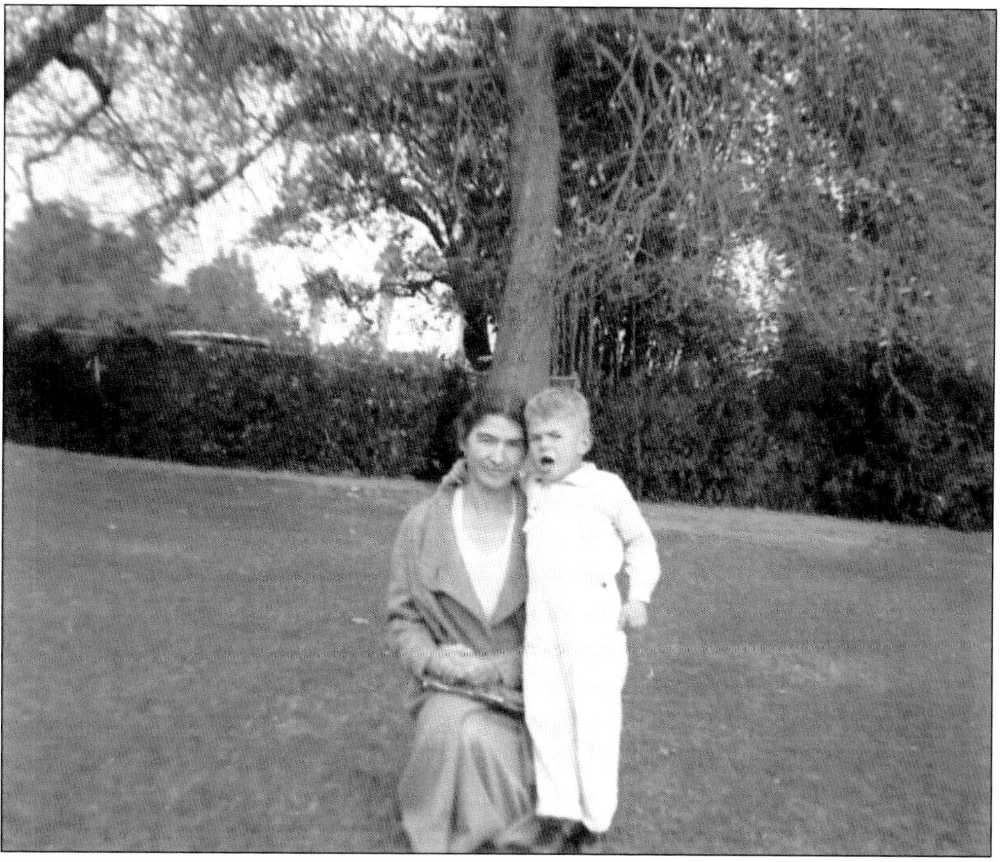

Many families are well known in the Denair area. Several of them lived here well before it was called Denair. Pictured here are early residents of the area Christine Hollingsworth-Chance and her son John Chance Jr. Christine compiled a lot of the history of Denair that is included in the book *Streams In A Thirsty Land*, published in 1972. John helped gather many of the photographs included in this book. (Courtesy of John Chance.)

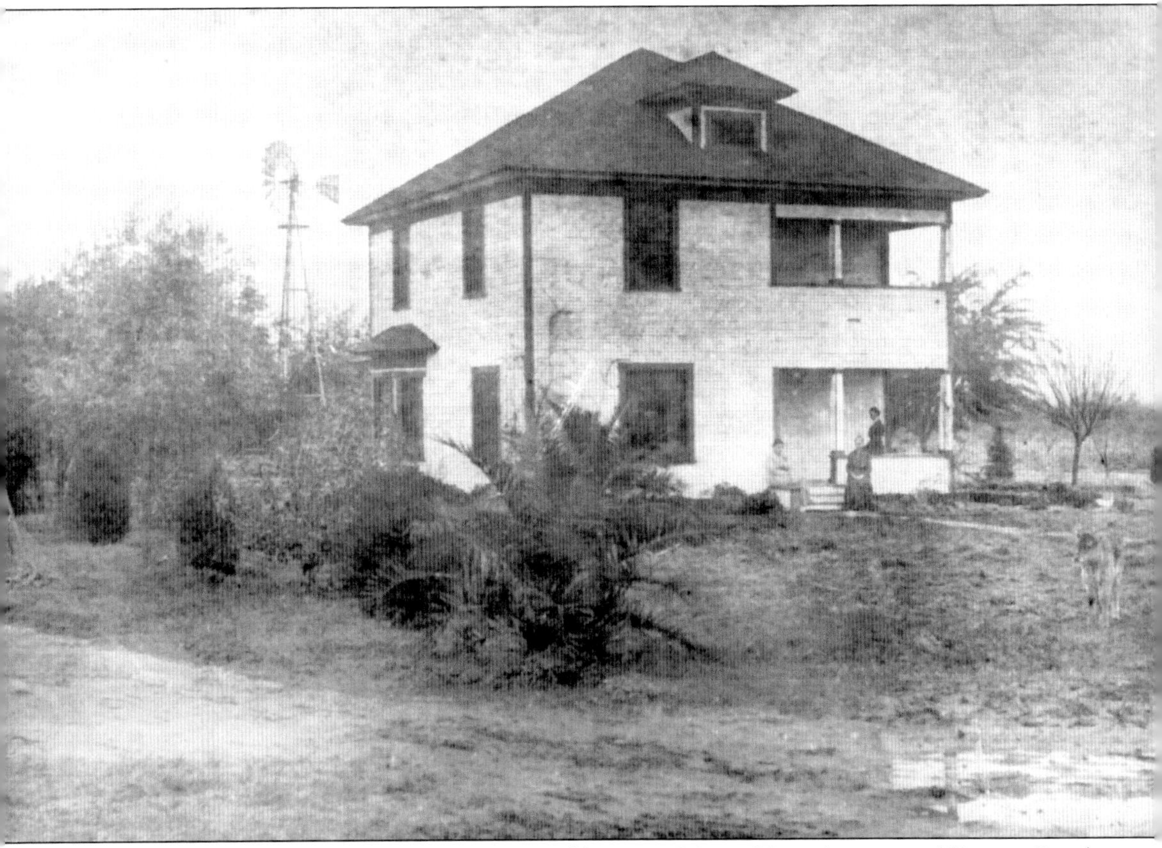

The Hollingsworth home sits on Lester Road between Monte Vista Avenue and Zeering Road. Built in 1909, it and the Lester House were the only homes on that street for many years. (Courtesy of John Chance.)

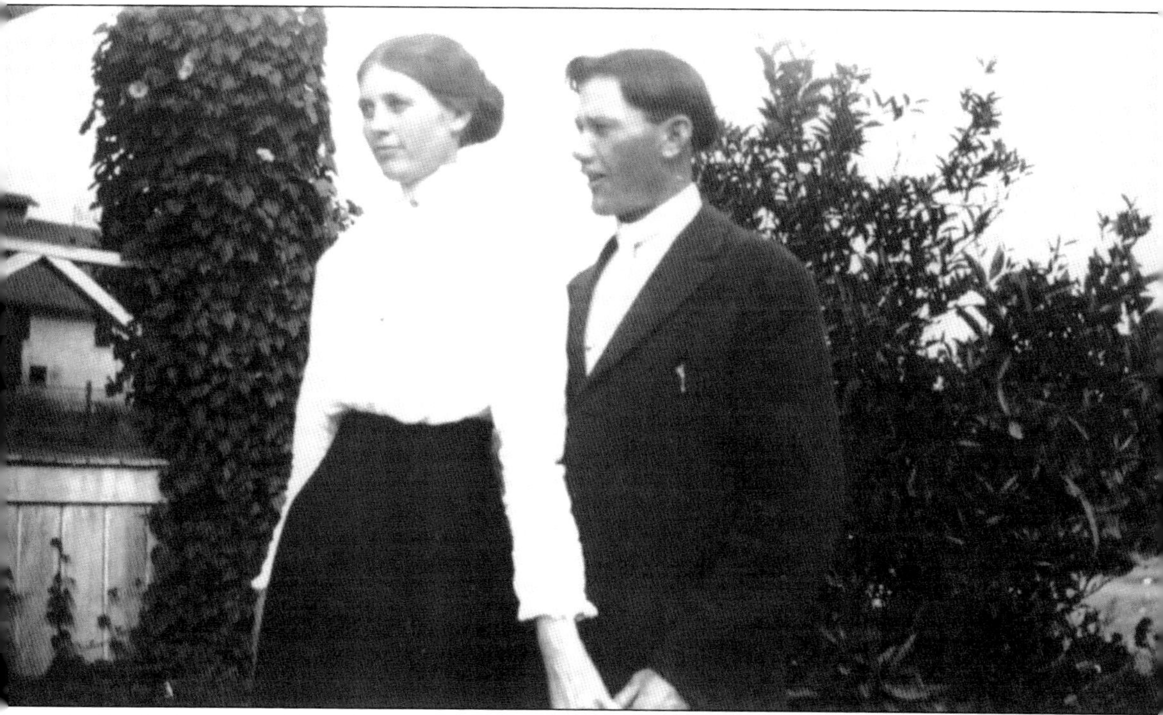

Earl J. Snider married Mary Morrison in July 1912. They lived on Keyes Road. The Snider land on Keyes Road housed many different businesses as well as crops over the years, including a lumberyard, honey operation, and others. (Courtesy of Cheryl Cline.)

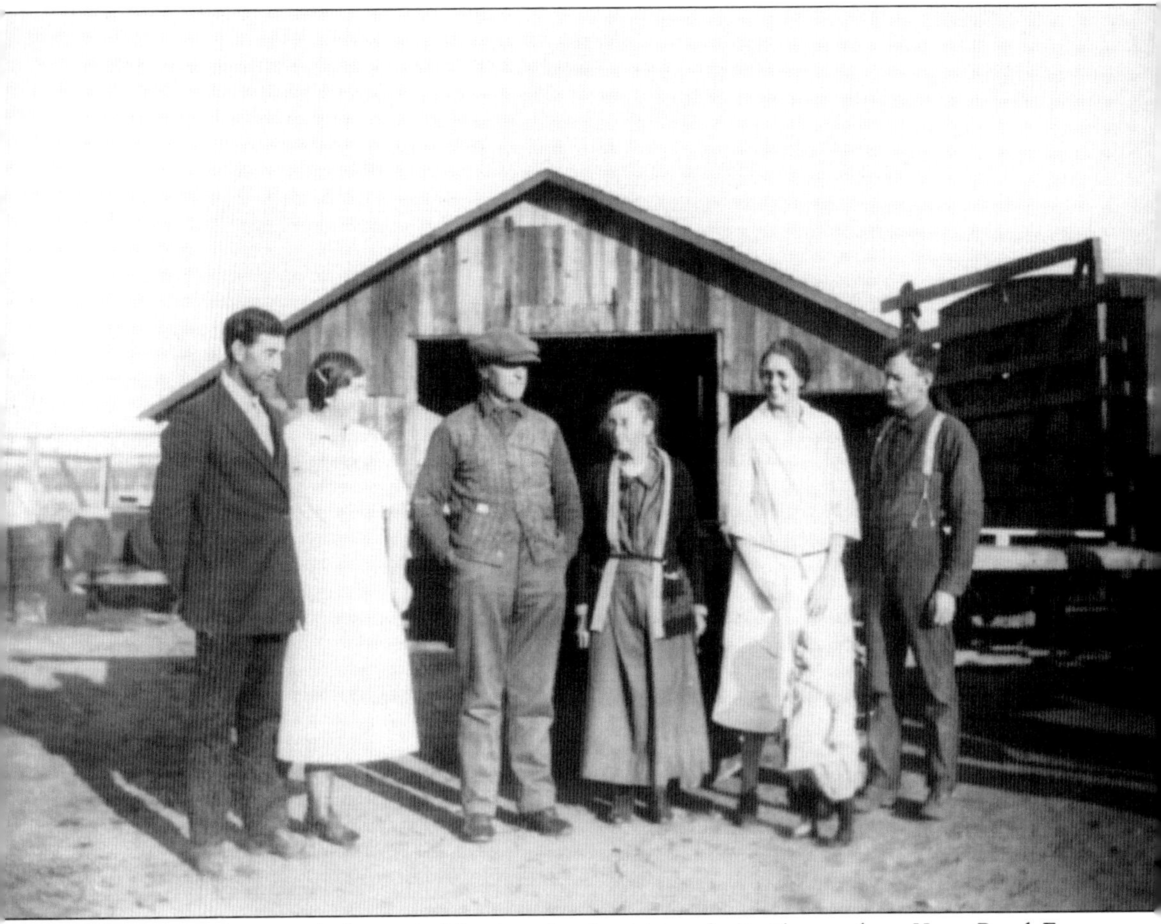

This 1919 photograph shows the Morrison family visiting the Snider ranch on Keyes Road. From left to right are Ed Morrison, Ethel Morrison, Daniel Morrison, Hannah Morrison, Mary Snider, her daughter Eileen Snider, and Earl Snider. (Courtesy of Cheryl Cline.)

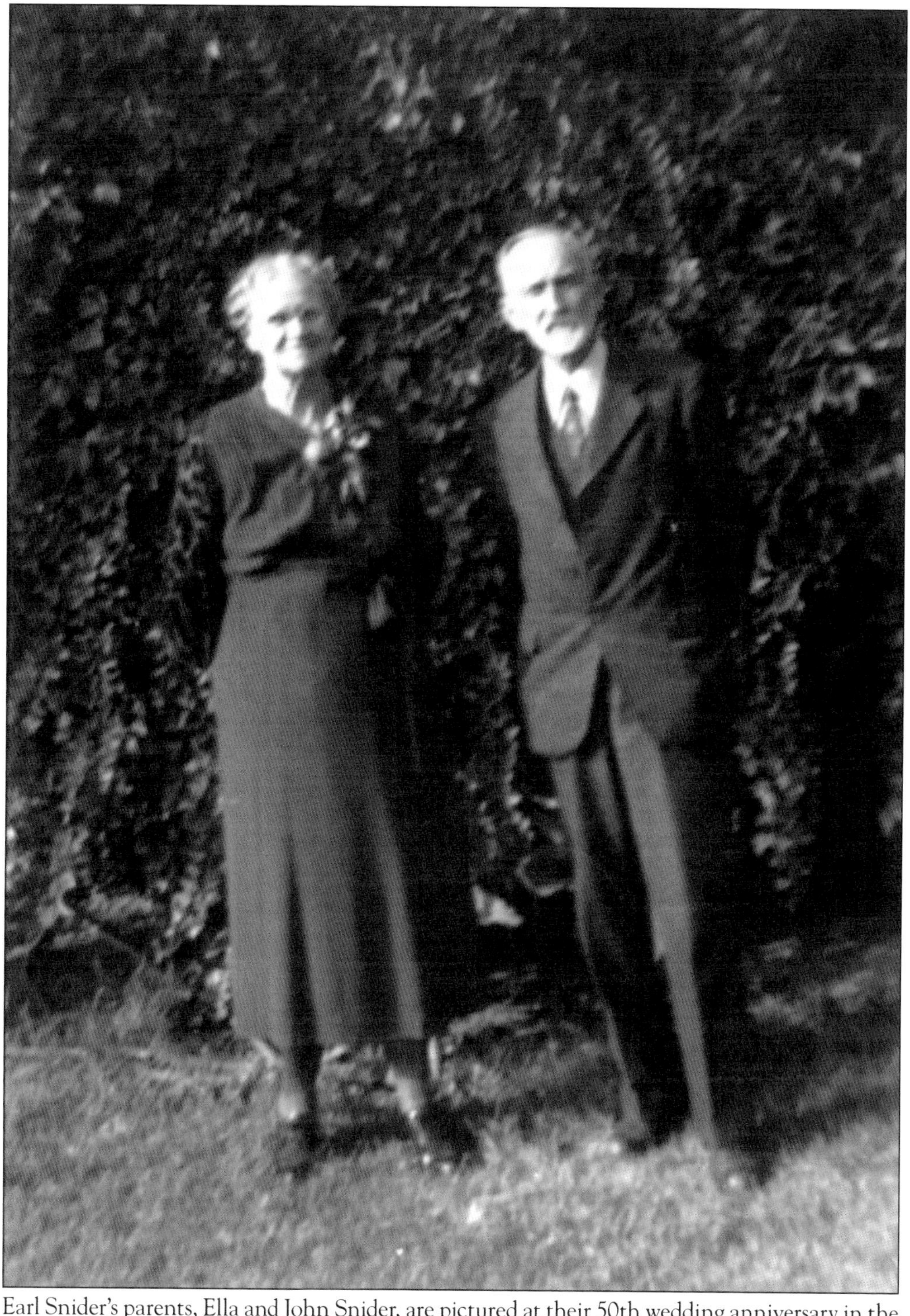

Earl Snider's parents, Ella and John Snider, are pictured at their 50th wedding anniversary in the 1940s. (Courtesy of Cheryl Cline.)

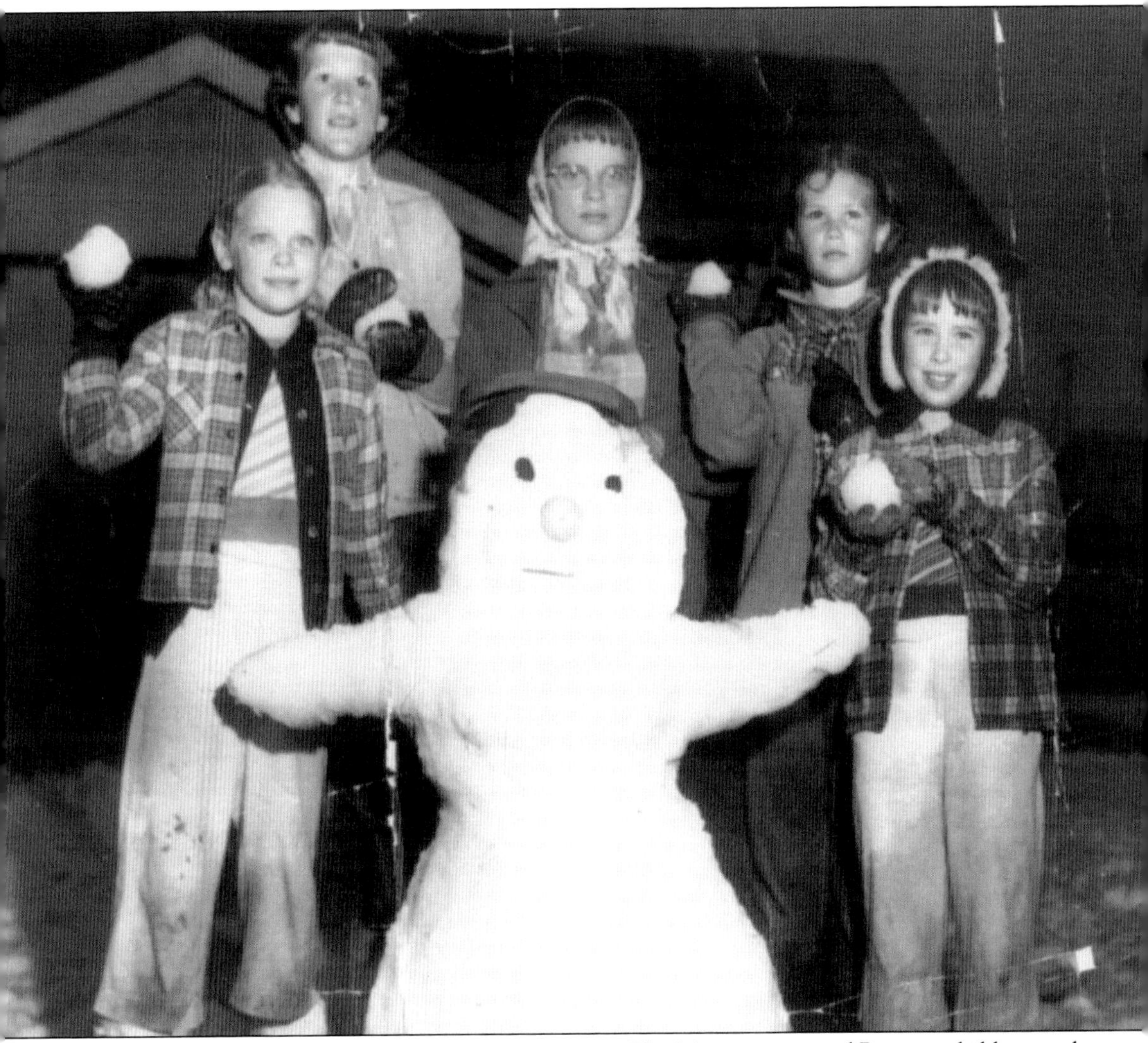

This 1952 photograph shows snow in Denair again. The Montgomery and Berman children took advantage of the rare event. The photograph was later used for an article in the *Turlock Daily Journal*. Pictured are, from left to right, Marcella Berman, Cheryl Montgomery, Loretta Burman, Diana Montgomery, and Janet Burman. (Courtesy of Cheryl Cline.)

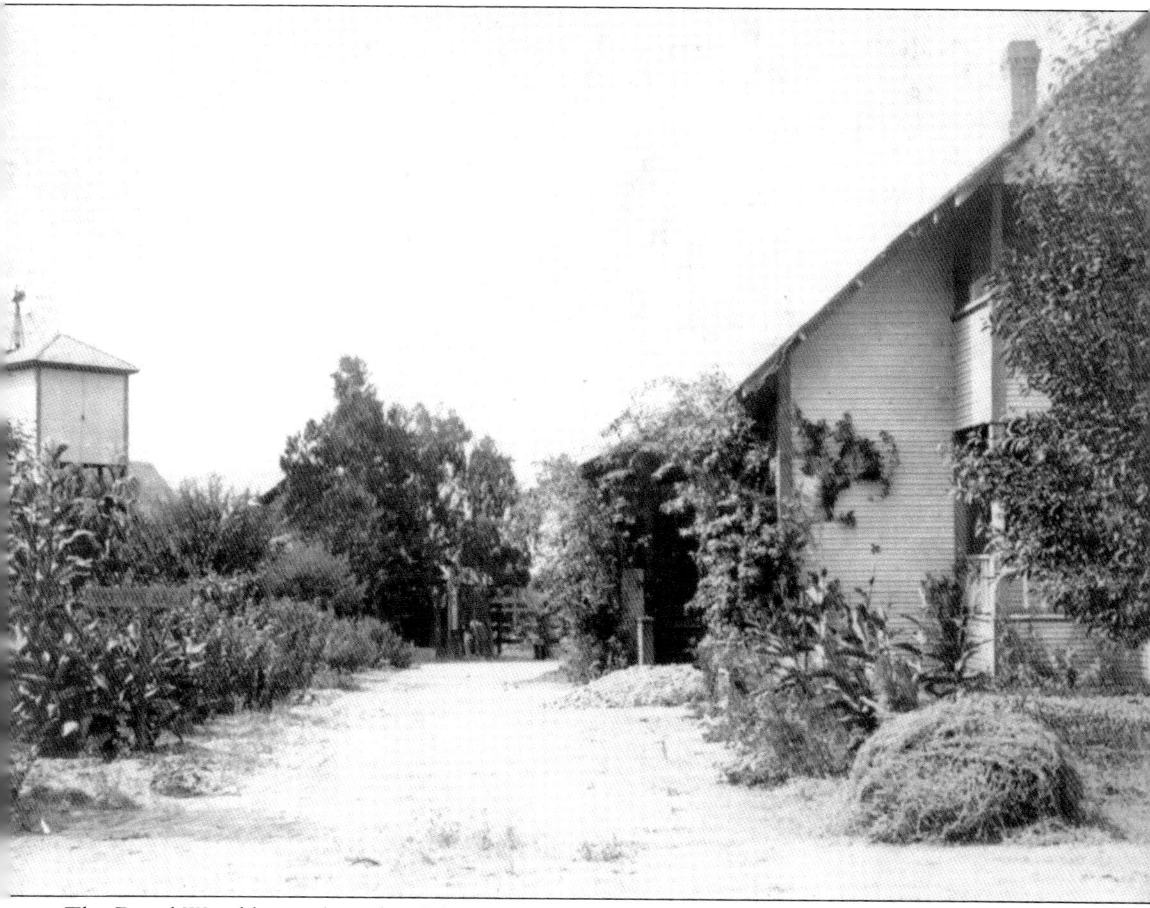

The David Wood house (seen here) located on Zeering Road was built in 1905. The house still stands today. (Courtesy of John Chance.)

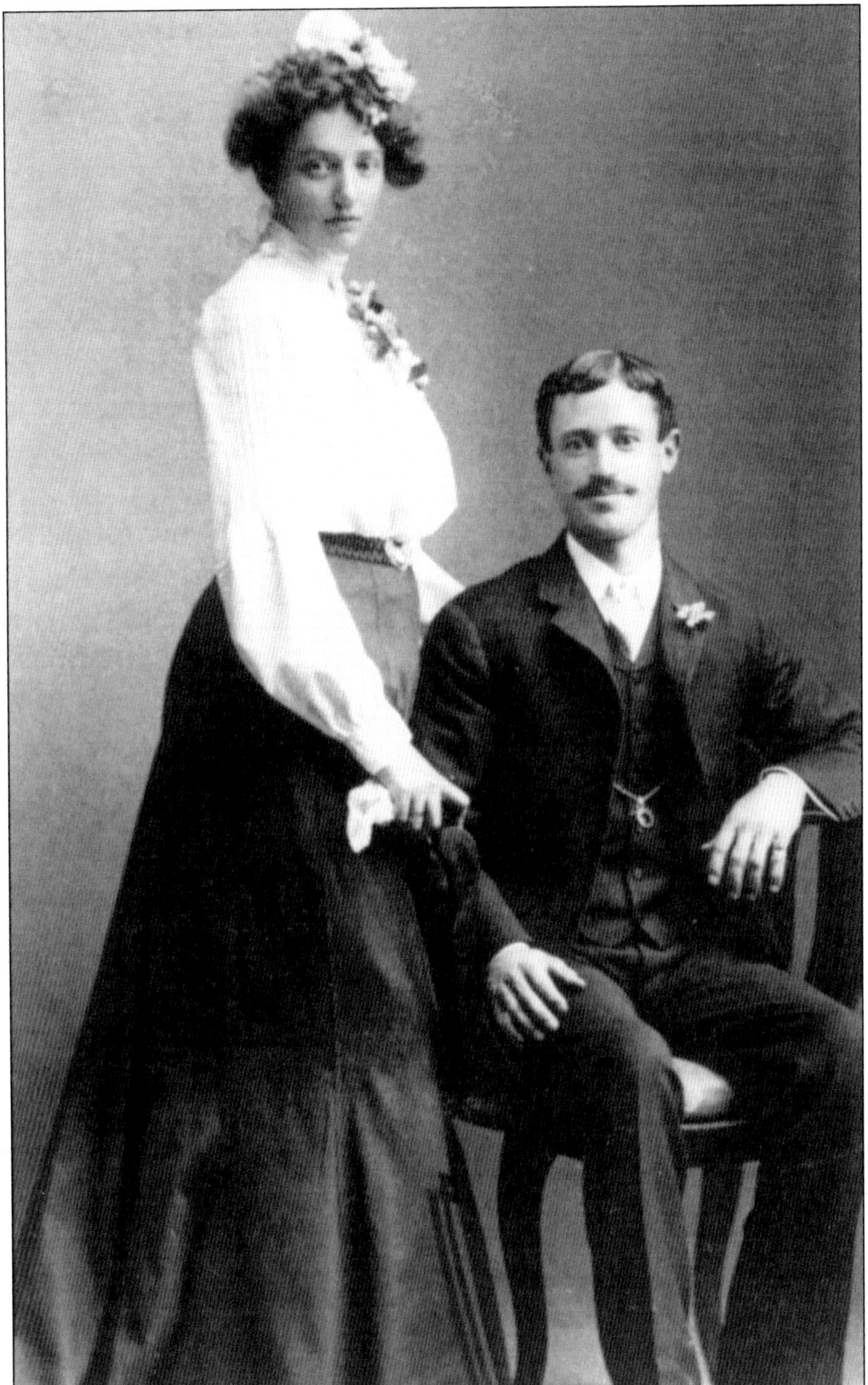

Louis Guillaume Domecq and Sarah Ethel Rouanzion were married in 1903 in Oregon. They moved to Denair in 1910 from Southern California. Ethel died in 1924, leaving behind her husband and nine children, ranging in age from 2 to 18 years old. Many will remember their children and grandchildren as members of the community. (Courtesy of Louis Domecq.)

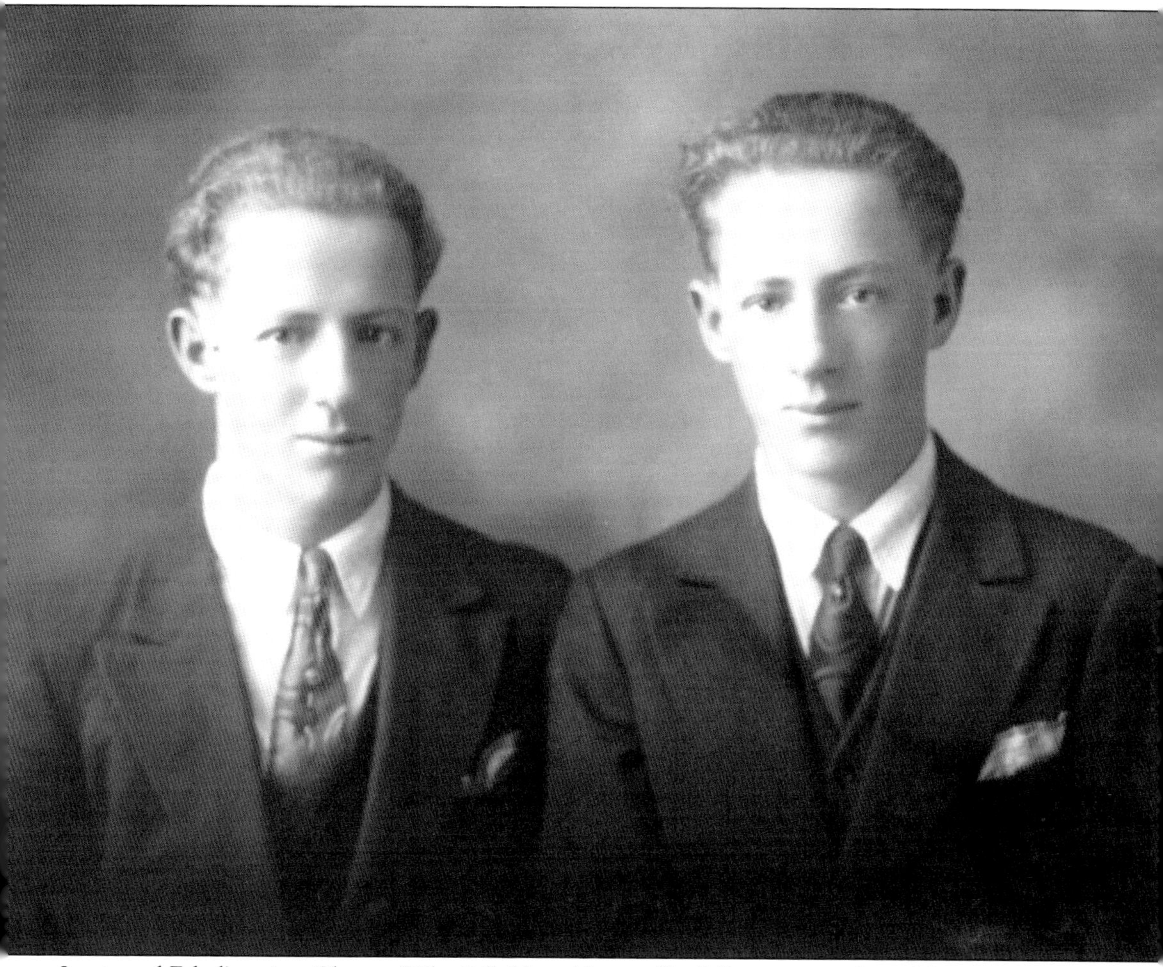

Louis and Ethel's twins, Chester "Chet" (left) and Lester "Let" Domecq, graduated from Denair High School in 1927. Both went on to hold many different positions in the community. (Courtesy of Louis Domecq.)

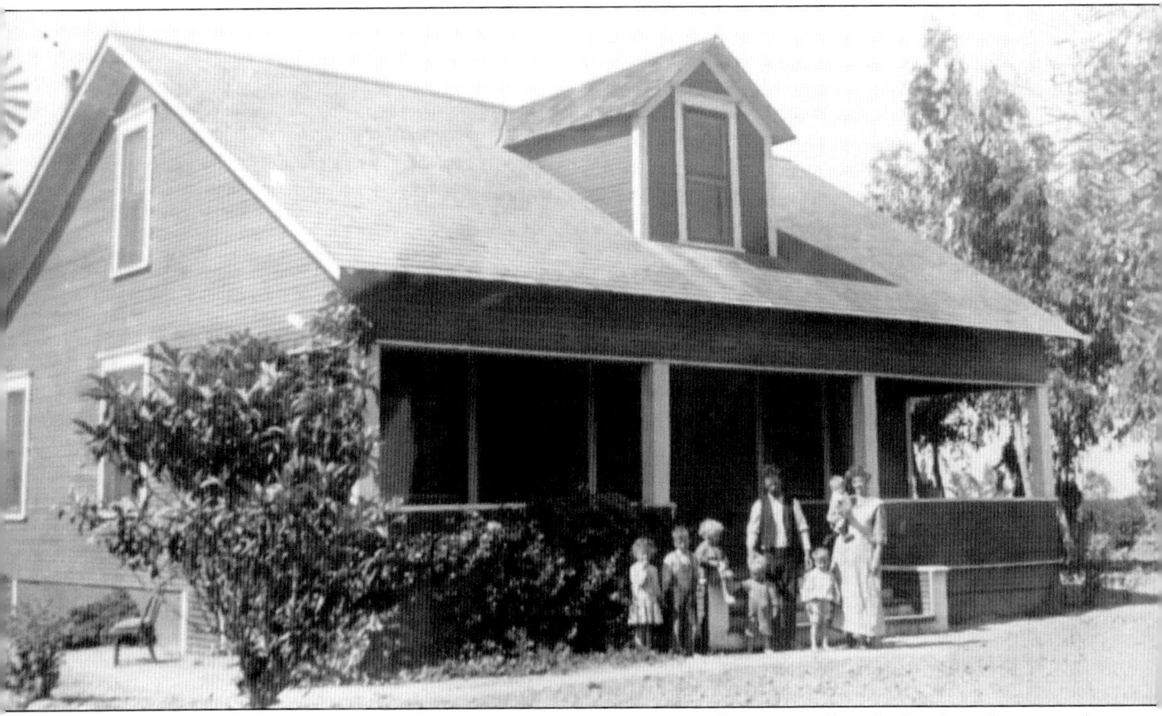

The Domecqs lived on Tuolumne Road between Lester and Gratton Roads. In this photograph are, from left to right, Marguerite, Elwood, twins Lester and Chester, Louis, Joe, and Ethel (with Bob in her arms). In September 1913, only 10 days shy of his ninth birthday, Elwood unfortunately died of pulmonary tuberculosis, possibly a form of valley fever. Obviously, before the advent of antibiotics, this was the fate of quite a few children in the area at the time, causing many children to suffer for months until finally succumbing to their illness. (Courtesy Patricia Moore.)

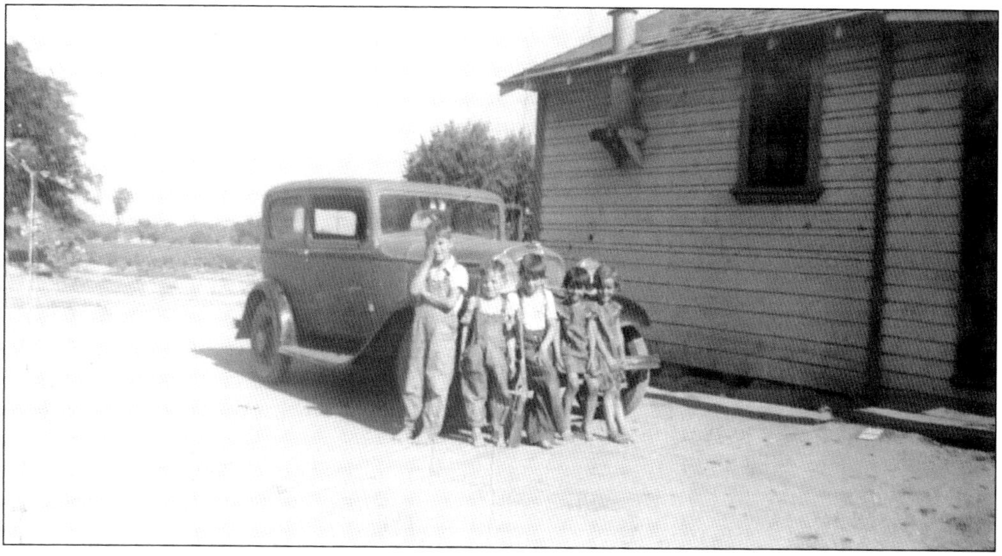

The Mills family and cousins are photographed at their Grandma Patterson's home in 1939. Pictured above, from left to right, are Bill Mills, George Haddock, Bob Haddock, Alma Jean Mills, and Barbara Mills. Below, Ruth (left) and Anna Patterson are shown sitting in front of Grandma Patterson's home on Mills Street. (Both, courtesy of Alma Jean Mills Coleman.)

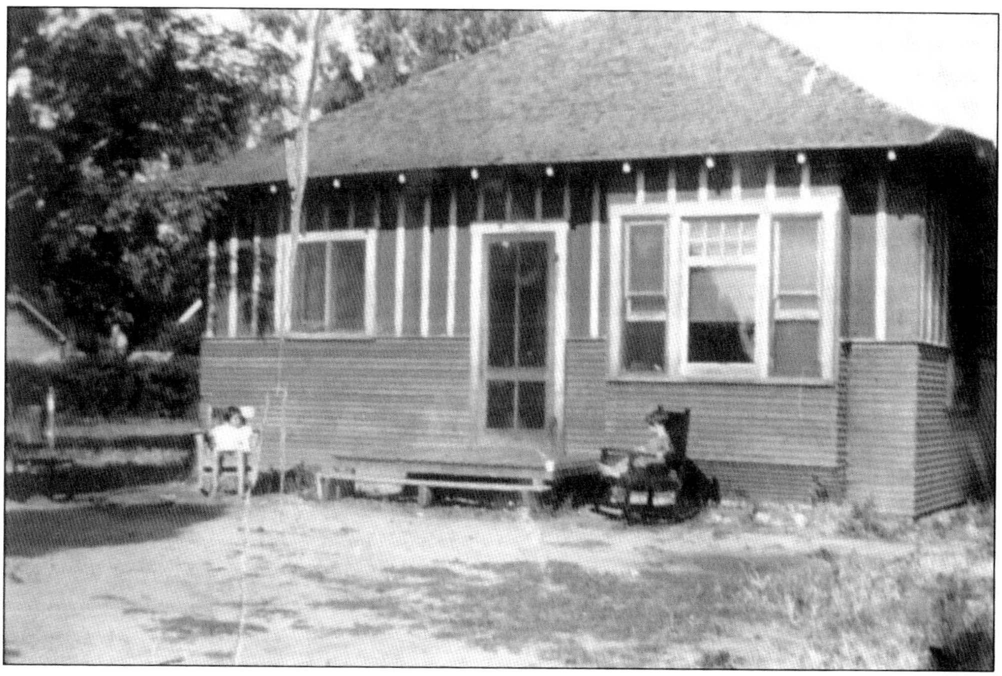

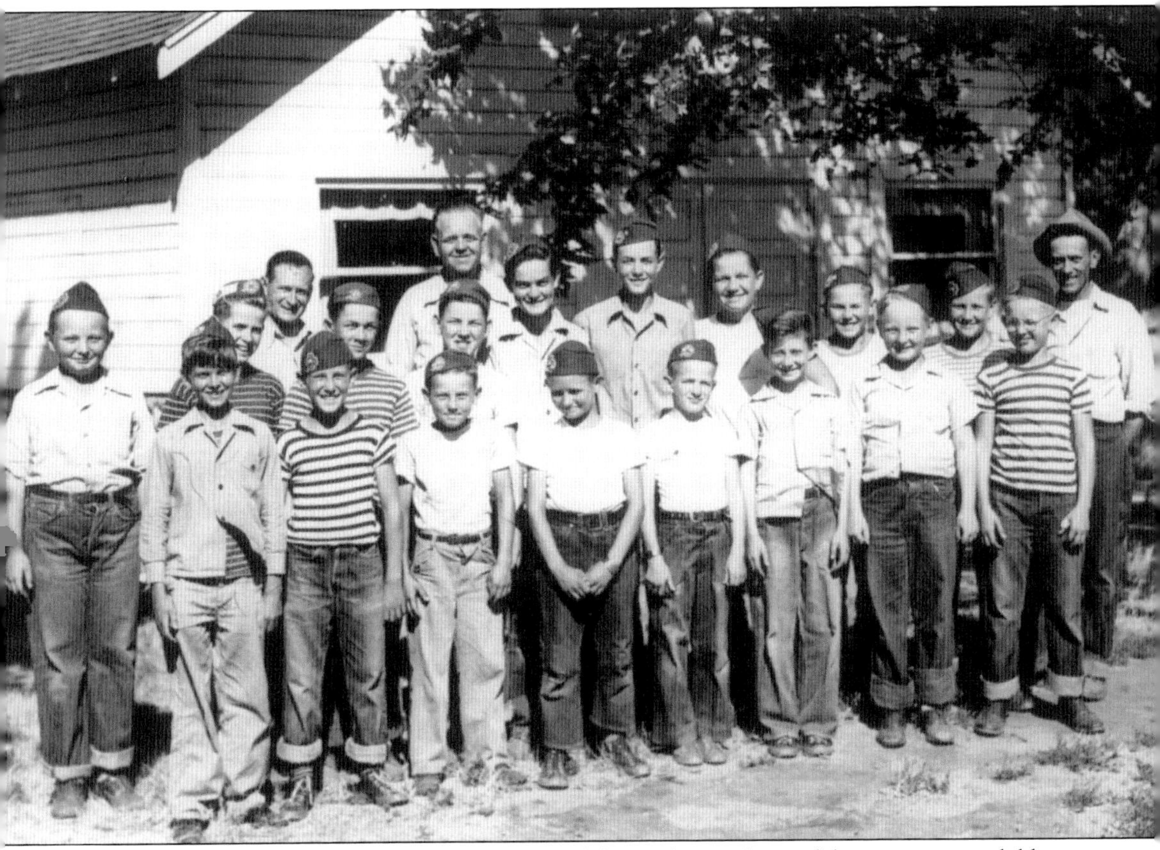

This 1947 photograph shows the Denair 4-H Club standing in front of the community clubhouse. (Courtesy of Louis Domecq.)

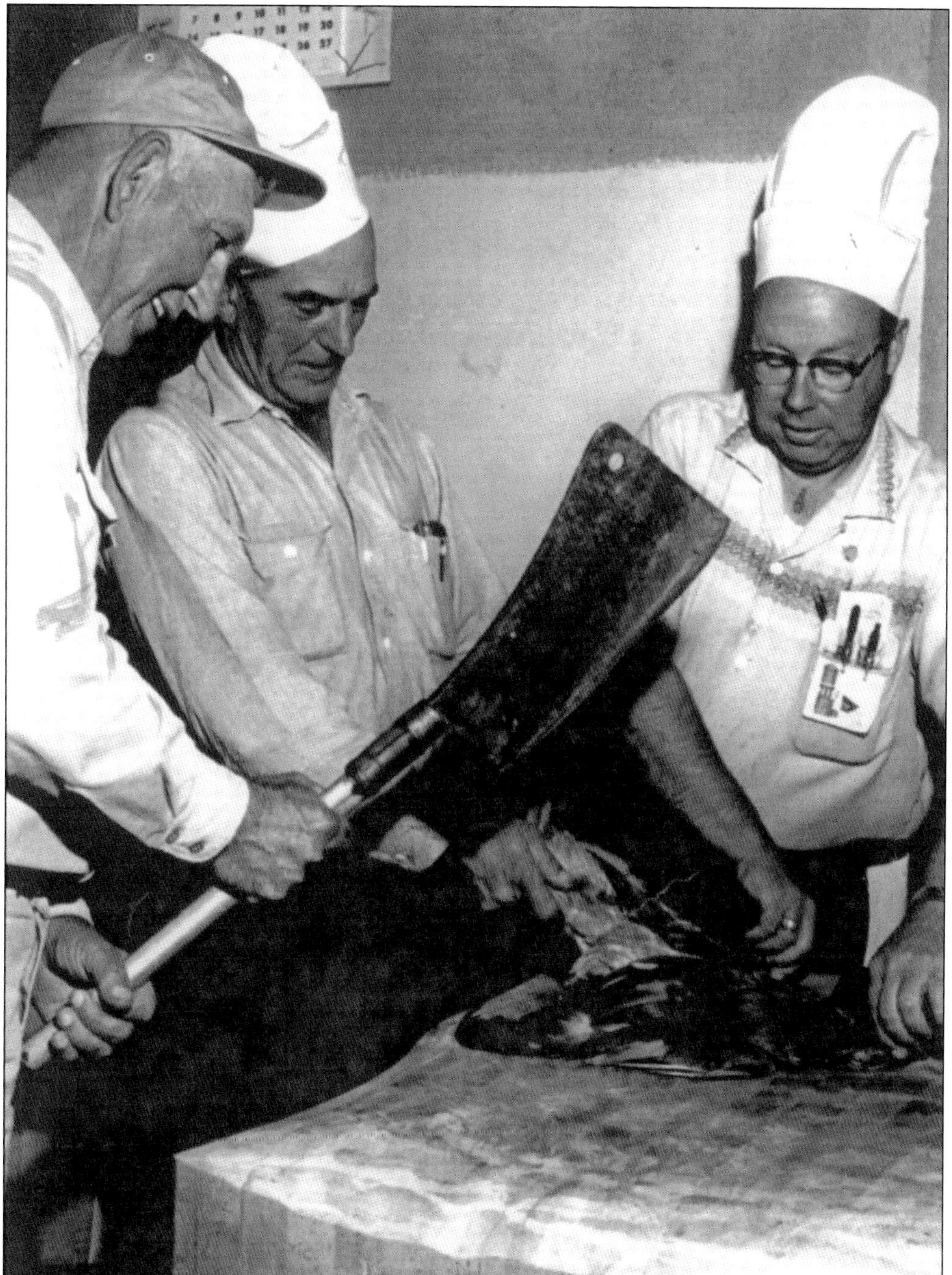
Perry Haworth (left), Jack McCauley (center), and Bob Heans prepare chicken for a fire department dinner around 1947. (Courtesy of Carole Royster.)

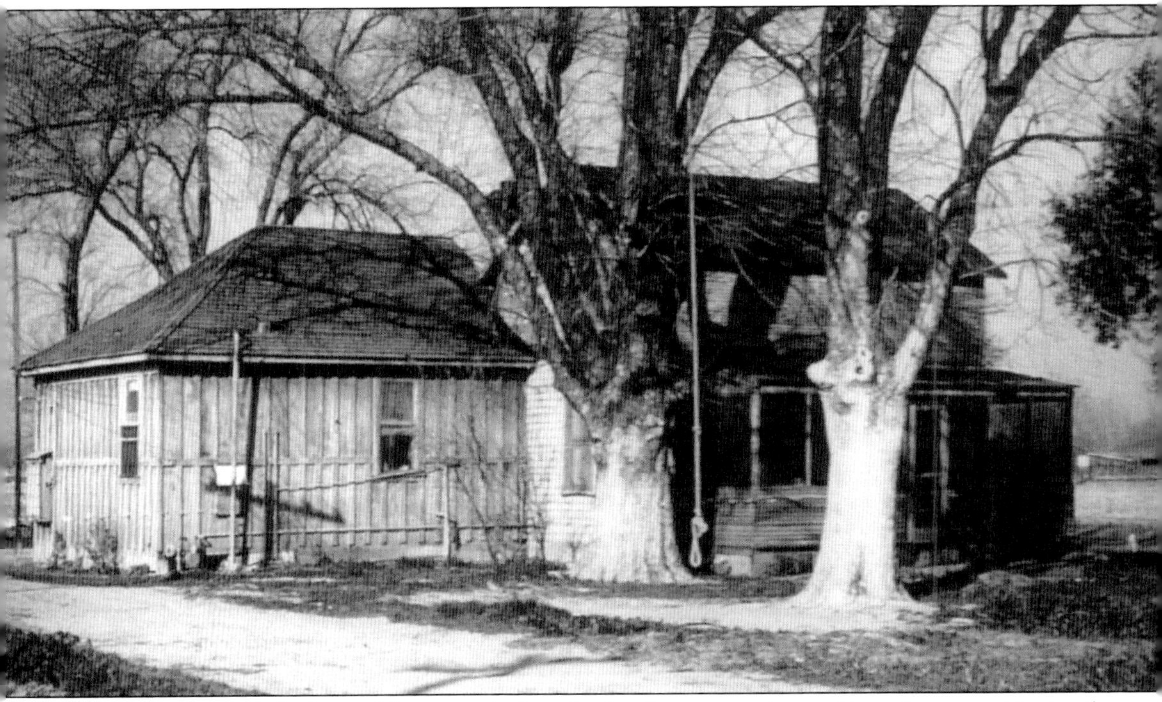

Pictured here is the Lester House just before the fire department burned it to the ground in April 1964 to make way for the new Denair High School on Lester Road. The home, as seen on the cover of this book, was built by John Davis. It was nearly 100 years old when it was destroyed. (Courtesy of the Turlock Historical Society.)

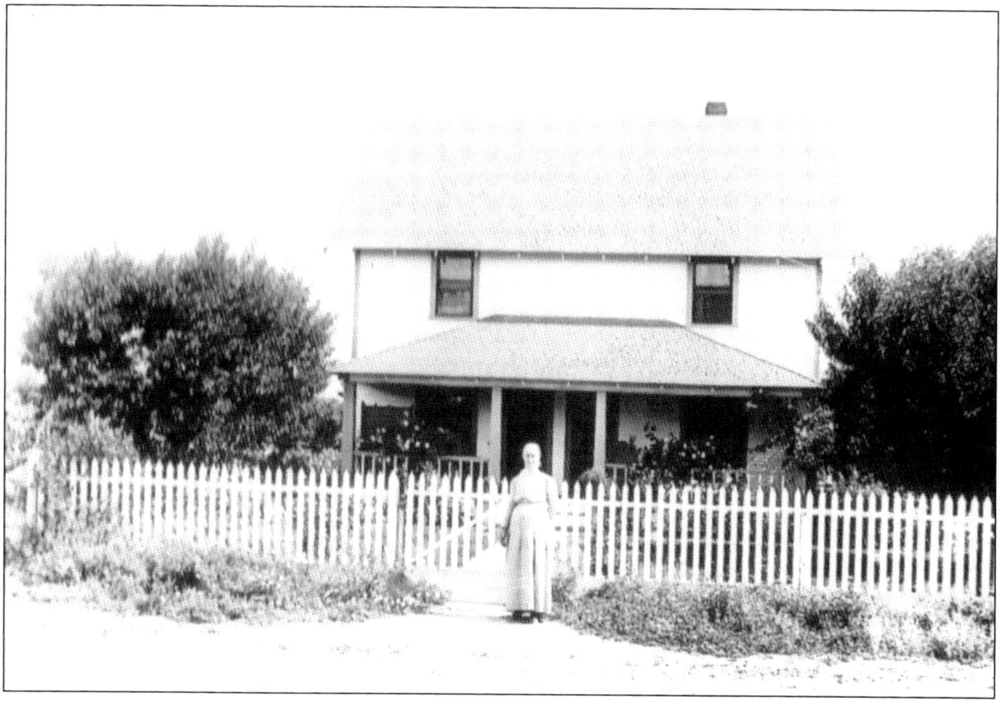

Katherine Yaggy stands in front of an unknown home in Denair. Katherine was married to Jacob Witmer. Pictured below is the Jacob Witmer house on Sperry Road around 1912. (Both, courtesy of the Witmer family.)

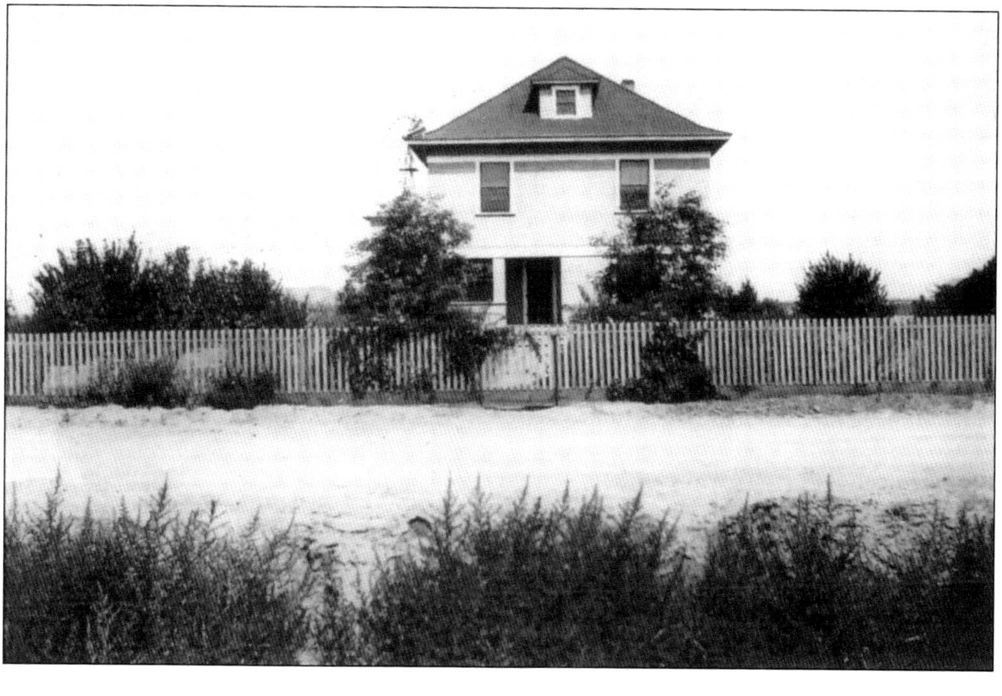

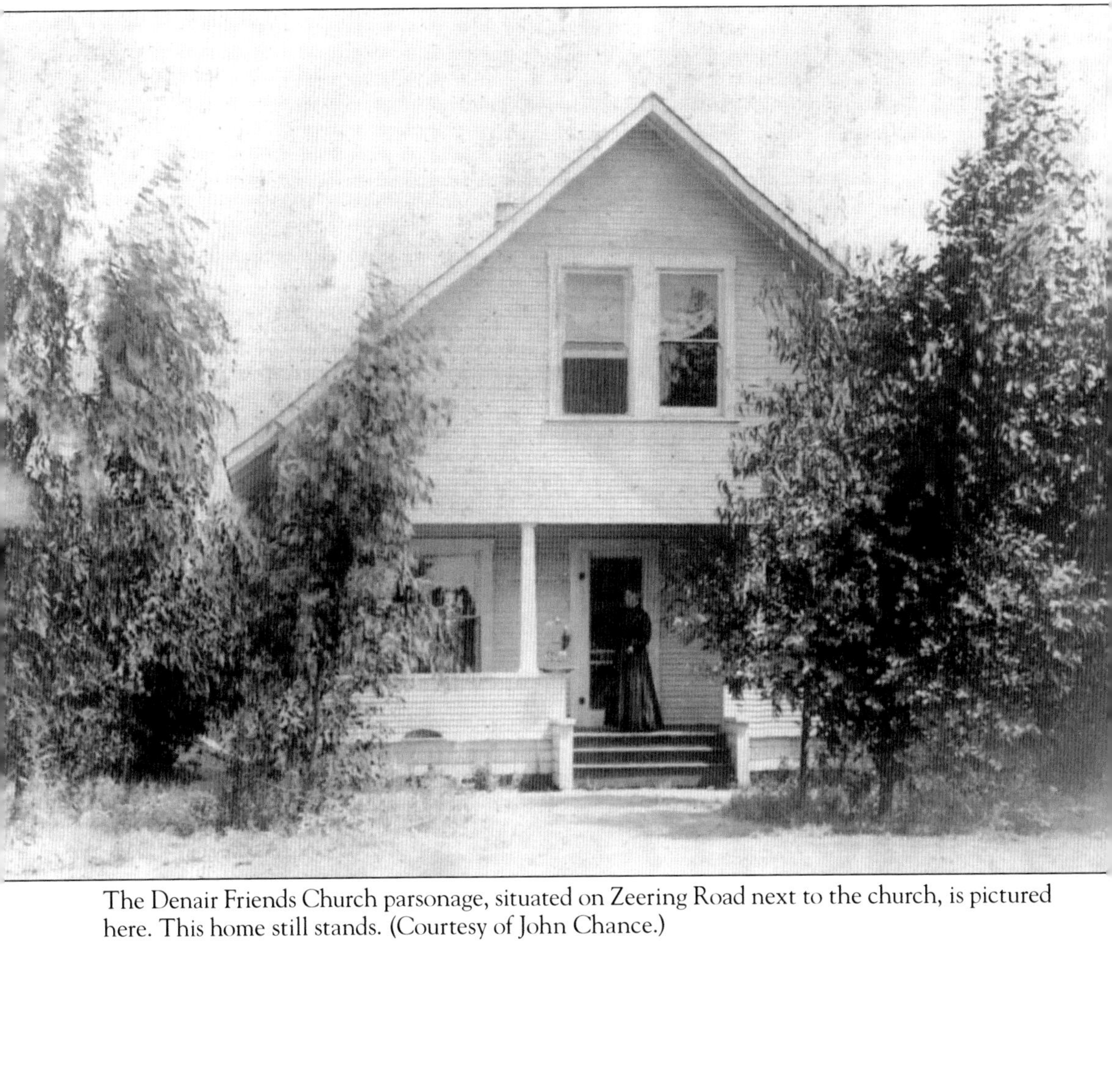

The Denair Friends Church parsonage, situated on Zeering Road next to the church, is pictured here. This home still stands. (Courtesy of John Chance.)

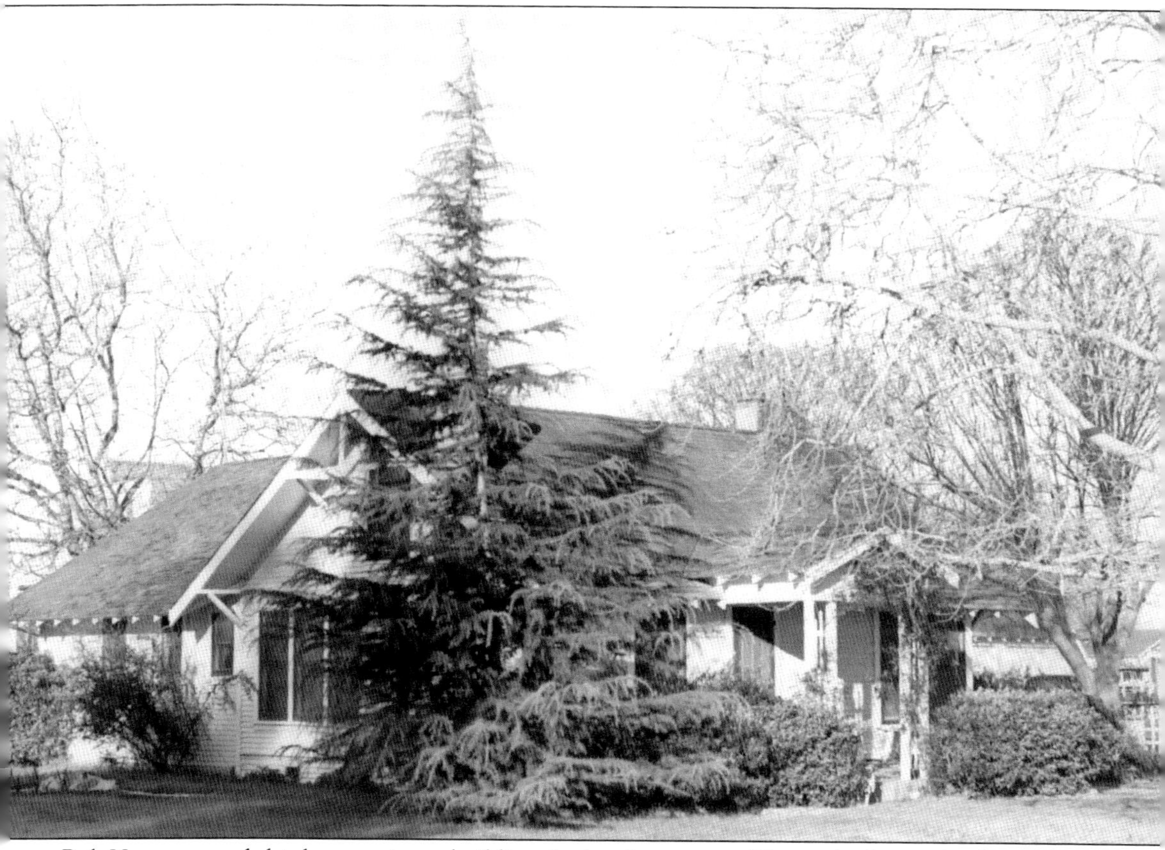

Bob Heans owned this home prior to building the hardware store. This is the house that he sold in order to buy out his partner and move into the apartment over the store. This structure sits on Alameda Avenue, across from the existing Denair Library. (Courtesy of Carole Royster.)